ICETE Series

Towards Vital Wholeness in Theological Education

Global Hub for Evangelical Theological Education

GLOBAL LIBRARY

God's truth is holistic, impacting all aspects of his creation. So also is his will and agenda for his world. Therefore his ministers in the world should be trained holistically through an integrated program in a wholesome community. That is the challenge that is posed before us in this masterful work by one of India's most innovative theological teachers. It calls for courage to totally transform, not just patch up, our method of training and assessment in our efforts in the formation of candidates. Its ideas and guidelines are profound, perceptive and practical arising from an earnest mind and a heart passionate for more effective theological education. For all those who have a hunger for the renewal of theological education, this work is an invaluable and indispensable resource.

Saphir Athyal, PhD
Formerly President of Union Biblical Seminary, Pune, India
Director, Christian Commitments, World Vision International
Deputy Chairman, Lausanne Committee
Founder-Chairman, Asia Theological Association

Towards Vital Wholeness in Theological Education by Jessy Jaison is a prophetic call to nothing less than the "conversion" of the contemporary world of seminary training. Jaison's call to "wholeness" is a frank acknowledgment that much of what happens today in ministerial formation is fragmented and lacks many of the key features necessary for vitality and health. This book patiently surveys the entire landscape of higher education and, in the process, gives us a much-needed call for spiritual awakening and for a dramatic reassessment of what has heretofore been called theological education.

Timothy C. Tennent, PhD
President, Asbury Theological Seminary, USA

A new benchmark in theological education has arrived! *Towards Vital Wholeness* is a must-read for all linked with theological education in this twenty-first century who seek a comprehensive approach to the equipping of men and women for Christian ministry. Jessy writes with both a burden and a passion – to see lives changed and transformed as they walk through the portals of any theology school – so that the church might be strengthened in her witness and service at large. Absolutely well done!

Dr Alexander Philip, MBBS
Director, New India Evangelistic Association
South Asia Facilitator, Transform World Movement

Global theological education has suffered compartmentalization and the fragmentation of learning since the Enlightenment. This has resulted in an emphasis on academia rather than on formation for the wholeness of students in our educational pursuit of theology. Dr Jessy Jaison brings a breath of fresh air of wholeness to the very core of theological education. Her emphasis on the students' learning, faculty's involvement in formation and assessment of the community life of the seminary breaks new ground for integral theological education.

Ashish Chrispal, PhD
Regional Director, Asia, Overseas Council

Dr Jessy Jaison's book touches on training philosophy, governance, curriculum, faculty formation, teaching and learning, community, assessment and much more, but it has a unified aim: to help theological schools understand and deliver wholeness in theological education. Nothing could be more vital. It is easy to read, clear as to theory and summarizes key discussions and issues in useful tables and diagrams. But, fundamentally, it is a book of practical wisdom. It wants to help schools deliver wholeness in their calling by explaining the best theory, inculcating the right attitudes and indicating the best ways forward. Every chapter, every main issue, has a self-assessment guide for schools and a list of suggested activities to realize the goals. Above all, it pulses with a passion for a wholeness in theological education built around the goal of mission, the needs of the church and the transformation of students.

Teachers, staff and governors, you need this book.

Graham Cheesman, PhD
Founder, Centre for Theological Education (CTE), Belfast, UK
Formerly Principal of Belfast Bible College, Northern Ireland
Council Member, European Evangelical Accrediting Association (EEAA)

All trustees, administrators and faculty in theological education ought to consult this book regularly in order to be reminded about the important questions that we need to return to again and again. This will ensure that our efforts in this important vocation are continuously recalibrated according to the most important commitments that should drive our endeavors – for these matters Dr Jessy Jaison leaves no stone unturned and will repeatedly probe our work and prod us to educational excellence in light of our higher calling!

Amos Yong, PhD
Professor of Theology & Mission
Director of Center for Missiological Research
Fuller Theological Seminary, USA

Towards Vital Wholeness in Theological Education

Framing Areas for Assessment

Jessy Jaison

Global Hub for Evangelical Theological Education

GLOBAL LIBRARY

© 2017 by Jessy Jaison

Published 2017 by Langham Global Library
An imprint of Langham Publishing
www.langhampublishing.org

Langham Publishing and its imprints are a ministry of Langham Partnership

Langham Partnership
PO Box 296, Carlisle, Cumbria CA3 9WZ, UK
www.langham.org

ISBNs:
978-1-78368-293-5 Print
978-1-78368-294-2 ePub
978-1-78368-296-6 PDF

Jessy Jaison has asserted her right under the Copyright, Designs and Patents Act, 1988 to be identified as the Author of this work.

All rights reserved. No part of this publication may be reproduced, stored in a retrieval system or transmitted, in any form or by any means, electronic, mechanical, photocopying, recording or otherwise, without the prior written permission of the publisher or the Copyright Licensing Agency.

All Scripture quotations, unless otherwise indicated, are taken from the Holy Bible, New International Version®, NIV®. Copyright ©1973, 1978, 1984, 2011 by Biblica, Inc.™ Used by permission of Zondervan.

British Library Cataloguing in Publication Data
A catalogue record for this book is available from the British Library

ISBN: 978-1-78368-293-5

Cover & Book Design: projectluz.com

Langham Partnership actively supports theological dialogue and an author's right to publish but does not necessarily endorse the views and opinions set forth, and works referenced within this publication or guarantee its technical and grammatical correctness. Langham Partnership does not accept any responsibility or liability to persons or property as a consequence of the reading, use or interpretation of its published content.

Contents

Foreword ix

Acknowledgments xi

List of Figures xv

Introduction: The Vital Wholeness in Theological Education. 1

1 Wholeness in the Goal, Mission and Training Philosophy 19

2 Wholeness in Theological Curriculum 35

3 Wholeness in the Formation of Faculty 51

4 Wholeness in the Overall Learning Experience 73

5 Wholeness in the Community Life of the School 91

6 Wholeness in the Interworking of Departments 103

7 Wholeness in Quality Assessment. 115

8 Wholeness in the Governance of the School 137

9 Transformative Methodological Trends in Teaching
   and Learning. 153

10 Treading the Path of Wholeness 177

Conclusion 189

Appendix 1: Detecting Points of Innovation through
Needs Assessment 191

Appendix 2: Mission Statement, Core Values and
Value Definitions: A Model 193

Appendix 3: Four Dynamics of Holistic Formation:
ConneXions Model 195

Appendix 4: Overseas Council International Program
Values and Standards for Theological Education 2014. 197

Bibliography 201

Foreword

In the past four decades theological education around the world has been under close scrutiny. The emphasis, for the most part, has been on the various ills plaguing the system. Thus, curricular design, integration, learning methodology, faculty competence, seminary–church relations, theory versus praxis, governance and administration, and a host of other issues are frequently the point of discussion and debate. Not many suggest a practical and workable way forward, and those that do are more conceptual and theoretical in nature. Jessy Jaison, however, brings to serious-minded theological educators practical recommendations to address the problems that afflict theological education.

What Jaison has done in this remarkable book is to address the crucial aspect of "*wholeness*" in theological education. The general trend (with very few exceptions!) is that theological training is troubled by several gaps in the areas specified earlier. Theological education is rarely viewed as a composite whole, from foundational vision statements to the objectives and actual training that takes place. Jaison paves the way for a holistic understanding of theological education keeping in mind the struggles that institutions face around the world.

Jessy Jaison draws upon her rich experience at the New India Bible Seminary (NIBS) in Kerala, India, where much of what she recommends has already been implemented. The result is a passionate call for wholeness based upon the results that are the fruit of several years of serious soul-searching and implementing change. She does not leave any stone unturned as she covers all the areas that bring life to the training of women and men for the various ministries of the church.

The uniqueness of this book is twofold. First, it covers the entire breadth of the different aspects that make up the life of a theological institution. This is a clear reminder that vision, objectives, governance, policies, curriculum, learning methods, faculty, mentor groups, library, academics and infrastructure are all equally needed to impart sound and relevant theological education. Second, it treats, in great depth, each area that must be evaluated and assessed if an institution is serious about holistic growth. Probing self-evaluation questions at the end of each chapter give boards and administrators a ready-made tool to embark upon a journey towards wholeness and excellence.

I personally am grateful to Jessy Jaison for this much-needed work. This is a book that brings hope to those who want to break out of the existing mold and begin to make a real difference in the church and the wider community she serves. *Towards Vital Wholeness in Theological Education: Framing Areas for Assessment* is a must-read for all those who have a stake in the equipping of men and women for the work of the kingdom – from church and mission leaders to boards, principals/presidents, faculty, staff and students!

Paul Cornelius, PhD
Regional Secretary, India
Asia Theological Association

Acknowledgments

Theological education is the indispensable design at the core of the church's life and mission. The task of theology is intrinsically holistic and therefore the call on theology schools is for formational wholeness. Based on this proposition, this book envisions a sustainable revitalization within theological education amidst the massive changes and innumerable disconnections. To share this vision as openly and plainly as possible is my task. It is my hope that we, the leaders and educators, will embark on an exciting and most rewarding journey, asking ourselves difficult questions in response to the divine call towards *vital wholeness*.

I take this opportunity to thank everyone for extending genuine support in this endeavor, and to mention the key experiences and persons that guided me into this theme.

First and foremost, it is the help, grace and wisdom of God Almighty that made this short-term intensive writing project possible.

My personal conviction that theological education, being central to the mission of the church, needs to be assessed and improved at every point to ensure that it nurtures wholeness in the indispensable pursuit of the knowledge of God laid the foundation for this venture. Increasing discontent with the fact that theology schools are becoming mere *centers for abstract knowledge that leads to a degree* fueled this exploration on wholeness. Every sentence in this book is profoundly impacted by the expressed agony of several educators that the formation of the whole person is getting sidelined in training and that the unity of purpose in the church's mission is being forgotten. I have referred to ideas on this wavelength from around the world throughout the book.

Over two decades, New India Bible Seminary (NIBS), the pivotal theological institution of the New India Evangelistic Association, has been my ministry base in India. This mission shows an authentic dissatisfaction with the slide of theological education into mere professionalism. Vigorous discussions are held on the persistent questions around the unmet ministry needs in the world today. This has instilled in me a fervent quest for holistic impact.

My academic mentor, Dr Graham Cheesman, influenced my vision for the critical balance of theory and practice in theological education. His conscientious efforts in empowering theological institutions in the global South have made an enormous impact.

The unswerving ministry endeavors of my husband, Dr Jaison Thomas, in interacting with practitioners in churches and missions inculcated in me a genuine appreciation for efforts in advancing the church–seminary relationship. Having been associated with his diligent formulation and implementation of the Context-Based Transformative Learning (CBTL) model at NIBS in Kerala, India, I found this prospect even more persuasive.

My teaching tenure at the South Asia Institute of Advanced Christian Studies (SAIACS) presented me with a rare opportunity to work alongside different academic departments. The scope for sustainable theory-praxis integration was increasingly evident in the distinctive learning approaches I explored with the research students in critical correlations among academic disciplines, intensive dialectical hermeneutics, and problem-posing and context-based learning methodology.

My team of colleagues explored the ConneXions Model of Building Healthy Leaders (BHL) by Dr Malcolm Webber and Dr Robert Walter in a months-long curricular revisit. The 5Cs in the model refer to the goal of training (5Cs: Christ, Community, Calling, Character and Competency) and the 4Dynamics, to transformative learning (4Ds: Spiritual, Experiential, Relational and Instructional). This intensive exercise built confidence in developing formational frames to resolve many practical puzzles in transformative curriculum design.

The *Journal of Theological Education and Mission* (*JOTEAM*), which I edit, received multiple queries from theology schools seeking guidance and assistance in curriculum revision. This earnest responsiveness and desire for guidance from theological educators was a major impetus for this book.

A qualitative open-ended survey of February 2016 among principals/academic deans in India gathered important evidence of the disconnections in theological education and the need for concrete deliberations. My sporadic academic engagement with the Overseas Council (OC) and the Asia Theological Association India (ATAI) were also inspirational in this task.

My profound appreciation goes to the Overseas Council International and Asbury Theological Seminary, Kentucky, USA, for their invaluable support for this project. In addition to all the excellent facilities for research and writing, the Asbury campus blessed me with the professional exposure and spiritual rest and awakening that were central to reflective thinking. Thanks go to Dr Thomas F. Tumblin and all the members of faculty at Asbury for cordially and devotedly supporting me in my writing task.

I gratefully acknowledge that this writing project would not have been possible without the continual support of New India Evangelistic Association and the Executive Director of NIEA, Dr Alexander Philip.

I am greatly honored to have this book published by the ICETE and Langham Partnership. Thanks go to the Series Editor, Rev Dr Riad Kassis, and his team for their wholehearted support.

My deepest sense of gratitude goes to Dr Saphir Athyal for his motivation and mentoring in my life. Also, my heartfelt appreciation to Dr Paul Cornelius, the Regional Secretary, ATA India, for kindly writing the Foreword. I owe a special word of thanks to Dr Timothy C. Tennent, Dr Alexander A. Philip, Dr Graham Cheesman, Dr Ashish Chrispal and Dr Saphir Athyal, for adorning this book with their words of endorsement.

Words cannot express my appreciation for Jaison, my incredible companion in life and ministry, and for my wonderfully loving sons, Abraham and Aquil. Their delightful hearts deserve the best gestures of appreciation.

In closing, I offer a special word of thanks to my students faithfully toiling in mission around the globe, and to all my colleagues in theological education who are passionately pursuing God's call to serve and strengthen his church in his world by his Word.

Jessy Jaison, PhD
E-mail: jessyjaison12@gmail.com

List of Figures

Figure 1: Jesus's Model of Holistic Formation 8
Figure 2: A Candid Perception of Theological Education 13
Figure 3: A Complex Portrayal of Theological Education 14
Figure 4: Distinct Persons in the Making in Theological Education 15
Figure 5: Multiple Aspects of Balance to Facilitate Wholeness in Theological Education 16
Figure 6: Edgar Portrayal of Models of Theological Education (2005) 20
Figure 7: Cronshaw Diagram of Theological Education and Missional Spirituality 21
Figure 8: ConneXions Model Leader-Development Structure 24
Figure 9: Ford's Curriculum Design Process 24
Figure 10: *Goal* or *Goals*? 25
Figure 11: Degree-Centered Approach and Student-Oriented Holistic Process 39
Figure 12: Who Prepares the Syllabus? 40
Figure 13: The Faculty Reality: Good and Bad Models 54
Figure 14: Divergence of Priorities in Theological Education 74
Figure 15: ConneXions Model of Holistic Formation 75
Figure 16: Facets of School Assessment 124
Figure 17: ConneXions Design of Assessment 125
Figure 18: A Systematic and Comprehensive Approach to Assessment LDQ® 126
Figure 19: Contemporary and Traditional Ways of Student Learning Assessment (from Suskie) 131
Figure 20: Dynamics in Teaching-Learning Methodology 156
Figure 21: Knowles' Six Assumptions of Adult Learning 165
Figure 22: Pivotal Procedural Considerations in the Path of Wholeness 180
Figure 23: Characteristics of Good Assessment (Suskie) 184

Introduction

The Vital Wholeness in Theological Education

The Vision and Contents of the Book

Drawing from both literary and experiential evidence, we assume that the global clarion call on the theological educational scene is for *vital wholeness*,[1] which denotes *integral balance*, *healthy integration* or *holistic formation*. Wholeness in our own self, society or church is considered to be unrealistic in the twenty-first century's uneven social climates. This work, however, represents a specific invitation to the theme of wholeness in the philosophy and practice of theological education. It explores key aspects to enable theology schools[2] to actualize their existence as God-centered, Bible-based communities to serve and strengthen the church's mission.

> "That which was from the beginning, which we have heard, which we have seen with our eyes, which we have looked at, and our hands have touched – this we proclaim concerning the Word of life." 1 John 1:1

---

1. The terms *wholeness* and *holistic* will be spelled thus throughout this book: *wholeness*, to maintain the emphasis on healthy integration and balance, and *holistic*, to identify with the mode in which the term is commonly used in literature today.

2. *Theology school* is used as a synonym for seminary, Bible college, training institute or any other term that denotes a place that offers theological training, while *theological education* is used as an inclusive expression that covers the variety of on- and off-campus education.

The primary aims of this book are to:
- Facilitate critical-constructive thinking on the current practice of theological education;
- Expose certain dimensions that are willfully neglected or unintentionally disunited;
- Motivate leaders and educators for systematic thinking and assessment towards unity of vision and action; and,
- Create solid awareness of the need for transformative theological training.

This book acknowledges and builds on the relentless contributions of many scholars who have dreamed of restoring theological education to its vital purpose and unity. However, these educators took different paths in their vision towards the unity of purpose in the learning experience. Efforts to advance the missional impact and formational insights have been commendable in many contexts. While some of them chose to do this by advancing the mission focus, others worked around other areas, such as Christian education, theological inquiry and practical theology, according to their formational emphases. Nonetheless, theological educators and schools still persevere with the ongoing challenge of multiple forms of internal fragmentation.

> "If a student should learn a thousand things, and yet fail to preach the gospel acceptably, his College course will have missed its true design. Should the pursuit of literary prizes and the ambition for classical honors so occupy his mind as to divert his attention from his life work, they are perilous rather than beneficial."
> C. H. Spurgeon, *Lectures to My Students*.

Most of our fundamental assumptions on which theological education was built have been slowly disintegrating into mere theories in different contexts. The essential reciprocity between church and theology school is increasingly diminishing in spite of the literature produced on the issue. Despite being the theological and practical foundation for the church's mission, theological education is often disposed to conserve mission as a separate entity, in some way detached from the *professional* setting of training. Closer inquiry reveals that the form taken by the delivery of theological education over the past decades is such that it exists for itself. This is a disobliging and hollow prospect.

To provoke change in this situation with theologically grounded thinking and viable procedures is the task at hand.

The gap between the church and the theology school seems to be widening. Churches and missions still wish to outsource a major part of their training to the seminary. But they often rapidly realize that their expectations of discipleship training or mission formation, or even theological grounding, are not so central to the theology school's vision. This makes the church and missions revert to their own modes of training. At the same time, we see the endless strivings of theology schools to become universities themselves or to get accredited by secular universities. The nature and extent of these shifts may vary, but they are tangible in our training contexts. In outlining the important areas for assessment in theological education, this book argues that there is much more to theological education than infrastructure, library resources and qualified faculty. The primary proposition suggests that the holistic formation of a student can be examined only in view of the goal and mission of the institution. Considering the changes that have occurred in theological education over the decades, this book sets out a multi-dimensional argument on the intrinsic unity of theological education through the following topics:

- Goal, mission and training philosophy
- Theological curriculum
- Formation of faculty
- Overall learning experience
- Community life
- Interworking of departments
- Quality assessment
- Governance of the school
- Methodological trends in learning
- Foundational steps towards wholeness

This book demonstrates that theological education, being central to the mission of the church, needs to be assessed and improved at every point to ensure that it nurtures wholeness in the pursuit of the knowledge of God. Theology schools are unique places that hold theoretical knowledge, spiritual discipline, affective wisdom, reflective skills and ministerial competencies in crucial balance. Having identified particular disconnects in training, this book calls for a comprehensive and cogent convergence of the goal, mission and practice of theological education. It also charts possible assessment trajectories towards this vision.

The layout of this book may well correspond to certain expectations of readers. The chapters represent conceptual pointers to the topic of *wholeness in theological education*, presenting it through key areas for assessment. In order to facilitate genuine thinking on integration in contexts from local schools to higher bodies of accreditation, this book intends to ignite the strategic commitment in leaders and educators to revisit, review and reform the way theological education is done in their institutions. The proposition is that each institution should take its unique path towards wholeness, aligning with the espoused mission statement of the school. Therefore, the book provides pointers for self-assessment, but not quick fixes. Chapters close with questions for self-assessment of the school and a few practical recommendations to act upon. It is hoped that accrediting bodies will steer their service into premeditated steps towards shared learning on these issues so that constructive changes may not be limited to certain pockets of training. The discussion here takes a qualitative bearing rather than a quantitative one. In spite of the multiple concerns laid out, this book is designed to provide an enlightening note and be a guide to any transformational initiative towards the wholeness of theological education.

Let me address what not to expect. There is no exhaustive theoretical treatise in this book on *theological education* or on the theme of *wholeness*. Rather, by addressing several vital areas for assessment, it intends to serve as a practical guide to leaders and educators in theological institutions. This book does not deliver ready-to-use curriculum or design structures for training institutions; it rather envisions that progressive and transformative initiatives will stream forth, shared and implemented from within the local contexts of training. This book does not limit its scope geographically, but seeks to address issues in general, stimulating constructive self-assessment in any context of theological education. This is not an answers book. Aiming to identify critical facets that need revisiting in theological education, it believes that training should achieve its intended purpose and hence impact God's mission.

Understanding *Wholeness*

What concerns us is the form and essence of theological education. Is our pattern of theological education an integrated whole? If not, what procedures will guide our thinking in that direction? Difficult questions of self-assessment are usually the right place to start for locating the disintegrations in the training process. My own studies in the Indian context of theological education[3] point to the following particular scenarios of mismatches in training:

- Academics vs. mentoring
- Infrastructure development vs. espoused goal
- Professionalism vs. spirituality
- Programs vs. purpose
- Training vs. church's expectation
- Partnerships vs. quality enhancement
- Accreditation vs. ministry formation

Ted Ward unequivocally articulated the need for wholeness thus: "Lacking integration – intellectual wholeness – the individual Christian and the institutions of Christianity are vulnerable to apostasy."[4]

A general meaning of the term *wholeness* is the state of being united and undivided. In other words, *wholeness* denotes the state of forming a harmonious whole. As a prominent philosophy of education in this century, *holistic education* denotes a multi-leveled experiential journey of discovery, expression and mastery in which students and teachers learn and grow together. It upholds every student's innate potential to think creatively, reflectively and innovatively. Holistic learning is organized around relationships within and between learners and their environment while empowering learners to live fully in the present and to co-create the future. It guides all students to active engagement in learning and doing, and to grow fully in their potential intellectually, spiritually, emotionally, socially, creatively, physically and artistically. Engagement may indicate a variety of approaches to providing for learning in terms of being cognitively engaged (I understand and want to know more), physiologically engaged (I am paying attention), emotionally engaged (I have a vested interest) or strategically engaged (I am in the action). Evoking engagement in a learning design is a challenge; each learner may have different ways in which he or

---

3. See Appendix 1 "Detecting Points of Innovation through Needs Assessment." Taken from Jessy Jaison, "Evaluation and Innovation: Possibilities of Theological Education," paper presented in Colombo, Sri Lanka, at the Overseas Council International Institute of Excellence, 8 August 2014.
4. Ted W. Ward, "The Lines People Draw," *Common Ground Journal* 10, no. 1 (Fall 2012): 26.

she is engaged.⁵ A holistic curriculum is inquiry-driven, interdisciplinary and integrated, and is based on explicit assumptions of interrelatedness, wholeness and multi-dimensional being. Contextual, moral, political, social and interdisciplinary values in education are blended in it in a healthy manner as students approach the body of knowledge.

In *Integral Education* Gunnlaugson stated,

> We believe that in future years integral education will gradually move toward participatory pedagogical approaches in which all human dimensions are actively encouraged to participate creatively at all stages of inquiry and learning. The explicit inclusion of all human attributes in the inquiry process will naturally reconnect *education* with its root meaning (edu-care: "bringing out the *wholeness* within") and, therefore, with transformative healing and spiritual growth, both of which involve a movement toward human *wholeness*.⁶

The essence of this wholeness is explained thus: "this is where the term *integral* comes in – where your most deeply felt values are being acknowledged and honored and in a process where you are able to make meaning out of what you are doing. The meaning-making part of this really began to emerge as a key thing."⁷ In theological education, this meaning is weaved in together on the centrality of God and the wisdom of his Word communicated to human situations in timeless relevance towards the mission of the church in God's plan. Very helpful literature is currently available on integral ministry training. Multiple areas of holistic learning and formation are addressed in these materials.⁸

---

5. Patricia McGee, "Learning Objects: Bloom's Taxonomy and Deeper Learning Principles," Paper for the Department of Interdisciplinary Studies & Curriculum and Instruction, University of Texas at San Antonio, http://faculty.coehd.utsa.edu/pmcgee/nlii/LOBloomsMcGee.doc; accessed 23 March 2017.

6. Sean Esbjörn-Hargens, Jonathan Reams and Olen Gunnlaugson (eds.), *Integral Education: New Directions for Higher Learning* (Albany, NY: SUNY, 2010), 99.

7. Ibid., 335.

8. For example, Robert Brynjolfson and Jonathan Lewis (eds.), *Integral Ministry Training: Design and Evaluation* (Pasadena, CA: William Carey Library, 2006); David P. Gushee and Walter C. Jackson (eds.), *Preparing for Christian Ministry: An Evangelical Approach* (Grand Rapids, MI: Baker, 1998).

Wholeness as a theme has been manifest in theological deliberation for decades. The three related terms echoed repeatedly in the discussions are *unity*, *integration* and *balance*. Wholeness is God's design and vision. *Wholeness in being* is not only God's essence but also is his will for his people in creation, salvation and the entire kingdom project. Scholars have looked keenly into the theme of wholeness in theological education. Graham Cheesman advocates and uses the Trinitarian concept of *perichoresis* or dynamic co-inherence, an ontology from ideas of the Trinity that the circulation of the divine life between and through the three persons brings each to fullness of deity. That sort of indivisible unity whereby encountering one person is encountering all three persons of the Trinity is, he believes, central to theological education, where all dimensions of formation are perfectly blended towards knowing God. James Brandt said how deeply the vision of wholeness influenced his service to pedagogy in theological education:

> A theological conviction undergirding all my work in theological education is that God wills wholeness, shalom for all of creation . . . This means that spiritual, relational, aesthetic and material-economic needs matter; and we who have caught a vision of God's future, a future of shalom for all, are called to live into that shalom. I am often renewed in this vision, as I labor in theological education. Hope begets hope as we catch visions of human beings fully alive – the glory of God.[9]

This wholeness is vital in theology, as we understand God and his purpose for the restoration of all creation. And the foremost call on theological institutions is to realize that they exist in and for the will of God and not for technical and temporary human accomplishments.

Attempts to analyze and integrate theological education are as old as theological education itself. Each center of learning in history, consciously or otherwise, tended to emphasize certain formational aspects over the others. The image of the minister has kept changing. In principle, theological education as a learning experience presupposes a holistic and transformative goal in

---

9. James M. Brandt, "Student Formation through Experiential and Transformative Learning: Pedagogical Insights from/for Contextual Education," in *Proleptic Pedagogy: Theological Education Anticipating the Future*, edited by Sondra Higgins Matthaei and Nancy R. Howell (Eugene, OR: Cascade Books, 2014), 67.

equipping persons to be rooted in their faith in God, passion for the Word of God, commitment in service to the church and vision formation for God's mission in the world. The travail of current theological education is attributed to multiple dimensions whereby genuine integration is missing between theology and experience, or theory and practice. Nonetheless, we often forget that Jesus's model paints the best picture for a training environment in which every formational component is held in balance. Everything Jesus did with his disciples had a holistic formational vision, although it was too deep for them to understand at the time (see Figure 1). About the holistic and communal training approach of Jesus, Banks says, "This took place partly through verbal instruction such as in the Sermon on the Mount and the parables, partly through such actions as healing miracles and exorcisms, exercising forgiveness, as well as undergoing persecution, and partly through their eating, drinking, and praying together."[10]

Figure 1: Jesus's Model of Holistic Formation

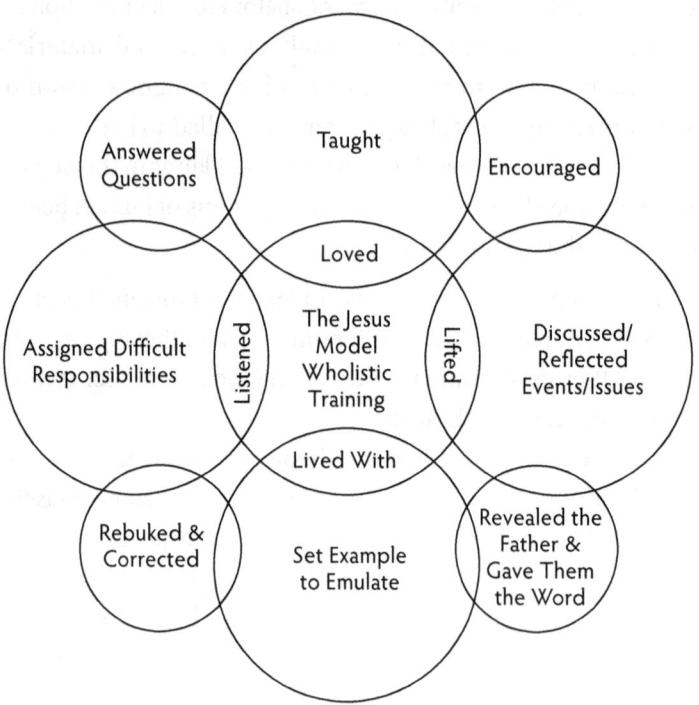

---

10. Robert Banks, *Re-envisioning Theological Education: Exploring a Missional Alternative to Current Models* (Grand Rapids, MI: Eerdmans, 1999), 110.

From Fragments to Wholeness

Identification of the disconnections is a global and continuing endeavor.

1. Friedrich Schleiermacher (1768–1834) is considered as the key contributor to the categorization of theological studies in the modern academy. He attempted to justify theological education in the modern German universities in terms of the professional educational needs of German Protestant clergy. Schleiermacher's vision for theological education as a preparation for a professional Christian vocation and as an academic discipline in the university contributed to the neglect of personal and spiritual formation in training.
2. Edward Farley attempted to center theological education in a broader theological habitus or sapiential knowledge of God that went beyond the "clerical paradigm." He explained[11] the danger of "theological study moving from an initial grounding in *theologia* – sapiential knowledge, understanding rooted in faith in God – to its dispersal into independent disciplines pertinent to ministerial practice, the clerical paradigm." Farley argued against the specialization of disciplines, the technical transformation of knowledge into strategic "know-how" techniques, and the clericalization of theological education. He called for theological education to be reformed around a recovery of *theologia* as a reflective wisdom of faith.
3. David Kelsey's book *Understanding God Truly*[12] attempted to deal with the concreteness of all the diverse forms of theological education by finding a unity based on the ideal of the common goal of understanding God more truly. He discussed the Athens Model (*paideia* – the cultivation of the soul) and the Berlin Model (*Wissenschaft* that focused on disciplined critical research and professional clerical education), exploring the integral theological core of theological education as knowing God more truly.

---

11. Edward Farley, *Theologia: The Fragmentation and Unity of Theological Education* (Philadelphia, PA: Fortress, 1983).
12. David H. Kelsey, *To Understand God Truly: What's Theological about a Theology School?* (Louisville, KY: Westminster John Knox, 1992).

4. Hough and Cobb[13] argued that it is precisely the task of the seminaries and schools of divinity to provide theological education, if not solely for ordained ministry, at least for those preparing for the "leadership of the church," which definitely would include preparation for ordained ministry. Hough and Cobb wanted to replace the image of the minister or Christian leader with the image of the minister as Practical Christian Thinker or Practical Theologian.

5. Max Stackhouse in *Apologia*[14] observed, "It is likely that the modern theological education has to discern those things that are merely contextual in the narrow, limited and parochial sense, and those things that are translocal, perennial and transcultural in a new way, so that the latter can be properly transposed into new places and times." According to him, theology is undermined in all arenas, not only in academia, but in the life of the church and society.

All these theologian-scholars identified crises in issues around the absence of "theology" in theological education, deficiency in the organization of the curriculum, the lack of Christian identity, and/or the confusion of theory and praxis.[15] In sincere attempts to resolve the discontent in the way theological education is conceptualized and practiced, many ended up in further compartmentalizing rather than synthesizing the system. The African, Asian and other contexts too have made invaluable contributions to the theme of vital wholeness in theological education.

The field of practical theology made crucial interventions into the issue of fragmentation within theological education. For example, Kathleen Cahalan gives an account of the key contributions and seminars on the theme. Seminars by the Association of Seminary Professors in the Practical Field in the USA were held from 1950 to 1984 (records not preserved), and by 1984, the organization became the Association of Practical Theology. "Over the thirty years, scholars framed the question of integration in two ways: First, as an

---

13. Joseph C. Hough Jr. and John B. Cobb's publication in 1985 titled *Christian Identity and Theological Education* (Atlanta, GA: Scholars) provoked heated discussions on the nature and purpose of theological education.

14. Max L. Stackhouse, *Apologia: Contextualization, Globalization and Mission in Theological Education* (Grand Rapids, MI: Eerdmans, 1988), 10.

15. Rebecca S. Chopp, *Saving Work: Feminist Practices of Theological Education* (Louisville, KY: Westminster John Knox, 1995), 9.

issue within professional education, understood as integrating knowledge and skill, second, as the relationship between theory and practice, or between the classical theological disciplines and the emerging practical fields."[16]

John Paver addressed the continuing problem for theological education in achieving a genuine integration between theory and practice, theology and experience. He explains the term *wholeness* and makes recommendations for structural integration within theological institutions. For him,

> Integration is related to wholeness and comes from the base word, "whole," meaning completeness, not divided up; containing all its elements or parts; that which is not broken, damaged or injured; in sound health. *Wholeness* describes the state of one's being, the quality of a person's life. By integrating or bringing together all the parts one becomes whole. In this context; "*Wholeness*" defines the state of the student and the goal for *theological* education that would have all the parts of the student's life come together within a whole, healthy person.[17]

The holistic formation of the learner presupposes a holistic training philosophy and design. This triggers the question of how we define *theological education*.

Assumptions That Immobilize an Effective Practice of Theological Education

Many assumptions gradually took root and adversely affected the practice of theological education. The long list below shows certain assumptions that immobilize the transformative practice of theological education. They include several facets in training, such as the educational philosophy, mission, faculty, students, spirituality and governance.

- Theological education is like any professional program that focuses on knowledge development.

---

16. Kathleen A. Cahalan, in *The Wiley Blackwell Companion to Practical Theology*, edited by Bonnie J. Miller-McLemore (Chichester: Blackwell, 2012), 387.

17. John E. Paver, *Theological Reflection and Education for Ministry: The Search for Integration in Theology, in Explorations in Practical, Pastoral and Empirical Theology* (Aldershot: Ashgate, 2006), 13.

- As an academic body that generates, shapes, expands and shares knowledge, the theology school can stand on its own, independent of the church.
- Theological education takes place entirely through lectures in the classrooms and literature in the library.
- Outstanding academic profiles guarantee an effective faculty team.
- All faculty members naturally get aligned with the doctrinal position and represent the vision of the school.
- Schools with their heavy academic load cannot afford spiritual and ministerial mentoring; that is the duty of churches and missions.
- Students join theology schools with a clear purpose and foundational knowledge of ministry.
- Students join the institution with the same level of faith formation and intellectual orientation.
- Students do their best when they are pushed to stressful schedules of reading and writing.
- Chapel is not as important as the classroom.
- Devotions, Holy Communion, prayer and fasting are not very conducive to a highly academic environment.
- There is no space for spiritual and personal mentoring in a rigorous university-accredited curriculum.
- Governance is all about functional administration; it has nothing to do with the formation of the school community.
- All that the dean does is deal with the institution's schedules, disciplinary issues and a few hours of teaching.
- A rigorous secular administrative pattern will ensure a better function of a theology school.

Scores of such damaging assumptions pervade the system through unexamined pathways. These make our institutions fall prey to mediocrity and functional failure. They lose purpose and divert from the goal and mission. This is creating the biggest hurdle in our path of development.

Figure 2: A Candid Perception of Theological Education

Facilitating Wholeness in Theological Education

The historical commitments of theological education, described by Larry McKinney as the "embedded immutables to be perpetuated in evangelical theological institutions," are as follows:

1. Commitment to Biblical Training: A thorough knowledge of the Bible has always been central to our institutions' educational goals. Serious devotion to the Word of God as the authority for all of life, both in respect to how we think, and how we live, has always been a hallmark.
2. Commitment to the Great Commission: The spread of the Gospel has been a primary desired outcome for our educational programs. A desire to produce world changers and infect students with a passion to win the world for Christ has been paramount.
3. Commitment to Holy Living: Issues of character, lifestyle, integrity, and godliness have always been important. There is a concern about belief and behavior, right thinking and right living.

14 Towards Vital Wholeness in Theological Education

4. **Commitment to Ministry Formation:** This has been the *raison d'être* of evangelical colleges and seminaries to equip students for meaningful church-related ministries. Most, if not all, of the characteristics of the institutions associated with ICETE could be summed up with the word "training."[18]

Figure 3: A Complex Portrayal of Theological Education

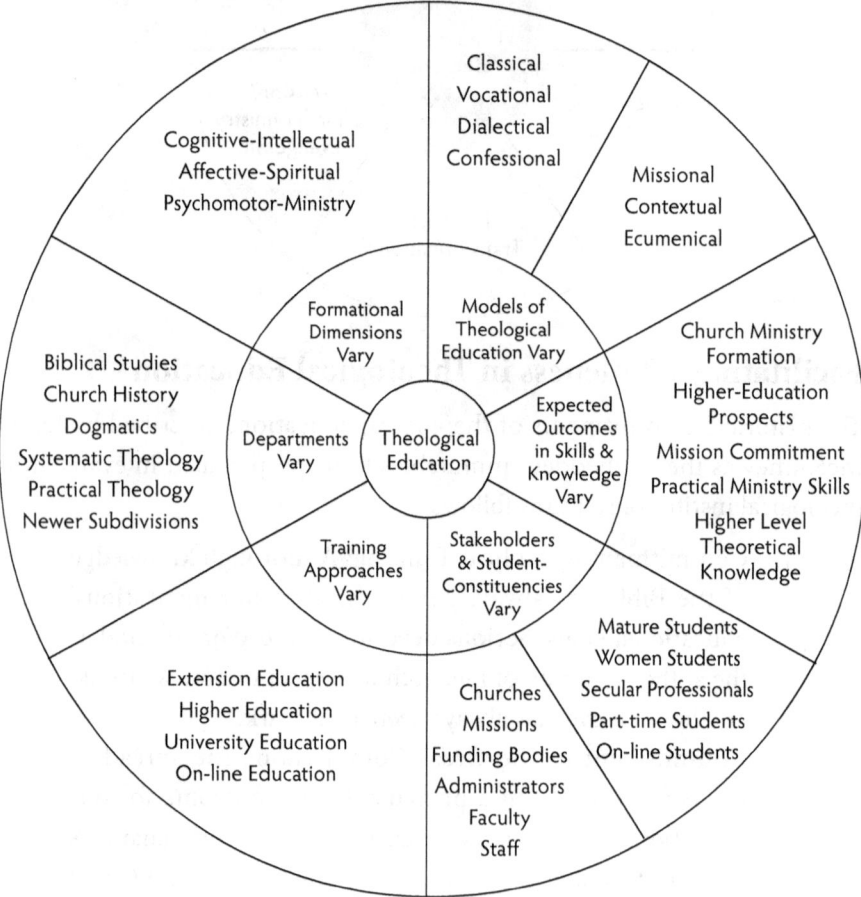

A group of theology students in India were asked to formulate an honest and comprehensive definition of theological education. Among the wide

---

18. Larry J. McKinney, "Evangelical Theological Education: Implementing Our Own Agenda," paper presented at the ICETE International Consultation for Theological Educators, High Wycombe, UK, 20 August 2003, 2. http://www.icete-edu.org/pdf/0%2003%20McKinney%20Our%20Own%20Agenda.pdf; accessed 19 April 2016.

variety of answers given, one undergraduate's comprehensive response was: "Theological education refers to the systematic learning of God's Word and the training that deepens faith in God and intimacy with him, as the result of which a person is being built in spiritual formation, character vitality, scholarship and service to those inside and outside the church." Figure 2 portrays this. A more intricate depiction of the multiple components of theological education is given in Figure 3.

Figure 4: Distinct Persons in the Making in Theological Education

An objective analysis of the make-up of the student community raises a number of issues around the *wholeness* prospect. When the student community represents diversified ministry aims and learning preferences, how can a theology school design a holistic formational pattern in training?

A bird's-eye view of theology schools points us to multiple dimensions that need nurturing towards wholeness. Figure 5 displays four main domains that need to be brought to a functional whole.

Infrastructure, student enrollment and faculty status are crucially important. But the greatness of a theological institution lies in the holistic transformational impact of training and tangible results in the mission of the church. The principal or president, being the chief visionary, is to visualize the large picture for the school. Many a time our schools suffer a critical lack of direction as the leader is away in another country for extended periods, or the leader chooses to focus only on the financial and administrative matters while being indifferent to the espoused mission of the school. When the leadership fails to recognize the significance of guiding the school to its intended purpose, the detour becomes increasingly evident year after year. A first substantial sign of a school's downfall is the absence of strategic personnel in governance/administration to critically analyze the impact of the ministry itself. But when there is a deep-felt realization of the need for a constructive change and the leadership allows this to happen in secure structural settings, the system begins to experience life within. These changes are to take place in the most natural setting rather than as a result of heavy prescriptions and programming. Still, only a team of innovators and strategists to follow-up this path of renewal and reform can help the school realize a sustainable transformational effect. Below are a self-evaluation questionnaire and a few recommendations for action.

Figure 5: Multiple Aspects of Balance to Facilitate Wholeness in Theological Education[19]

PERCEPTIONAL/GOAL-DIRECTED WHOLENESS	ACADEMIC WHOLENESS
• Goal-Training Design Balance • Academic Objectives–Mission Statement Balance • Governance Structure–Goal Balance • Need in Church and Society–Programs Balance • Curriculum–Stated-Objectives Balance	• Theory–Practice Blend • Theology–Experience Blend • Classroom–Field Blend • Philosophy–Practice Blend • Text–Context Blend

---

19. Some aspects of this chart may seem to overlap, but they are included to emphasize balance.

STRUCTURAL WHOLENESS	PERSONAL/DOCTRINAL WHOLENESS
• Church–Seminary Relation • Seminary–University Relation • Governing Body–Faculty Relation • Faculty–Students Relation • Expectations–Infrastructure Relation	• Intellectual–Spiritual Integration • Rational–Emotional Integration • Cultural–Biblical Integration • Extreme–Conservative Integration • Liberationist–Evangelical Integration

A School's Self-Assessment Guide on Wholeness in Theological Education

- What is the main purpose of the school's existence? To what end are students trained?
- What has the school actually achieved over the years of its existence as a theological institution?
- How well does every member of your community know the core purpose of the school?
- Does the *mission statement* of the school fit well with the *program and procedures*?
- What is not going well at the school? What are the main functional gaps identified?
- Is there a clash between the purpose of the school and the pressure from governing boards or academic bodies?
- How often do the leadership, academic administration and the faculty get together to review the goal, function and future direction of the school?
- Who gives the theological and ministerial leadership to the school and takes initiatives in periodical quality assessment?
- Against the backdrop of the changing cultural and socio-political scene in society, what perceptible changes during the past three–four years have been made in the way theological education is offered?
- As far as *wholeness* is concerned, where is the school particularly vulnerable – spiritual formation, academic theological core, ministry formation, character formation, community, mentoring or modeling in mission, or anything else?

Practical Recommendations: Wholeness in Theological Education

- Seek God's wisdom as individuals and as an academic team, that the school would perfectly align with God's vision for wholeness in serving the church.
- Identify a core team that has genuine concern for the holistic development of the school, and explore ways and means for collaborative learning in this matter.
- Organize informal talks with the executive board, administrative personnel and faculty, rethinking the key dimensions for the self-assessment of the school.
- Plan progressive learning procedures for the faculty to create interest and awareness of the centrality of theological education in the church's mission and the need to tackle the breakups along the way.
- Arrange for open talks on the most challenging areas of imbalance at the school without appearing to be a drastic change-agent. Facilitate thinking within the community and stand by them as deliberations on the need for reformation take place.
- The leader of the school (principal/president) should initiate recurrent communication of the goal and mission of the school with the community.
- Listen intentionally to the hopes, anticipations and goals of students.
- Orient the faculty and staff towards the mission and vision statement every year and together discuss concrete ways to get it saturated into everyday learning and teaching.
- Explore and implement new patterns and procedures to assist the school to achieve the goal more effectively each year.
- Prepare an assessment process of the outcome and impact of training at the school and use it as a guidepost for further development.

1

Wholeness in the Goal, Mission and Training Philosophy

Varied Notions of Theological Training

> What else is the goal of theological education than to bring us closer to the Lord our God so that we may be more faithful to the great commandment to love Him with all our heart, with all our soul, and with all our mind, and neighbor as ourselves (Matt. 22:37). Seminaries and divinity schools must lead theology students into an ever-growing communion with God, with each other, and with their fellow human beings. Theological education is meant to form our whole person toward an increasing conformity with the mind of Christ so that our way of praying and our way of believing will be one.

These words of profound wisdom are from Henri Nouwen.[1] Here we ask the following pertinent questions: Why theological education? What does it accomplish? Does it fulfill what it is supposed to fulfill? Ebeling pointed to the current predicament by saying, "The study of theology is beset by a crisis in orientation. Because our access to the unity and totality that constitutes the subject matter of theology is disrupted, the main domain of its subject matter and task has broken apart and crumbled into a bewildering conglomeration

---

1. Henri J. M. Nouwen, *The Way of the Heart* (New York: Ballentine, 1989), 39.

of individual items."² Apparently, when the goal stops being the goal, then the multiple individual subsidiary items try to occupy its place.

Those who are keen about the unity of theological education will encounter the multiple models and philosophies that have given distinct flavors to the enterprise. David Kelsey argued that there are two normative types of theological education, which he referred to as the Athens Model (education that transforms the individual) and the Berlin Model (education that prepares competent professionals for the ministry of the church). Robert Banks added to this polar model another type, namely the Jerusalem Model (a community-based education that trains missioners for the world); Brian Edgar added the fourth one, named the Geneva Model (seminary education which is exclusively confessional); Darren Cronshaw added the New Delhi Model (education that engages other spirituality worldviews); and we also have the Auburn Model (education that is contextual and local), and many more. The pertinent questions are: Are schools thinking through these frames or concepts? What difference would it make if training was assessed through these visions and philosophies? Figures 6 and 7 show some of these notions and their emphases.

> "We proclaim him, admonishing and teaching everyone with all wisdom, so that we may present everyone perfect in Christ."
> Colossians 1:28

Figure 6: Edgar Portrayal of Models of Theological Education³ (2005)

CLASSICAL	Transforming the individual	Knowing God	CONFESSIONAL
	ATHENS Academy	**GENEVA** Seminary	
	THEOLOGIA	DOXOLOGY	
	MISSIOLOGY	SCIENTIA	
	JERUSALEM Community	**BERLIN** University	
MISSIONAL	Converting the world	Strenghening the church	VOCATIONAL

---

2. Gerhard Ebeling, quoted in Bernhard Ott, *Beyond Fragmentation: Integrating Mission and Theological Education* (Oxford: Regnum, 2001), 235.

3. Edgar portrayal of models of theological education. Reproduced from Brian Edgar, "The Theology of Theological Education," *Evangelical Review of Theology* 29, no. 3 (2005): 213.

Figure 7: Cronshaw Diagram of Theological Education and Missional Spirituality[4]

Training models always held distinct focuses in philosophy and practice, as the following section shows. This list is not exhaustive continentally or regionally. The names given represent only a few key contributors whose names appear frequently in the literature on these models.

- *Classical:* Farley,[5] Cannon et. al.[6] and the Neuhaus symposium 1992.[7] Theological education for the whole church; formation

---

4. Reproduced from Darren Cronshaw, "Reenvisioning Theological Education and Missional Spirituality," *Journal of Adult Theological Education* 9, no. 1 (2012): 13.

5. Edward Farley, *Theologia: The Fragmentation and Unity of Theological Education* (Philadelphia, PA: Fortress, 1983); *The Fragility of Knowledge: Theological Education in the Church and University* (Philadelphia, PA: Fortress, 1988).

6. Mud Flower Collective, Katie Geneva Cannon and Carter Heyward (eds.), *God's Fierce Whimsy: Christian Feminism and Theological Education* (New York: Pilgrim, 1985).

7. The Neuhaus Conference 1992 identified moral and spiritual formation as priorities in theological education. Cited by Willem Petrus Wahl in "Towards Relevant Theological Education in Africa: Comparing the International Discourse with Contextual Challenges," *Acta Theologica* 33, no. 1 (2013): 266–293. See also http://www.scielo.org.za/pdf/at/v33n1/14.pdf; accessed 23

towards acquiring a certain disposition, i.e. a habit of correct thinking patterns that interpret the whole of life in a theological way.
- *Confessional:* George P. Schner[8] and Richard A. Muller.[9] Also known as neo-traditional; clergy/the ordained gain theological information and hence cognitive knowledge of the doctrinal and ethical content of the Christian revelation.
- *Vocational:* Joseph Hough and John Cobb[10] and the apologetic circle of Stackhouse.[11] This model is also known as *Professional*. Theological interpretation by which skill is acquired; cognitive discernment and reflective and practical goal.
- *Dialectical:* Charles Wood,[12] David Kelsey[13] and Rebecca Chopp.[14] Synthesis between the Classical and Vocational philosophies towards an overarching vision or practice; practical insights surpassing the cognitive understanding.
- *Missional:* Robert Banks.[15] Whole church in mission; partnering reflection and spirituality in concrete ministry.
- *Blended:* Combination of models to assist the rounded purposes of the school.
- *Formational:* Cheesman (Trinitarian), Lindbeck, David Tracy. Spiritual and personal formation is key in theological education; training as discipleship and mentoring (Hall, Cheesman).

March 2017.

8. George P. Schner, "Formation as the Unifying Concept of Theological Education," *Theological Education* 22, no. 2: 94–113. Also George P. Schner (ed.), *The Church Renewed: The Documents of Vatican II Reconsidered* (Lanham, MD: University Press of America, 1986).

9. Richard Muller, *The Study of Theology*, Vol. 7 (Grand Rapids, MI: Zondervan, 1991).

10. Joseph C. Hough, Jr. and John B. Cobb, *Christian Identity and Theological Education* (Atlanta, GA: Scholars, 1985).

11. Max L. Stackhouse, *Apologia: Contextualization, Globalization and Mission in Theological Education* (Grand Rapids, MI: Eerdmans, 1988).

12. Charles M. Wood, *Vision and Discernment: An Orientation in Theological Study* (Atlanta, GA: Scholars, 1985).

13. David H. Kelsey, *Between Athens and Berlin: The Theological Education Debate* (Grand Rapids, MI: Eerdmans, 1993).

14. Rebecca S. Chopp, *Saving Work: Feminist Practices of Theological Education* (Louisville, KY: Westminster John Knox, 1995).

15. Robert Banks, *Re-envisioning Theological Education: Exploring a Missional Alternative to Current Models* (Grand Rapids, MI: Eerdmans, 1999).

Wholeness in the Goal, Mission and Training Philosophy   23

- *Contextual:* Barbara Wheeler and the Auburn Center for the Study of Theological Education.[16] Theological education reflecting and responding to contextual realities.
- *Church-focused:* Linda Cannell.[17] Theology school as an instrument to serve the church.
- *Distance and online:* Theological education by extension. ETE (WCC), TEE, DTE. Learning without detaching from the real-life context of the student. Learning theology online, using technological advancement; students learn in their own time and in their preferred modes.
- *Practical wisdom:* Robert Ferris,[18] Harvie Conn[19] and Gordon Smith.[20] Theological wisdom as the unified principle and goal in theological education; a wisdom that transforms a person into maturity in both understanding and behavior.
- *Discipleship:* Sylvia Wilkey Collinson.[21] Making disciples is the prime directive of Jesus Christ and has to be dominant in contemporary methods of teaching.

Knowing the Goal of the Theological Institution

Knowing the goal[22] of the institution is primary in assessments and reforms. The goal informs and shapes the curricular process and design so that assessment of the multiple layers of training can be done effectively. The ConneXions Model

---

16. Barbara G. Wheeler and Mark N. Wilhelm, *Tending Talents: The Cultivation of Effective and Productive Theological School Faculties* (New York: Auburn Theological Seminary, 1997): reports from a study of theology school faculty by Wheeler, President of the Auburn Seminary. See also Jackson W. Carroll, Barbara G. Wheeler, Daniel O. Aleshire and Penny Long Marler, *Being There: Culture and Formation in Two Theological Schools* (Oxford: Oxford University Press, 1997).
17. Linda Cannell, *Theological Education Matters: Leadership Education for the Church* (Newburgh, IN: EDCOT, 2006).
18. Robert W. Ferris, *Renewal in Theological Education: Strategies for Change* (Wheaton, IL: Wheaton College, 1990).
19. Harvie M. Conn, *Evangelism: Doing Justice and Preaching Grace* (Grand Rapids, MI: Zondervan, 1982).
20. Gordon T. Smith, "Academic Administration as an Inner Journey," *Theological Education* 33 (Autum 1996): 61–70.
21. Sylvia Wilkey Collinson, *Making Disciples* (Milton Keynes: Paternoster, 2004).
22. This chapter uses the terms *goal* and *mission* fairly synonymously.

of Leadership Development[23] uses this vision in facilitating transformative learning praxis, as shown in Figure 8.

Figure 8: ConneXions Model Leader-Development Structure

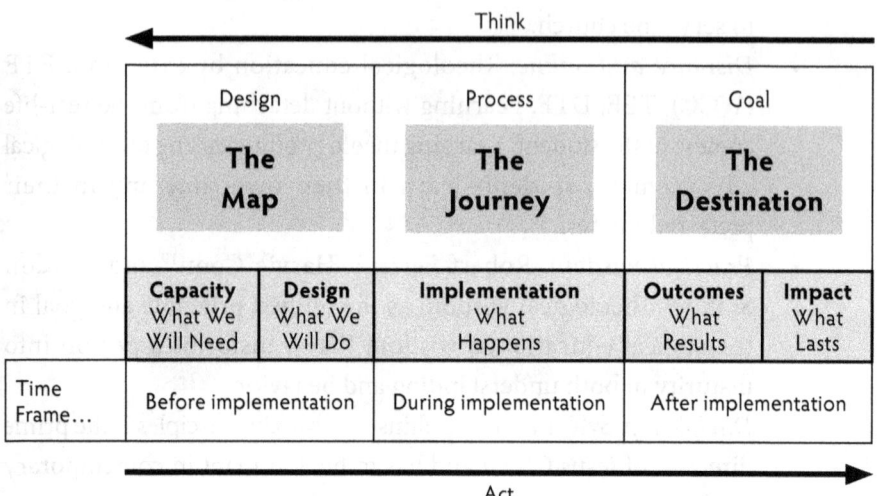

As Leroy Ford portrays in Figure 9,[24] the task of curriculum design also starts from the goal or the purpose and proceeds from there.

Figure 9: Ford's Curriculum Design Process

The challenge for many institutions is in defining the goal clearly. It is often said, "We are operating not on one goal, but on many." Sometimes the overall goal of theological education and the goal of the school may be in conflict; or these may not be aligning with the goals of the programs or courses. On other occasions there can be too many goals within the school, making the direction unclear to the constituencies (see Figure 10).

---

23. Malcolm Webber, *Building Healthy Leaders: Spirit-Built Leadership Series, 4: Transforming the Way Leaders Are Built* (Elkhart, IN: Strategic, 2011), 14. Diagram used with permission.

24. For the full version of the diagram, see Leroy Ford, *A Curriculum Design Manual for Theological Education: A Learning Outcomes Focus* (Nashville: Broadman, 1991), 84.

Figure 10: *Goal or Goals?*

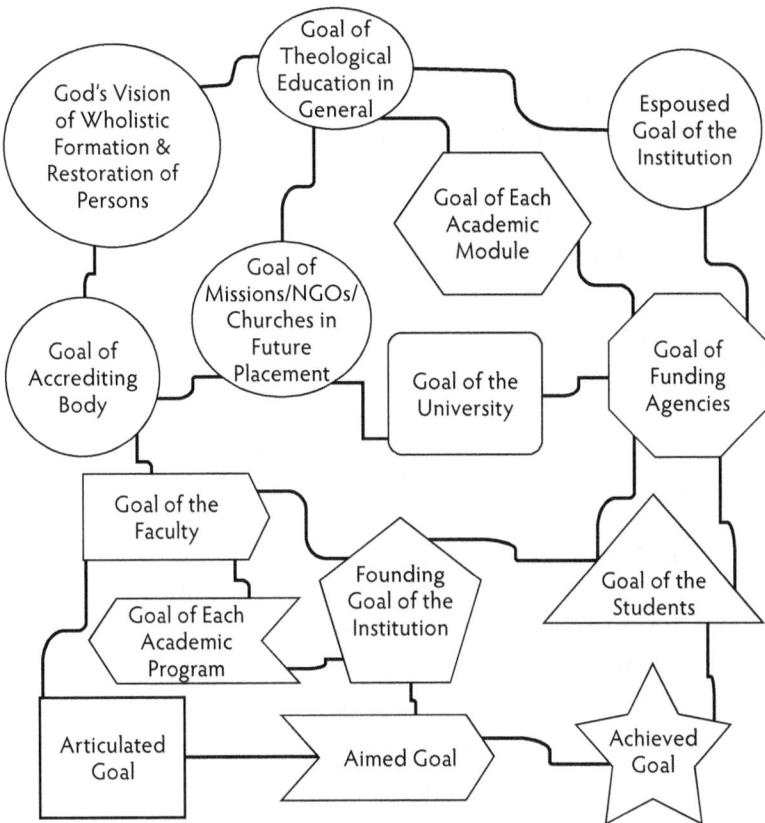

The School's Mission as Serving and Strengthening the Church

Do all theology schools see *church* as their central goal? The answer is probably "No." Empirical studies show that many schools would not see it that way. It is not rare to hear principals/presidents say with seemingly firm conviction, "We are the intellectual centers. The church can surely depend on us for what it needs. Otherwise, we have our own existential purpose as an intellectual base for theology in professional academia." However, efforts to uncover these "existential purposes" are not successful apart from the vague claims made about the schools' contributions to academia. Most practitioners wrestle with the catastrophe that theological education is delivered with no specific goal to identify with or feed into. Jesus affirmed his mission thus: "I will build my church; the gates of hell shall not prevail against it." And anything we call *ministry* or *mission* is about the gospel of salvation and redemption, and hence the building up of the church in the world God wants to be saved. This goal has to determine everything else we do in theology schools, be it exploring theological wisdom, engaging in mission or empowering ministry skills. The goal of serving the church and strengthening its mission helps a theology school in many ways:

- It sets the right direction theologically and educationally;
- It raises specificity, realism and relevance within the educational endeavor;
- It enables a tangible assessment of the outcome and impact.

In the philosophy of theological education, impact assessment always has *church* at the core. The ICETE "Manifesto on the Renewal of Evangelical Theological Education" emphasized the "churchward orientation"[25] of the schools:

> Our programmes of theological education must orient themselves pervasively in terms of the Christian community being served. We are at fault when our programmes operate merely in terms of some traditional or personal notion of theological education. At every level of design and operation our programmes must be visibly determined by a close attentiveness to the needs and expectations of the Christian community we serve. To this end we must establish multiple modes of ongoing interaction between programme and church, both at official and at grassroots levels, and regularly adjust and develop the programme in the light of these contacts. Our theological programmes must become manifestly of the church, through the church and for the church. This we must accomplish, by God's grace.

The Overseas Council "Values and Standards" document opens with the statement: "We believe that theological schools exist to strengthen the Church," and it adds specific *values* to determine how the schools uphold this vision. The values are:

---

25. "ICETE Manifesto on the Renewal of Evangelical Theological Education," 2nd ed., 1990. http://www.icete-edu.org/manifesto/; accessed 8 April 2016. Also see "Manifesto on the Renewal of Evangelical Theological Education," in *Renewal in Theological Education: Strategies for Change*, by Robert Ferris (Wheaton, IL: Wheaton College, 1990).

Wholeness in the Goal, Mission and Training Philosophy 27

- Commitment to biblical, historical, orthodox Christianity;
- Training of leaders who strengthen the church in all of its ministries and functions;
- Fostering of mutually beneficial partnerships with churches, church bodies and Christian professionals through continuing dynamic dialogue;
- National or regional ownership, both legal and psychological.

The Asia Theological Association (ATA India) document "Values Esteemed by ATA Educators"[26] unequivocally establishes "Church Orientation" as the first of its "Relational values": "Our institutions must orient themselves in terms of the Christian community being served. Our theological education must serve the church." The "Theological and Missional Value" consists of the affirmation that "All ministerial training ought to be oriented towards fulfilling the mission mandate of the Church." Likewise, examples of value documents from theology schools can inform our thinking considerably. For instance, the mission and goal of Asbury Theological Seminary has been laid out in a Strategic Map that lists the Ten Core Values of the school with value descriptions to guide assessment.[27] Appendix 2 provides an overview of the document.

How far theology schools actualize their focus on the church is an ongoing inquiry. Often it appears to be an add-on. It takes diverse forms. There are cases of schools that exist completely for the church and its ministry. In other situations it may be about managing to include the term *church* in the value documents, connecting a church with the practical ministry department for occasional student internships, or inviting the ministers of a church to teach or preach at the theology school. The definition of reciprocity varies greatly from school to school. The structure of theology schools as denominational, nondenominational or interdenominational determines their commitment to the church to a large extent. However, value indicators are essential to decide on the outcome and impact of the commitment between both institutions. If the school exists for the church, its entire mission will serve and strengthen the church. In a school that sets church as its core goal and mission, the student

---

26. Asia Theological Association, "Values Esteemed by ATA Educators," revised May 2006, http://www.ataindia.org/uploaded_files/uploads/documents_32.pdf.

27. For the full version of Asbury Theological Seminary "2023 Strategic Map," go to http://asburyseminary.edu/wp-content/uploads/2023StrategicMap011012.pdf.

is trained to represent grounded theological wisdom in the church, personify active discipleship in the church, exemplify mission involvement with the church and epitomize leadership advancement for the church. This sort of definition does not eliminate the wide variety of commitments in formal academia, the marketplace or the corporate world, but rather upholds them.

> "An institution which does not have a statement of educational goals and objectives for learners is like a ship without a rudder. It may have a lot of 'sail' but no sense of direction." Leroy Ford, *A Curriculum Design Manual for Theological Education: A Learning Outcomes Focus* (Nashville, TN: Broadman, 1991), 97.

The Inevitable Crisis: Defining, Establishing and Pursuing the Goal and Mission

Is it possible for a theology school to be unable to define its goal? Might it be the case that a school does something very different from its stated goal? Possibly, yes. When the goal is not defined, established and tracked, inevitable divides follow, because it is the goal that spells out the process of education and the relevant design that appropriates it. Obviously, in many contexts *church* is no longer the central unifying factor of theology schools. A school can function purely as an intellectual center where theology is just another academic subject. It can also function like a parachurch agency that does different types of ministry of its own. Schools need to grapple with the continuing challenge of defining their mission and goal. The following are pertinent issues:

Not Knowing the Goal of the School

Theology schools may have their distinct goals on the formal documents. Two schools may not have exactly the same goal statements, which is fine. But each school is expected to define its goal and mission clearly and pursue it authentically. Not knowing the goal entails a high level of risk in the life of the institution. Having functioned for years in the same routines of training, many schools experience mediocrity creeping in, making members in the community unaware of and unconcerned about their founding goals. Key questions are: Has the goal been stated with clarity so that the school can cling to it for focused direction? How many in the school community know reasonably well the specific goal the institution is striving towards? How many members in the community are able to articulate the goal of the institution? How would the leadership know if the school is achieving the espoused goal?

Duplicating Programs and Curricula from Elsewhere

The goal informs our process. With no goal to pursue, the learning process grows vague and the community lacks direction. An institution can only duplicate from others if good thinking is not given to the goal and design of the training. When a school shrinks its mission to pointlessly copying what other schools do, it mislays purpose and impact. Key questions to ask are: Why are we existing? Do we function for the sake of functioning? What is the relevance of this school at this time in this society? What are we doing here differently from other schools?

Lack of Clarity about Setting the Goal for the School

Schools encounter several layers of *goals* in training:
- Goal of theological education as understood by the leaders, faculty and students
- Goal of the school
- Goal of the church
- Personal goal of the student
- Goal of each academic program
- Goal of each course/module
- Goal of the sending agencies

My own qualitative survey in 2016 in India showed that there is much ambiguity in elucidating the goal of theological education in general and of the institution in particular. Many schools are found seeking authentic help in defining or refining their goal statements. Michael Jinkins made this emphatic comment on mission statements: "The process of developing mission statements is widely recognized as helping schools to clarify their purpose and goals so they can plan for the future. The mission statements themselves can also provide an indispensable focus of a school's purpose that can help its leadership avoid 'mission creep.'"[28] Apart from the governing bodies, the office

---

28. Michael Jinkins, "Mission Possible: Making Use of the School's Mission Statement in Curriculum Review," *Theological Education* 43, no. 1 (2007): 17.

of the academic dean holds a vital practical role in providing clarity in this matter. Deans are to constantly evaluate the relationship between the mission statement and the curriculum of the school and strengthen the strategic bond between the goal and the impact.

Lack of Competent Personnel to Scrutinize the Structural Concerns of the Educational Environment

Not many are competent to process strategic thinking on the vision of the school and to make objective judgments of its procedural limitations or strengths. Most leaders could speak, at least vaguely, of the founding goals of their institutions; but very few could explain how each of their academic programs is geared conspicuously to achieve that goal. In other words, the contents and teaching-learning methodologies of the academic programs should be pointing towards the distinct goal of the institution. If a goal is unique, it has to be enhanced with unique procedures and designs. Theological communities have to seriously rethink their goals to see if the process is suitable for the goal. The more clearly the goal is stated and communicated, the more vibrantly the community will capture the outcome and impact. The end result may not be tangible otherwise.

Lack of Confidence in Precisely Stating the Mission of the School

Consider the genuine purposes that can be further shaped into a theological institution's goal statement. Do we struggle to specify our training philosophy? For the sake of clarity, some prefer to portray the school as a *community* or *center*, serving a unique purpose. How would we define the core identity of the school from this list?

- Center for discipleship
- Center for denominational ministry formation
- Center for evangelism
- Center for church planting
- Center for mission
- Center for practical theology
- Center for theological higher education
- Center for advanced theological wisdom

- Center for the university
- Center for church administration
- Several of the above, or something else?

Lack of Reciprocity with the Church

In the present climate where many theology schools are turning into mere intellectual centers or degree-granting bases, we keep asking ourselves about the theological purpose of our existence. A growing detachment of seminaries from the church raises concerns on the ultimate theological bearings of our institutions. It is increasingly evident that faculty recruitments are based more and more on higher degrees and less and less on theological standpoints and ministerial impact. The same might be true for student admissions. Theological convictions or ministry commitment are sidelined, while degree-based qualifications and financial stability matter the most. The graduate profile often gives little indication about what the student is capable of rendering to the mission of the church.

How do we define the purpose of theology schools that function independently of the church? What is the God-ordained, biblically directed aim of a theology school? Is there a mutually relating, nourishing interaction between the church and the theology school? Is the school a detached intellectual center, where abstract knowledge is set as the highest value? If knowing God is relegated entirely to an intellectual exercise, what is the essence of Christian faith?

A School's Self-Assessment Guide on Goal, Mission and Training Philosophy

- What is the primary philosophy of the school?
- Is it biblically grounded and ecclesiastically oriented? How?
- Has the school been getting rooted in this philosophy or shifted from it over the years? Explain.
- How often do we communicate the philosophy of training with the members of the community?
- What ways and means help the school in affirming and upholding this philosophy within the school community?

- Does the vision and mission statement of the school adequately reflect the training philosophy?
- How does the accrediting agency evaluate the philosophy and purpose of the school?
- What essential considerations and values does the school uphold in faculty appointments?
- How does the school ensure that every member in the governing/administrative bodies and on the faculty aligns well with the training philosophy and purpose of the school?
- How well do the ministry placements of the alumni reflect the purpose the school served?
- Are the publications, seminars and consultations adding strength to the philosophical grounding of the school?
- What tools and methods will assist the task of assessing the outcome and impact of the vision, mission and training philosophy?

Practical Recommendations: Goal, Mission and Training Philosophy

- Do a quick verbal survey on the understanding of administrative leaders, faculty and students on the training philosophy of the school.
- Organize a leadership/faculty seminar exclusively for the school and study the stated goal, vision and mission statement of the school as recorded in documents since the start of the institution.
- Organize exclusive times for prayer and devotions for the members in administration and on faculty to focus on the calling of the school.
- Initiate an open forum to discuss how far the school affirms the vision, mission and philosophy in day-to-day functioning, in theory and practice.
- In separate teams of governance, academic administration and faculty, initiate indepth discussions about what is happening and what should be happening about the mission of the school.
- Then come back to the larger group, where each team shares their observations and recommendations for wholeness.
- Make strategic plans on how to go forward with clarity in training philosophy and practice.

- Write these plans down and assign responsibilities to specific persons/groups.
- Schedule review meetings.
- Assess outcomes and impact.

2

Wholeness in Theological Curriculum

The Curriculum

When we want high-value outcomes in training, we design our curriculum accordingly. Ted Ward defines *curriculum* as "the planned, charted-out and workable path toward worthy and reachable learning objectives."[1] The word *curriculum* began as a Latin word that meant "a race" or "the course of a race," which in turn derived from the verb *currere*, meaning "to run" or "to proceed." *Curriculum* refers to all that happens in the learning context – "a sum of all learning experiences resulting from a curriculum plan . . . directed toward achieving objectives."[2] With a *theological curriculum*, our task is to design and revise the entire learning plan in terms of purpose, procedures, expected outcomes and the future impact. Perry Shaw emphasizes curricular assessment as central to the integration of the multiple dimensions of learning.[3] Curriculum denotes the training in

> "All scripture is God-breathed and is useful for teaching, rebuking, correcting and training in righteousness, so that the man of God may be thoroughly equipped for every good work."
> 2 Timothy 3:16–17

---

1. Ted W. Ward, "Curriculum: The Path to High-Worth Outcomes," *Common Ground Journal* 10, no. 1 (Fall 2012): 42.
2. Howard P. Colson and Raymond M. Rigdon, *Understanding Your Church's Curriculum* (Nashville, TN: Broadman, 1981), 39.
3. Perry Shaw, *Transforming Theological Education: A Practical Handbook for Integrative Learning* (Carlisle: Langham Global Library, 2014), 51–106.

its entirety, including syllabi, social environment, relationships, expectations and challenges. Therefore, we see that the curriculum of an academic program is not the same as the course syllabus. The term *lesson plan* is also connected to this. It denotes faculty's detailed plan for daily or weekly teaching. This has to perfectly align with the program curriculum and course syllabus and, at the same time, clarify the minute details of teaching and learning that take place in each lesson or unit. Absence of a realistic lesson plan reflects poor time planning and management. It might eventually lead the faculty to a situation where they leave much of the syllabus ignored. Absence of a firm lesson plan results in confusion about the entire process of teaching-learning and the annual revision of the course design.

A significant level of thinking has gone into the formulation of a definition for *theological curriculum*. The Association of Theological Schools defines *theological curriculum* as

> the means by which teaching and learning are formally ordered to educational goals . . . In a theological school, the over-arching goal is the development of theological understanding, that is, aptitude for theological reflection and wisdom pertaining to responsible life in faith. Comprehended in this over-arching goal are others such as deepening spiritual awareness, growing in moral sensibility and character, gaining an intellectual grasp of the tradition of a faith community, and acquiring the abilities requisite to the exercise of ministry in that community. These goals, and the processes and practices leading to their attainment, are normally intimately interwoven and should not be separated from one another.[4]

This definition focuses on the development of theological understanding, from which everything else develops. It is evident that the mission and philosophy of the accrediting body or school forms the foundation of the curriculum.

Assessing the nature and effectiveness of the curriculum should be an ongoing practice in the life of the school. However, sustainable assessment is possible only when the learning environment is conducive, with quality

---

4. The Association of Theological Schools in the United States and Canada, "Standard 4: The Theological Curriculum, Statement 4.1.1," *Bulletin* 45, Part 1 (2002): 54. Quoted in Gordon T. Smith and Charles M. Wood, "Learning Goals and Assessment of Learning in Theology Schools," *Theological Education* 39, no. 1 (2003): 25.

envisioned, faculty cooperative and the purpose defined and agreed on. Curriculum assessment presupposes a comprehensive analysis, as (1) curriculum means *everything* in a learning environment; (2) assessment of curriculum is ongoing; (3) new methods and improved tools are needed to guard against lethargy and stringency; and (4) every facet of assessment may present us with a distinct call to improvement or change.

Theological Curriculum: A Hurdle

- There is much ambiguity as to what a theological curriculum is.
- The curriculum is often misunderstood as a course outline.
- Theological educators need training in educational principles (teaching-learning dynamics) for efficient curriculum design and implementation.
- Many schools have not attempted a curriculum-design seminar or curriculum assessment.
- Learning about the design and revision of the curriculum is not a priority for schools.
- Schools sometimes uncritically emphasize one aspect of the curriculum and ignore all else.
- Theological education in general lacks experts, practitioners, learning resources and funds to address the vital needs around curriculum.

Fourfold Dimensions of Curriculum

Theoretically, the scope of a learning curriculum is fourfold:[5]

- *Explicit curriculum:* The espoused vision and mission of the school, courses taught, and knowledge and skills that the school expects successful students to acquire make up the explicit curriculum.
- *Implicit/hidden curriculum:* This is the unofficial, unwritten and unintended curriculum, learning that arises from the culture

---

5. Mark K. Smith, "Curriculum Theory and Practice," *The Encyclopedia of Informal Education* (1996, 2000), www.infed.org/biblio/b-curric.htm. See also John Dewey, *The Child and the Curriculum* (Chicago: University of Chicago Press, 1902), 1–31; and A. V. Kelly, *The Curriculum: Theory and Practice*, 6th ed. (London: SAGE, 2009).

of the school and the behaviors, attitudes and expectations that characterize that culture.
- *Excluded/null curriculum:*[6] Topics, lessons or perspectives that are specifically and thoughtfully excluded from the curriculum.
- *Extra-curriculum:* This includes school-sponsored programs that are intended to supplement the academic aspect of the school experience. Community-based programs and activities such as sports, academic clubs, performing arts, social services and many others fall into this category.

Assessing the Implicit and Null Curricula

We follow conventional methods of tests and examinations to assess the explicit curriculum and leave the rest of the learning mostly undefined and imprecise. A few reasons for this are as follows:

1. Theology curricula, apart from the "explicit," vary greatly from school to school based on their distinct goals and ethos, and therefore cannot be duplicated.
2. It takes time, effort and focused teamwork to realize our own implicit/hidden and excluded curricula.
3. There might be areas in the implicit curriculum that are not viable for quantitative assessment.
4. Setting the desired outcomes, deriving specific questions from the transformational indicators, designing the procedure of evaluation, processing the results and carrying out follow-up require a substantially higher level of commitment and competency.
5. We must design the evaluation tools separately for different constituencies at the school to match their level of comprehension of the issues represented.

---

6. David J. Flinders, Nel Noddings and Stephen J. Thornton, "The Null Curriculum: Its Theoretical Basis and Practical Implications," *Curriculum Inquiry* 16, no. 1 (Spring, 1986), 33–42. Published by Blackwell Publishing on behalf of the Ontario Institute for Studies in Education/University of Toronto Stable. URL: http://www.jstor.org/stable/1179551. Accessed 10 July 2015.

The Traditional and the Holistic Curricula

The educational environment is changing dramatically around the globe. The primary focus in education is no longer on the output, but on the outcome and impact. Teachers are not the sole owners of a knowledge deposit, but lifelong learners. The focus is shifting from the teacher to the learner. The teacher facilitates the learning process and the students become active participants. The classroom is no longer the elite center of learning. The entire experience of the learner in the school nurtures growth. The affective domain in learning is gaining a central focus. Leroy Ford said, "One of the greatest weaknesses in curriculum design is the failure of designers to include the affective domain in designs and in the curriculum plans which follow."[7] We encounter newer discernments that turn our long-held educational perceptions upside-down. Figure 11 distinguishes between the degree-centered and holistic curricular models.

Figure 11: Degree-Centered Approach and Student-Oriented Holistic Process[8]

Degree-Centered Approach	Transformative Holistic Process
Passive learning	Active engagement
High dependency on teacher/technicalities	Personal responsibility and initiative
Get-it-done; certificate-oriented	A process; experience
Impersonal or individualistic	Responsive and life-in-community-focused
Irrelevant	Vital; life-giving
Curriculum	Collage of relationships and experiences
Conformity	Reality
Head/intellect	Holistic/the whole person
Temporary thinking	Permanent change
Informing	Transforming
Teaching	Learning
Us and them (adversarial attitude to teachers)	Us (togetherness and mutuality)

---

7. Leroy Ford, *A Curriculum Design Manual for Theological Education: A Learning Outcomes Focus* (Nashville, TN: Broadman, 1991), 91.
8. Malcolm Webber, *Building Healthy Leaders: Spirit-Built Leadership Series, 4: Transforming the Way Leaders Are Built* (Elkhart, IN: Strategic, 2011), 167.

Required/mandatory	Choice
Possible disintegrations (in subjects/departments)	Unity of purpose
Disengaging	Engaging and interactive
Competition	Teamwork and cooperation
Scholarship	Scholarship and relationship
Knowledge in	Knowledge in and out
Humanistic	God-centered

Contextually Designed Curriculum or Syllabus Given?

Who should define and revise the curriculum – the school, the accrediting agency or an external team of expert consultants? Who decides what to teach and how to assess learning? A ready-to-use curriculum might make the job easy for the school, enhance uniformity across the schools and do a noticeably better job than what could be accomplished by an individual faculty. Nonetheless, numerous questions arise regarding the visional direction of the school, flexibility of the given curriculum, the process of curricular revision and the subsequent checks on outcomes and impact (see Figure 12).

Figure 12: Who Prepares the Syllabus?

Syllabi Designed Elsewhere and Given to the Faculty	
Advantages	**Disadvantages**
A commonly known format is available for faculty and students	Less flexible for innovation and new directions
A centralized point of direction, standardization and control	Faculty might not own the syllabus
Control over indiscreet alterations and deletions	Develops a fixed mindset
Faculty gain confidence when they fulfill requirements	Might not have scope for *content beyond syllabus*
Student knows the exact content of the course and can be competent with anyone instructed in the same path	Might limit the responsibility of students and additional contributions of the faculty

| Even with a lethargic teacher, students can make up learning by working hard themselves | Ultimate responsibility for learning exposure may fall on the student in the case of centralized assessment |

Syllabus Solely at the Discretion of Individual School/Faculty

Advantages	Disadvantages
Faculty have freedom to keep on improving, moving to *content beyond syllabus* relevantly	No common ground; the content and approach might change from faculty to faculty or school to school
Flexibility inherent and innovations welcome	Possible indiscipline; individual freedom could be misused
Freedom to work towards institutional ethos, doctrinal position and ministerial philosophy	If the team and the individual faculty are not intentional, quality enhancement is at stake
Transformative collage of learning experiences can be incorporated year after year	No guarantee for revisions and progressions, as it depends more on self-motivation
Faculty member owns the syllabus	If faculty is not committed to excellence, it is wasted time for students
Faculty member can draw from contextual realities and keep on improving	Accountability measures are not clearly defined; student may be getting less than the minimum input

At some point, we have to pause and examine how far our schools have grown in addressing these concerns. The scope for setting the core directives on the syllabus and shaping it contextually with learning experiences could be explored. Most importantly, the visionary leadership and faculty at the school have to own the curriculum and syllabus, and keep improving it for the healthy formation of students. As "outcome–impact assessment" is seizing the focus in the educational process, schools might need to initiate strategic deliberations on curriculum, syllabus and the lesson plan.

> "Only through taking context seriously can we hope to develop an integrative curriculum that touches our changing world." Perry Shaw, *Transforming Theological Education: A Practical Handbook for Integrative Learning* (Carlisle: Langham, 2014), 103.

Wholeness in Curriculum by Centering on the Core Vision

The long-debated question is: What is the integrative center in theological education? Farley's critique began the debate on *fragmentation and integration* in theological education. He argued that the problem of fragmentation in theological education is not merely structural but theological in nature. If the problem is theological in nature, the solution will also be theological. However, that *theological solution* can doubtlessly be created with pedagogical implications, including curriculum development on the basis of educational theories. The call for re-orientation and wholeness since the early 1960s was accompanied by numerous attempts towards the formulation of new paradigms of integration, by picking one of the three core objectives of theological education – such as academic, spiritual and ministry formation – and using it as the integrating factor. For some, the decisive factor for wholeness was theological wisdom, while for others, it was discipleship, spiritual formation or mission. Unwittingly, by taking one formational aspect out of the three, thinkers (and practitioners) perpetuated the mistake of making that one dominant, resulting in another level of fragmentation. By projecting one over the other, we cannot advance integration. These dimensions have to be held in creative tension and each has to express the others. Let us see how some of the paradigms framed the missional objective into a curriculum. Bernhard Ott's four-dimensional paradigm for an integrative curriculum consisted of (1) *missio Dei* as the central agenda of theological education; (2) people-oriented andragogy; (3) integration of theory and practice; and (4) the church's participation in mission. It was held that this sort of mission curriculum could be the prospective unifying core of theological education. Robert Banks's study exploring a missional alternative to the other models in theological education advocated the *missional paradigm* in which teaching is reconceived as a missional practice and the theological curriculum is thoroughly based on practical mission.[9] Generally field work, reflective practices and cohort approaches in learning are to be advocated in the reshaping of the theological curriculum. Besides these scholars, many others searched into the theme of wholeness in curriculum, advocating as the core unifying factor spiritual formation, church-ministry formation or practical

---

9. Robert Banks, *Re-envisioning Theological Education: Exploring a Missional Alternative to Current Models* (Grand Rapids, MI: Eerdmans, 1999), 223–245.

theology. Deep thinking has gone into each of these. In any move towards wholeness, we must make sure that the unifying factor does not become *a separate* or *the outstanding element*. It is rather the one that *serves* and *underpins* the others, uniting, holding and strengthening everything together to assist the school in achieving the essential balance.

Wholeness in Curriculum by Suiting Learning to the Context

The strength of a curriculum does not hinge exclusively on academic meticulousness, as some would assume. It is determined by the integration of the curricular elements in fulfilling the goal and mission of the school and the impact it makes on the context of learning. The curriculum is affected by the context of the school, the church and the society. Students and faculty absorb the contextual packages of goals, knowledge, skills, expectations and traditions in their construction of learning and ministerial practice. Therefore, the curricular intersections between the contextual correspondences of the student and the objectives of training require cautious treatment. A transformative curriculum reflects the needs and hopes of the context. We make the objectives of the academic program responsive to the pertinent needs of the context and require the active engagement of students in the context in structured processes of reflection and action. This is an acid test for the effectiveness of the curriculum, whereby the outcome of our training is assessed in the specific context it intends to serve. Such a curriculum demonstrates wholeness by effecting tangible and positive changes in the context of training. When context is absent in the curriculum, learning is restricted to mere abstractions, however good the syllabus may be.

How can we facilitate wholeness in the curriculum and the overall learning exposure? What are the most vital areas to consider? Laudable amounts of thinking have gone into this matter in the Asian context of theological education. *Tending the Seedbeds*, a compilation of writings from Asian theological education, reaffirmed the need for theological and biblical grounding in every aspect of theological education. The book cited Asia Theological Association's core value of biblical grounding and contextual rooting thus: "We must together take immediate and urgent steps to seek, elaborate and possess a biblically informed theological basis for our calling and engagement in theological education and allow every aspect of our service to become rooted and nurtured in this soil."[10] This core value is non-negotiable for curricular wholeness. Instead of shutting off all cross-fertilizing learning from other contexts, it actually upholds interaction and reciprocity. The book discussed multiple facets in nurturing wholeness in theological curriculum, such as cultural grounding, gender consideration, pastoral formation, adult education principles, mentoring, leader development, spiritual disciplines, social concern and engagement, problem-based learning, and interactive and reflective principles in learning. In the National Conference on Theological Education organized in 2013 on the theme "Theological Education: Ploughing the Field for New Life to Sprout" numerous concerns were expressed over the present system and the syllabus. An ideal theological education was expected to be "integrative, contextual, communitarian, transformative, gender-sensitive, prophetic, crucial, innovative, interdisciplinary, inter-linked, ministry-oriented and based on sound pedagogy and spirituality."[11]

Foundational Curriculum for Real-life Experience

The curriculum is not merely "an accumulation of courses and other sorts of academic experiences but . . . an overall process of critical reflection and integration. The curriculum itself, understood in this holistic manner, is 'formative' in the full sense of the term."[12] Curriculum as the design for wholeness in the formation of a theology student, faculty and the school reflects the goal, philosophy and mission of the school. The following is a list of things for an educator to consider in shaping an overall curriculum for the school. These help shape a vision-directed, corporately driven theological community, perhaps combined with more components bonded well into the learning environment:

---

10. Allan Harkness, "Introduction," in *Tending the Seedbeds: Educational Perspectives on Theological Education in Asia,* edited by Allan Harkness (Quezon City, Philippines: Asia Theological Association, 2010), 7–22 (here, 12).

11. Felix Wilfred, "Foreword," in *Theological Education: Ploughing the Field for New Life to Sprout,* edited by G. Lawrence Jebadoss and P. Mohan Larbeer (Bangalore: BTESSE; Chennai: CLS, 2014), iii.

12. Donald Senior and Timothy Weber, quoted in Robert Banks, *Re-envisioning Theological Education: Exploring a Missional Alternative to Current Models* (Grand Rapids, MI: Eerdmans, 1999), 223.

- Make the institution's goal statement clear.
- Discuss the history of the school, specifying founding goal, growth milestones, major shifts and challenges, and the panoramic future.
- Specify the overall learning process and programs with the core content.
- Make explicit the fundamental biblical assumptions, faith statements and traditional values of the school.
- Set out unambiguously the values of the institution in the spiritual and personal–moral dimensions.
- Establish activities in a holistic design for the overall life at the school (spiritual, intellectual, social, aesthetic, experiential, cultural).
- Design a variety of learning experiences that effectively blend the cognitive, affective and psychomotor aspects of development of the student.
- Build feasible interconnections between the seemingly disparate procedures within the school.
- Elucidate how the vision of the institution fits into larger avenues of God's mission in the world.
- Explore a systems view of the institution with local, global and cosmic perspectives.
- Create focused occasions to deliberate on the paradoxes and dilemmas in theological thinking and ministerial practice.
- Outline the events, inspirational stories, biographies and films that endorse the mission and vision of the school, and create opportunities for the community to reflect on them.
- Develop innovative strategies to nurture value intuition, insight and imagination through poem composition, art, drama, exhibitions, publishing, outreach and so on.
- Frame multiple tracks of interactive learning to engage students in local and global realities.
- Prepare precise forms of mission engagement to lead students to deeper deliberations and refined praxis.
- Design events for open and free dialogue on theological issues.
- Write down practical procedures to enable students to clearly perceive and communicate their theological convictions and ministerial calling.

We design and build each academic program and the syllabus for each subject on this firm foundation:

Design Components of the Academic Program

- Title of the academic program
- Accreditation status of the program
- Goal of the institution
- Program purpose statement
- Program objectives
- Program description (goal, process, design, usefulness)
- Admission criteria/prerequisites
- Essential learning requirements for successful completion (holistic dimensions: academic, spiritual, personal, ministerial)
- Graduate profile
- Faculty members
- Mentoring services
- Fees, scholarships
- Ministry placements
- Higher-education prospects of the program
- Program-assessment procedures

Design Components of the Course Syllabus

- Course title and course number
- Sequential placement of the subject in the curriculum of the academic program
- Credit hours
- Espoused goal and mission of the school
- Goal of the course
- Course description (goal, process, relevance, usefulness, design)
- Course objectives: what the learning aims to provide in terms of cognitive, spiritual, personal and ministerial formation of the learner
- Course outline: unit titles and pattern of learning procedure; units organized according to key subdivisions; evidences of adequate background study; core content of the course; precise biblical and theological foundations; scope for contemporary reflection

- Course requirements: required readings, seminars, papers, research, participatory assignments; requirements on attendance in teaching sessions; expected level of involvement in the integral designs in spiritual, relational and experiential dynamics
- Expected learning outcomes: immediate results anticipated in learning; the expected transformation and growth of the learner in terms of knowledge, understanding, attitude, skill, behavior, reflection and application
- Course assessment methods: tests, examinations and all forms of assessment in learning
- Required reading: key texts and classics recommended for pre-course or through-term reading
- Bibliography: extensive list of texts, articles, documents, websites and other resources; including foundational and recent literature

There are underlying curricular intersections that determine wholeness in the learning process.

Curriculum designates the entire formational design, process and purpose, while *syllabus* serves as the guiding document that explains the learning content and requirements of the students. The syllabus is a key document of the whole curriculum of a program. The *lesson plan* is the personal document of the faculty member that elaborates the hourly/ weekly/ daily slots of the teaching-learning procedure. The list below sets out certain gauges in fostering curricular sustainability through the syllabus:

- The *course* makes a significant impact on the vision and mission of the school.
- The *course syllabus* makes a definite contribution to the goal of the program.
- The *course description* is well reflected in the *outline of the main units*.
- The *course objectives* are well represented in the *course outline*.
- The headings and subheadings in each unit are logically aligned.
- Themes in the course (e.g. biblical, theological, historical, ecclesial, literary, missiological or contextual) are precise.
- Components within the units are logically correlated.
- The course does not overlap heavily with other subjects in the program.
- The time frame is realistic.

- The learning design holds all formational dimensions in a critical balance.
- The *course requirements* are well defined.
- The *learning activities* are pertinent to the capacity and contextual needs of the students.
- The non-credited, participatory learning expectations in the course are listed.
- The practical essentials of the course are revised periodically with greater innovation.
- Resources for *required readings* are made accessible to students.
- Bibliographic resources are relevant, updated and accessible.
- The assessment designs for the course foster transformation of the students through critical, reflective thinking.
- The expected *learning outcomes* and the *graduate profile* of the course are known to the faculty and students.

All these together make the focused core of the program. Central to the task of facilitating wholeness is the critical revisiting of each of these facets in training.

A School's Self-Assessment Guide on Curriculum

- How do the faculty members perceive the terms *curriculum*, *syllabus* and *lesson plan*?
- Which of these types truthfully describes the curriculum at the school: degree-oriented or aimed at transformation?
- How often do the leadership team and faculty meet exclusively to discuss and revise the curriculum?
- Who coordinates the development and revision of the explicit curriculum by the faculty?
- Who is on the team in charge of the design, quality control and ongoing assessment of the curriculum?
- How reliably is the implicit curriculum enhancing the holistic formation of the school community?
- What procedures would help the school to assess a particular academic program (e.g. MDiv) in order to invigorate its holistic formational design and impact on the mission of the school?

- What are the major challenges in revisiting the curriculum and teaching-learning process at the school?
- What practical processes will assist the faculty in transformative curriculum design and its effective implementation?

Practical Recommendations: Curriculum

Based on Steve Hardy's "Broad Trajectory for Strategic Curriculum Revision/Development":[13]

- Revisit the core values/vision of the school.
- Review the Mission Statement.
- Reckon up relevant needs in church and missions (needs assessment).
- Reconsider the school's strengths, weaknesses and possible resources.
- Retreat to realistic first steps.
- Reexamine and improve the process, design and impact in light of the goal.

A Detailed Procedure for Curriculum Revisiting

The following is a detailed and ordered procedure for curriculum revisiting for schools that embark on a first serious attempt:

- Explore potential models for designing and assessing transformative patterns in training.
- Do a critical self-evaluation of the school in view of the stated goal and philosophy.
- Evaluate and reflect on the transformative nature of the overall learning environment.
- Critically revisit each academic program.
- Review each syllabus for formational goals.
- Make an unbiased assessment of campus life (school experience of the student).
- Identify potential areas for implicit learning experiences to foster personal transformation.

---

13. Adapted from Steve Hardy, "Strategic Planning for Theological Education," in *Educating for Tomorrow: Theological Leadership for the Asian Context*, edited by Manfred Waldemar Kohl and A. N. Lal Senanayake (Bangalore: SAIACS, 2007), 60–62.

- Identify necessary resources to help the task of assessing spiritual, attitudinal and behavioral formation.
- Strategically design a small-group project (fellowship group, cell groups or a ministry team) to impact all dimensions of holistic development.
- Organize well-designed off-campus community exposure.
- Revitalize the practical ministry design at the school.
- Design evaluation formats for the school, curriculum and outcomes.
- Revise annually the informal and non-formal learning experiences.
- Develop feasible measures to coordinate assessments across the programs and departments to see how they contribute to the goal and mission of the school.
- Introduce innovations/changes step by step (with ongoing assessment) for greater efficiency in training.

3

Wholeness in the Formation of Faculty

Ongoing Formational Predicament for Faculty

Faculty's role and attitude are pivotal in determining the nature of education offered in a theology school. Any attempt towards reformation of theological education will have to place a major focus on the faculty. Understandably, faculty's alignment with the ethos of the school is significant for wholeness in training. According to Ferris, "Alignment with ethos is the most important consideration when building or winnowing the faculty. Academic, scholarly and ministerial qualifications for appointment to the faculty must be honored, but never at the expense of alignment with the institution's ethos."[1] Governing teams in theology schools are often at fault in setting the criteria for faculty recruitment and assessment, perhaps due to multiple situational pressures. The following are some common flaws:

> "When they saw the courage of Peter and John and realized that they were unschooled, ordinary men, they were astonished and they took note that these men had been with Jesus."
> Acts 4:13

- Recruiting faculty exclusively on the basis of academic credentials, indifferent to their personal values, faith convictions and ministry involvement;

---

1. Robert W. Ferris, "The Work of a Dean," *Evangelical Review of Theology* 32, no. 1 (2008): 65–73.

- Assigning subjects without examining how their teaching aligns with the ethos of the institution;
- Not orienting the faculty to the vision and purpose of the seminary or discussing the expectations of them in the larger team of faculty and administrative staff;
- Not emphasizing the priority of spiritual disciplines for the faculty on and off campus;
- Overloading faculty with courses and other assignments and hence leading them to a lifeless existence at the school;
- Negligence in addressing issues considerately and strategically when faculty's attention is excessively divided between external jobs/ministry engagements;
- Insufficient provision for faculty to meet their basic needs, resulting in their need for earnings outside the school;
- Not igniting in faculty a desire for their own holistic formation in teaching and learning;
- Not coaching the faculty to shift from *preparing students for ministry* to *actively engaging students in ministry*;
- Not making *ministry engagement and reflective praxis* the integral part of their service;
- Not providing opportunities for ongoing informal development[2] (besides the *formal*) for the faculty;
- Not developing a working culture of teaching-learning assessment to strengthen the faculty.

Faculty's work is demanding. In their seemingly mundane function of teaching, it is not easy to get the faculty to think through the lines of transformation or integration of learning. As Edward Farley observes, "faculty members come out of graduate schools with a loyalty to a particular field, and it's very hard to get their attention or arouse their passion for larger sets of problems such as pedagogy or the reform of theological education."[3] He argues that as long as faculty members defend their respective specializations, genuine

---

2. Arun K. Sarkar, "Non-formal Faculty Development in Theological Seminaries," in *Tending the Seedbeds: Educational Perspectives on Theological Education in Asia*, edited by Allan Harkness (Quezon City, Philippines: Asia Theological Association, 2010).

3. "Toward Theological Understanding: An Interview with Edward Farley," *The Christian Century* 115, no. 4 (February 1998): 115.

reform for all practical purposes is next to impossible.[4] Calian articulated it this way:

> For Farley, the big question is, Are faculty willing to contribute to and participate in the academic program holistically to a greater extent than is thus far evident? Is there openness to change in how we carry on the business of educating in our theological schools? Are most revisions simply cosmetic dressing around the status quo that fail to harmonize our voices into a shared message? To what extent is theological education sensitive to the stresses and confusion found in local churches?[5]

Arun Sarkar's ideas correspond well with this discussion on the non-formal formation of faculty. He recommends the following individual avenues for faculty's non-formal development. The lists below, however, maintain an exclusive focus on intellectual–professional development:[6]

- Library research
- Orientation for new faculty
- Faculty mentoring (senior to junior)
- Meeting with the academic dean (fixing time-bound strategies for development)
- Faculty growth contract (guidance in self-directed goal-setting in learning)
- Supervised learning tutorials with experts for highly motivated faculty
- Distance education opportunities fostering ongoing development
- Research
- E-learning
- Learning from students
- Memberships in professional bodies

Faculty small-group avenues:

- Peer coaching
- Faculty study circles
- Field education

---

4. Ibid., 113.
5. Carnegie Samuel Calian, *The Ideal Seminary: Pursuing Excellence in Theological Education* (Louisville, KY: Westminster John Knox, 2002), 48.
6. Sarkar, "Non-formal Faculty Development," 136–141.

- Consultation with experts
- Networking with other theological institutions

All-faculty avenues:
- Seminars, conferences and workshops
- Projects
- Faculty meetings

In addition to these significant professional avenues, there are plenty of other dimensions we need to work on towards faculty formation. It is our contention that the faculty is a key determinant in the transformative growth assessment of a school (see Figure 13).

Figure 13: The Faculty Reality: Good and Bad Models[7]

Faculty Bad Model	Faculty Role Models
Does the minimum	Committed beyond the call of duty
Bound to classroom	Engages voluntarily in campus, church and mission
Not committed to the ethos of the school	Well aligned and committed to the ethos
Indifferent or hostile to students	Hospitable, humble and accessible to students
Uninterested, detached face	Smiling, welcoming face
No passion for faith and ministry	Teaching is delivered passionately
Lacks peer respect and motivation	Strengthens the team with a motivating presence
Monotonous monologues	Innovative adaptations, participatory exercises
Follows outdated syllabus	Revises the syllabus annually
Hurries to complete an extensive syllabus	Allows deep thinking and reflection
Lacks dynamic commitment to family	Family is a high priority
Shows favoritism among students	Affirms and appreciates everyone's unique identity
Hates certain cultures and languages	Loves and celebrates differences
No personal spiritual disciplines	Well-patterned spiritual disciplines
Neglects chapel and community services	Regular in chapel and community services
No continual learning, research or writing	Up-to-date with knowledge; self-directed research
Poor time keeping and time management	Punctual; makes the best use of time
Manipulative in assessments and grading	Always just in assessments and grading

---

7. Jessy Jaison, "Faculty Formation for Revitalizing Theological Education," *Journal of Theological Education and Mission (JOTEAM)* 6, no. 6 (February 2015): 1–11.

Little regard for God's Word and prayer	High regard for God's Word and prayer
Wants to take	Ready to give away
Divided attention; teaching is a side business	Single-minded devotion to the formation of students
Lacks careful design of learning experiences	Best learning experiences designed and improved
No respect for others on campus	Courteous to everyone on campus
Never owns the curriculum	Owns the curriculum in total fidelity to its purpose
Lacks insights into transformative education	Consistently growing in transformative education
Busy with own affairs; no time for campus community	Available and accessible for fellowship and mentoring

Faculty as the Owners, Designers and Improvisers of the Curriculum

The curriculum is deeper than the syllabus and broader than a list of contents. Curriculum refers to the overall learning environment that interconnects the formal, non-formal and informal learning experiences that help achieve the purpose of education. It is a process that impacts students beyond the classroom. The faculty members who know what is taught and why it is taught will approach the *how to teach* question realistically.

> We try to include too much. We mistakenly imagine that students absolutely must be acquainted with a massive volume of information. There is an ever-present tendency to confuse quantity with quality, resulting in many students suffering from overload – a kind of academic indigestion. The more serious outcome is that they have very little time to think issues through and therefore little opportunity to develop convictions of their own and to discover who they really are and what they want to accomplish.[8]

The core curriculum is the essential knowledge or set of topics that all students must receive in the program. We determine the curriculum in view of the contextual and ministerial realities of the students and breathe life into the

---

8. Graham Houghton, "Theological Education for Leadership Development," In *Educating for Tomorrow: Theological Leadership for the Asian Context*, edited by Manfred Waldemar Kohl and A. N. Lal Senanayake (Bangalore: SAIACS, 2007), 218.

curriculum by careful integration of relevant learning experiences to enrich their spiritual and relational life.

Many schools follow a borrowed curriculum and pass it on at every new faculty appointment. We often lack an administrative body that examines the coherence between the curriculum and the espoused goal of the school. This creates a huge obstacle on the path of growth. Several issues emerge as we consider faculty and curriculum. We see that faculty members:

- Fail to own the curriculum;
- Lack competence in designing the best learning experiences;
- Teach with no foundational knowledge on educational theories;
- Do not revise curriculum for transformative impact;
- Do not continue learning;
- Follow outdated methods in teaching and learning assessment;
- Do not take curriculum development as integral to formational wholeness.

> "When I do not know myself, I cannot know who my students are. I will see them through a glass darkly, in the shadows of my unexamined life – and when I cannot see them clearly, I cannot teach them well." Parker J. Palmer, *The Courage to Teach: Exploring the Inner Landscape of a Teacher's Life* (San Francisco: Jossey-Bass, 2007), 3.

We need to facilitate *self-change* in the faculty. Faculty–curriculum issues are always ambiguous in practical terms. This entails an intentional and intensive revisit of the curriculum. Faculty members who own the curriculum will naturally pay attention to the pattern of course delivery, learning activities and assessment procedures.

Faculty as Role Models Exemplifying Humility and Hospitality

The shift from *teaching* to *ongoing learning* invites faculty to continuing self-assessment. There is no doubt that faculty are role models to the students. According to Ferris, "The work of a theological faculty is the formation of students for ministry. This is achieved, first of all, through modelling a life of ministry and scholarship. It is modelling which touches the lives of students most profoundly and provides credibility for instruction."[9] Certain indicators can guide us towards the motif of investing life and wisdom in the younger generation. Barsness and Kim describe six sensitivities in the examined life of a faculty. These are critical test points for the faculty: privilege and power, tacit ethno-centrism, bias, micro-aggressions, shame and the need to be liked.[10] The way one handles these areas affects the transformation of persons positively or negatively. Five key dimensions of a faculty's praxis are scholarship, humility, relationships, conflict and dialogical space. Every aspect of the faculty's life is important in the learning environment.

Faculty exert a very high level of influence on the learner.

> To a degree, no tutor can escape the clutches of the discipleship phenomenon. The tutor has always been the medium and the medium has always been the dominant message. Looking back on our own student experience, it is the quality of life, attitudes and enthusiasm, of a few teachers that are remembered when much of the content of the teaching is forgotten – often 24 hours after the end of the exam. Conversely, the tutor who is ineffective as a person, uncommitted, unable to offer a clear message from his or her life, can have a devastating effect on the acceptance of the truths taught. This may not be an over-riding argument if the subject is Biology or History. But for the teaching of Biblical truth, it raises the issues of hypocrisy. As Martin Buber said, "The teacher must himself be what he wants his pupils to become." This calls the faculty to go beyond their focus on the particular knowledge of the academic discipline. William R. Myers puts it thus: "[The] faculty of a confessing seminary should be concerned about their common vocation as theological educators rather than to act solely as individual promoters of a particular discipline's academic wisdom."[11] The *discipleship paradigm* consciously harnesses this effect in a training college. Communication theory would suggest

---

9. Ferris, "Work of a Dean," 69.
10. Roy E. Barsness and Richard D. Kim, "A Pedagogy of Engagement for the Changing Character of the 21st Century Classroom," *Theological Education* 49, no. 2 (2015): 97–101.
11. William R. Myers, "Antecedents to a Hopeful Future: Challenges for Theological Faculty," *Theological Education* 50, no. 1 (2015): 83.

that discipleship is a far more efficient tool for learning than the standard information transfer by lecture. It relates learning to life and reality. Bonaventura wrote around 1257 in the Introduction to *The Soul's Journey into God* these words that set out eloquently the sort of learning that is required of a theological student, "First therefore, I invite the reader to the groans of prayer through Christ crucified, through whose blood we are cleansed from the filth of vice – so that he not believe that reading is sufficient without unction, speculation without devotion, investigation without wonder, observation without joy, work without piety, knowledge without love, understanding without humility, endeavor without divine grace, reflection . . . without divinely inspired wisdom.[12]

Faculty are role models and life-shapers in theological communities, and therefore formation of faculty is central to wholeness in theological education.

Theology classrooms increasingly represent the diversity of culture and philosophy. Detachment between the scholar and the learner emerged as the inevitable result of *professionalism* in its faulty connotation. In the power-laden cultural moves of the current era, how can theology faculty model a creative interchange between people, modeling humility and hospitality? How can strangers become friends? Nouwen portrays how students resist the pressurized learning process: "one of the greatest tragedies is that millions of young people spend many hours, days, weeks and years listening to lectures, reading books and writing papers with a constantly increasing resistance . . . We have lost our sense of surprise when men and women who are taking courses about the questions of life and death anxiously ask us 'how much is *required.*'"[13] Our model has to be different. Christlike humility covers the faculty as they start to see students as colleagues in ministry. Students recognize humility when the faculty set great examples in spiritual disciplines and avoid professional rivalry with colleagues, favoritism among students and excessive entertainment in their own lives. These faculty members reveal their constant need for God's presence and grace in life. Arrogance and pride has no place.

---

12. Cited in Graham Cheesman, "Competing Paradigms in Theological Education Today," *Journal of Theological Education and Mission* 2, no. 1 (2011): 10–28 (here, 23).
13. Henri J. M. Nouwen, *Reaching Out* (London: Harper Collins, 1976), 59.

Teaching is not about faculty pouring knowledge into the student. In order to recognize the power of students' reflections in the classroom, faculty should enter the classroom with humility. In other words, "Faculty entering the classroom must choose to enter with a sense of awe, not so much of what they have to give but of what they might also learn."[14] Humility and hospitality are not signs of weakness; they are great sources of transformative power. Jesus did not despise anyone; he accepted and served. Crowds followed him and listened to his words, drawn by the ever-present kindness and humility in him. These qualities marked his life. While himself being in the deepest agony, Jesus washed the feet of his disciples, fellowshipped with them around the table, let them talk to him and even lean on his chest.

Faculty as Living Documents of Theology and Theological Wisdom

Cheesman wrote, "If I was to give two fundamental reasons why teaching doesn't work, they would be a lack of passion for the subject and lack of peace in the teacher."[15] These words tell us that the dispositions, responses and reactions of faculty impact their teaching. Theology faculty are the living documents of what they teach. It is from them that the students receive faith with intellectual vitality. Students who passionately seek to serve the church always look up to the faculty who engage in the ministry of the church in one way or another. The highest form of appreciation of a faculty member echoes in the words of the apostle Peter to Master Jesus: "Where shall we go? The words of life are in you."

> Personnel-wise, theological faculties who mediate student learning are no longer merely depositors of head knowledge but are mentors and exemplars. Not every faculty can do all things equally well, but a theological faculty can as a whole provide a range of models for student emulation . . . faculty aim for their *telos* through a methodological model that integrates heads (academic or discursive knowledge), hearts (personal wholeness or sapiential

---

14. Barsness and Kim, "Pedagogy of Engagement," 103.
15. Graham Cheesman, "Kissing and Theological Education," blog post, 31 December 2012, http://theologicaleducation.org/category/blog/.

knowledge), and hands (missional service in church and society or practical knowledge).¹⁶

Students see the faculty as the sources of divine wisdom and this makes them trust the knowledge communicated in the classroom without bias. Students search for wisdom through profound interactions with faculty. They persistently seek to work out how the absolutes in the Bible maintain relevance in the social and ideological changes of the times. Every so often they wonder about living as Christians in a world that denies faith in God. Faculty who are busy finishing the syllabus regrettably have no time to address the deepest issues that trouble souls. Only teaching that unifies the content with the context can make lasting impact. Ted Ward outlines the interrelated complex processes in learning that ensure the essential engagement of the learner's mind as "perceiving," "remembering," "using" and "valuing." Do our students perceive the theology we teach? How much of it will they remember? What is it that they will use in life? What from our teaching will be valued in their future life and service? These are questions that matter. Students value the teaching that reflects concrete awareness of the changing world and its needs and the essential wisdom that makes relevant responses to it.

Faculty as Steadfast Worshippers and Persons of Prayer

There is nothing more demoralizing in theology schools than to see the faculty so deeply immersed in study that they scarcely find the time to join the corporate prayer and devotions. Never by force but by calling, faculty members must be part of the worshipping community. "Bifurcating academics from spirituality and placing those in different compartments are counterproductive. As far as theological education is concerned both should go side by side and are two sides of one coin," says Thomas,¹⁷ reflecting on the escalating level of mediocrity in theology schools both in academics and spirituality. What if fewer than 30 percent of our students experience some level of spiritual growth from their time at theology school? What if many lost their personal

---

16. Amos Yong, "Beyond the Evangelical–Ecumenical Divide for Theological Education in the Twenty-First Century: A Pentecostal Assist," *Theological Education* 49, no. 1 (2014): 92.
17. O. Thomas, "Editorial," *The Journal of Malankara Orthodox Theological Studies* 3, no. 1 (August 2015): 3–5.

disciplines and faith convictions while pursuing a theology degree? Dearborn referred to a study that reported the words of numerous graduates who said they were "feeling spiritually cold, theologically confused, biblically uncertain, relationally calloused and professionally unprepared"[18] as the result of their seminary education. A primary reason for this is the lack of spiritual foundation and practices in our delivery of theological education. Our faculty seminars must emphasize that modeling worship, prayer and love for God's Word are essential in transformative theological teaching. A significant amount of learning happens on the campus informally. Faculty who neglect chapel times and yet regularly engage in classroom teaching are in fact communicating something: that prayer and devotion are not as important as lecturing! If faculty's entire work is *for God*, it must be entirely *of God*. Theology itself is *knowing God*. Shaw says it plainly: "Too many of our professors teach without prayer or recognition of the need for the Holy Spirit's direction in theological teaching. By so doing we run the danger of communicating to our students that God does not care about what we are teaching, or even that God is not present in academic classes."[19] Great teachers of theology in Christian history guarded against conceptual perversion, hypocrisy and heresy, not by the assimilation of information, but by spending disciplined personal time in the presence of God and meditating on the Word. Amassing abstract theological information for two to three years will only result in producing graduates who are incapable of leading a basic Bible study or are insensitive to the needs of their contexts. We may verify this empirically. Students refer to multiple commentaries, texts and articles and prepare a twenty-minute sermon that has nothing to do with the heart. But information by itself is incapable of transforming lives and societies. Words lack power when they do not originate from devotion, meditation, silence and prayer. There is no greater impact upon theological education than when students see their teachers live a life shaped by the Word, worship and prayer. Above all, this was the model set by Jesus Christ.

---

18. Tim Dearborn, "Preparing New Leaders for the Church of the Future: Transforming Theological Education through Multi-Institutional Partnerships," *Transformation* 12, no. 4 (Oct–Dec 1995): 7–12.
19. Perry Shaw, *Transforming Theological Education: A Practical Handbook for Integrative Learning* (Carlisle: Langham Global Library, 2014), 89.

Faculty as Integrative Practitioners and Trend-Setters in Mission

God's design of salvation and discipleship essentially carries the aspect of service with it. Theology schools must serve the church in its multi-faceted ministry commitments. Sadly, many of our classrooms engage in endless debates on theological arguments or in criticism of the inconsistencies of accrediting bodies or of denominational catastrophes. Such experiences can never form effective servant-leaders for the church. Students rarely see their faculty serving on the mission field and returning to the classroom generating a passion for mission. A *"real mission focus of the school* (not just in theory)" is one indicator in Robert Ferris's list of the "Signs of Innovative Schools."[20] Mission, which was the driving force of theological education in the 1990s, has given way to other disciplines. Steven Studebaker and Lee Beach wrote, "The emerging paradigm thoroughly believes that practice informs theory. They believe that the pragmatic demands in ministry can and even should shape theology. Theology arises from the warp and woof of life. Credible theology, moreover, is functional."[21] Adult learners approach studies in the light of their contexts, problems, needs and capacities. In this regard, it is important to strongly affirm the balance within faculty as critical thinkers and reflective practitioners.

The questions for us are: Does theological scholarship serve the mission of the church in any way? Does our theological scholarship connect us with or disconnect us from the church? We are accustomed to define scholarship on the basis of higher degrees listed in the faculty profiles. But formation and transformation do not happen without practical integration in learning. This is not, however, to set one against the other. "Deep scholarship and integrated theological education are not mutually exclusive. Without serious scholarship, professors have little to say. Without integration, what they say matters little (at least to those beyond the academic guild). The problem is not digging deep, but rather returning to the light of the day."[22] Our training should enable students

---

20. Robert W. Ferris, *Renewal in Theological Education: Strategies for Change* (Wheaton, IL: Wheaton College, 1990), 107–118.
21. Steven Studebaker and Lee Beach, "Friend Or Foe? The Role of the Scholar in Emerging Christianity," *Theological Education* 48, no. 2 (2014): 51.
22. Ibid., 51–52.

to realize who they are; who their people are; what their world needs; and what their calling in mission is. Faculty, irrespective of their subject areas, have the responsibility of motivating and guiding their students into God's mission in and through his church.

Faculty Employing Adult Education Principles in Training

There are distinct demands in teaching and learning today. Theological education usually occurs in an adult environment. According to the principle of andragogy (adult education), learning has a simultaneous impact on the learner's life and on his or her contribution. The task of the faculty in a theology school is to create a conducive learning environment for adults, who approach life with more experiential wisdom and seek problem-based learning methods to equip them in ministry. Schools need to train their faculty to discover the multiple impacts of andragogy, including reflection, innovation, responsiveness and praxis-orientation. The theory of andragogy upholds connected and continuing learning.

> In order for us [educators] to prepare our students for what is without question a future filled with networked learning spaces, we must first experience those environments for ourselves. We must become connected and engaged in learning in these new ways if we are to fully understand the pedagogies of using these tools with our students. We cannot honestly discuss twenty-first-century learning skills for our students until we make sense of them ourselves.[23]

Learning becomes exceedingly irrelevant when ready-made answers are taught without the existence of a question. Students keep wondering why they are learning the subject. According to adult education principles, faculty facilitate students in meaningful engagement with the world with grounded theological wisdom and a compassionate lifestyle. Terming this method "the pedagogy of engagement,"[24] Barsness and Kim say that "Universities have

---

23. Will Richardson, *Blogs, Wikis, Podcasts, and Other Powerful Web Tools for Classrooms*, 3rd edn (Thousand Oaks, CA: Corwin, 2010), x.
24. Barsness and Kim, "Pedagogy of Engagement," 90.

historically relied on a model of education based on the transmission of formal knowledge, where learning has been content specific, framing knowledge as an achievement rather than as a process."[25] Pedagogy of engagement is defined as an experiential approach to education that invites faculty to meaningfully engage students in interpersonal relationships, rooted in the values of mutuality and dignity.

An excessive focus on the intellectual domain and endless pressures on academic achievement spoil the joy of learning.

> Learning occurs most effectively where learners are encouraged rather than coerced; where the natural motivations of curiosity and exploration are recognized; where a community of peers provides easy opportunities for sharing insights and questions; where a teacher carefully extends and expands the learners' interpretations; where the spirit of cooperation toward discovery and exploration is stronger than the motivation to compete and surpass others; and where teaching one another is motivated by a spiritual unity toward eternal values.[26]

In teaching, we may have to address the intrinsic academic debates and opposing viewpoints. Yet, in doing this, we should consciously safeguard our student community from being trained in ever-growing ideological and attitudinal conflicts.

Classrooms make great places to build students holistically. First, the theology classroom is the place where students and the faculty meet with God, who is the source of wisdom and life. On the other hand, these classrooms can also be places of constant intellectual chatter and complicated, lifeless debates. We need to make sure that our teaching touches the innermost quests or struggles of the students as they journey in the path of God. Virginia Cetuk describes the element of wholeness in teaching thus: "Our psychological, spiritual, emotional and cognitive make-up comes with us into the classroom and has a profound impact on our receptivity to new learning. Our relationship with God, in no small measure as a result of this make-up

---

25. Ibid., 89–90.
26. Ted W. Ward, "Understanding Teaching and Learning as Inseparable Processes," *Common Ground Journal* 10, no. 1 (Fall 2012): 52.

(as well as a determinant of it), is at the heart of the matter in the theological school classroom."[27]

Second, the classroom is the place where students get "world-oriented."[28] This frame is built on the theological nexus of "God so loved the world that He gave His only begotten Son that whoever believes in Him shall not perish, but have everlasting life" (John 3:16).

Third, classrooms must be places that foster wholeness and growth through designs for interactive learning. For example, Lee Wanak articulates the depth of integration and wholeness Jesus facilitated through just one of his methods, known as *asking questions*.[29] The kinds of questions Jesus used were:

- Questions that gave focus and clarifications (e.g. Luke 13:18)
- Questions that revealed Jesus's deep disappointment (e.g. Matt 26:40; John 3:12)
- Questions that challenged tradition and authority (e.g. Mark 3:4)
- Questions regarding Jesus's own nature and identity (e.g. Matt 16:13, 15)
- Questions that challenged existing values (e.g. Matt 16:26)
- Evasive questions (e.g. Matt 21:24)
- Questions to activate faith and commitment (e.g. Matt 9:28)
- Deeply penetrating questions (e.g. Luke 2:49)

Wanak argued for the kind of metamorphosis already being applied in teaching roles in the Asia Pacific context.[30] The primary shifts needed to occur as the faculty approach the curriculum are the following:

- Dispenser of Information to Resource Guide
- Depositor of Knowledge to Problem-Poser
- Low-tech to High-tech Teaching Style

---

27. Virginia Samuel Cetuk, *What to Expect in Seminary: Theological Education as Spiritual Formation* (Nashville, TN: Abingdon, 1998), 95–96.

28. Carnegie Samuel Calian, *The Ideal Seminary: Pursuing Excellence in Theological Education* (Louisville, KY: Westminster John Knox, 2002), 54–60.

29. Lee Wanak, "Towards Perspective Transformation: Adopting Jesus' Use of Questions in the Seminary," in *Tending the Seedbeds: Educational Perspectives on Theological Education in Asia*, edited by Allan Harkness (Quezon City, Philippines: Asia Theological Association, 2010), 285–306.

30. Lee Wanak, "Theological Education and the Role of Teachers in the Twenty-First Century: A Look at the Asia Pacific Region," in *Educating for Tomorrow: Theological Leadership for the Asian Context*, edited by Manfred Waldemar Kohl and A. N. Lal Senanayake (Bangalore: SAIACS, 2007), 173–194.

- Local Educator to Global Educator
- Generalist to Specialist to Interdisciplinary Focus
- Classical Theology to Holistic Theology
- Non-regulation to Accreditation and Credentialing

In the adult learning environment of theological education, students maintain their own perspectives and expectations of the faculty. The following ideas are extracts from Priyadarshini's expectations of a theological educator.[31] In her view, a faculty member:

- Should not maintain an unhealthy distance from the student community;
- Should not overburden students with syllabus content such that deep-level thinking is hindered;
- Should not set a pattern of non-availability and non-sharing;
- Should not be unconcerned about the needs of the church;
- Should not limit theological education to certain strands but make it accommodative of all situations;
- Should not assess all students by the same standards but rather consider individual capacities;
- Should not create or support gender-based isolations;
- Should not set bad examples in their ethical and moral lives.

Faculty as Mentors

As mentors, faculty focus on getting to know the students and aiding them to relate the knowledge that is shared to their lives. Teaching theology is a divine gift and assignment. Jesus summarized it this way: "I did not speak of my own accord, but the Father who sent me commanded me what to say and how to say it. I know that his command leads to eternal life. So whatever I say is just what the Father has told me to say" (John 12:49–50). The apostle Paul confidently stated in 2 Timothy 3:10–11, 14, "You . . . know all about my teaching, my way of life, my purpose, faith, patience, love, endurance, persecutions, sufferings . . . continue in what you have learned and have become convinced of, because you know those from whom you learned it." Students represent different cultures

---

31. Beena Priyadarshini, "What Do We Expect from Theological Educators: A BD Student's Point of View," in *Theological Education: Ploughing the Field for New Life to Sprout*, edited by G. Lawrence Jebadoss and P. Mohan Larbeer (Bangalore: BTESSC; Chennai: CLS, 2014), 205–211.

and they join the school with different expectations of ministry formation. They look for some form of mentoring or interaction where someone will listen to their voice and respond to their queries. Aleshire's expression "mining the wisdom of ministry practitioners"[32] echoes this yearning of students to draw from the pragmatic-theoretic proficiency of their teachers. The mentoring dynamic typically accomplishes two things: it benefits the student and transforms the faculty. This interactive formational pedagogy "creates a communal learning experience where information, knowledge gathering, and objective facts, though valued, are a means to a greater and deeper learning where both teacher and student are changed."[33]

Formation and transformation are processes that assume time and intentionality. Mentoring advances these processes significantly. Therefore, faculty's development in the mentoring ministry is important. In mentoring, the faculty create space for free communication in which students discover receptivity, growth and maturation. Shifting mentoring further into the congregation-based ministry context, Banks wrote,

> The field-based approach [in theological education] draws on what it sees as New Testament precedent; this stresses the seminal role of the congregation in theological education, especially by house groups within it. Ownership of the operation is in the hands of the local churches. Drawing fully on the best adult education principles, and the problem-positing approach to education developed by Paulo Friere, the program keeps classes small and focuses on students' learning rather than professors' teaching. At the heart of this model is the vision of personal discipleship, involving the development of "head, heart and hands" for ministry, which means formation in intellectual, emotional and behavioral dimensions. Since mentoring of students by professors is crucial to this, faculty must have spent at least five years in effective ministry and be spiritually mature. Some of the main features of this approach are: Every student has a supervisory team consisting of

---

32. Daniel O. Aleshire, "The Future Has Arrived: Changing Theological Education in a Changed World," lecture presented at ATS/COA Biennial Meeting, June 2010, http://www.ats.edu/uploads/resources/publications-presentations/documents/aleshire-the-future-has-arrived.pdf.
33. Barsness and Kim, "Pedagogy of Engagement," 94.

a faculty advisor, a pastor, and a member of the congregation and follow designed patterns for supervision; Spiritual and character formation is encouraged through students determining, with faculty help, what they most need to work on during a year and how this can be best assessed; One day each week, courses take place at a central church location in different regions; Assessment by the lay and ordained supervisory team is primarily to establish how far the student has developed relevant competencies and what he or she needs to learn next."[34]

This radically different form of ministry education is done in the context of the church.

The disciples followed Jesus literally. Jesus never taught his disciples anything that he could not exemplify himself. This is definitely not a comfortable idea for theological faculty in the twenty-first century. Could we call our students to follow us literally into at least some ministry facets of our lives? Could we let them watch closely the way we handle our lives' details and challenges? Jesus, in John 13:13, affirmed his relationship with the disciples thus: "You call me teacher." As their teacher he gave them an example by washing the feet of the disciples and calling them to follow in his footsteps. Closer observations reveal that Jesus's teaching mostly emerged from a preceding action that validated that teaching. Accompanying Jesus was much more than following a routine study program; it was training in ministry and ongoing progression in the perfect blend of practice and theory. Robert Banks makes a profound analysis based on Mark 8–10 of how Jesus's instruction was occasioned by events and how they created the blend of wholeness in the person. The events in sequence were:

- Feeding of the four thousand
- Question and answer sessions[35]
- Healing of the sick
- Challenge to say who he was
- Mount of Transfiguration experience
- The "who is the greatest" discussion
- Predictions of death

---

34. Robert Banks, *Re-envisioning Theological Education: Exploring a Missional Alternative to Current Models* (Grand Rapids, MI: Eerdmans, 1999), 230.
35. See Wanak, "Towards Perspective Transformation," 285–306.

The teaching design was rich and holistic. Banks adds, "In all this, we see the forethought and preparation, flexibility and spontaneity, versatility and directness, instruction and participation, verbal and non-verbal character of the teaching and learning that occurred."[36]

The apostle Paul, who presented himself as a teacher, always operated within a transformative context of ministry and reflective learning. Looking at this from a missional perspective, Banks emphasizes the following:

- Learners had different levels of association with the apostle.
- A significant degree of commitment was required to join the learning team.
- The core group of learners had to learn, eat and pray with the apostle, sharing in his whole life.
- The purpose was active service or mission in furthering the kingdom, and not mere academic, moral or spiritual formation.
- The apostle's role was only to enhance their learning that had started early in the learners' homes and in their local communities.[37]

A School's Self-Assessment Guide on Faculty

For the Leadership of the School

- How constant and deliberate is the institution in fostering continual development of the faculty through formal and informal programs?
- How well do the course syllabi reflect the challenges and needs of the contexts of the students? How and when does the school assess this?
- What procedures could ensure that the faculty engage in ongoing learning?
- How can we plan a faculty-formation program at the school? What resources are already available to assist this?
- How confident are our faculty members in employing the question-and-answer method in the classroom?
- What percentage of the faculty balances academic rigor with spiritual and ministry commitment?

---

36. Banks, *Re-envisioning Theological Education*, 105.
37. Ibid., 122–124.

- How does the school know if faculty engage in unhealthy debates on doctrinal or moral issues in the classroom? How will such situations be handled?
- Are faculty members accessible and available to students for research guidance?
- Do the faculty engage in any form of practical ministry with students?
- Is the function of the faculty united or individualistic as far as the curriculum and goal of the institution are concerned?
- What group-learning opportunities have been made available by the faculty in the past three to four years on curriculum and teaching methodology?

Based on the Conduct and Formational Development of the Faculty

- In what ways are the faculty members engaging in continuing learning?
- How often does the school organize seminars or discussions on teaching-learning enhancement?
- Do the faculty members write and publish?
- Are the faculty trained to mentor the research projects of students?
- How does the school assist the faculty to develop resources for their courses and programs?
- Do the faculty exhibit genuine compassion and respect for the learners?
- How often do the faculty revise their curricula with new learning experiences?
- Do they actively participate in the informal activities of campus life?
- How many members on the faculty are capable of employing andragogical principles in teaching?
- What particular approaches would foster humility and hospitality in teaching in the context of the school?
- How could the faculty motivate and guide students in lifelong learning?
- In what ways does the school provide space for creative communication that takes seriously the queries of the students?

- What examples can be given of faculty's extra-curricular and implicit-curricular initiatives in recent years?
- What are faculty's creative and innovative methods in transformative teaching/learning?
- Do students see their faculty as role models in interpersonal relationships and commitment to ministry?
- How effective and meaningful are the methods and procedures of learning assessment?

Practical Recommendations: Formation of Faculty

Faculty formation initiated by the school's administration
- Walk alongside the faculty. Make a careful assessment of the faculty's potential and formulate developmental plans. When we do this purposefully, the disparity between the lazy and the highly motivated will be lessened and the system will achieve equilibrium.
- Discuss with faculty the need to set the right thinking-direction in students. Safeguard the students from falling into redundant ideological and attitudinal conflicts.
- Warn the faculty about the risks involved in taking extreme doctrinal stands without a substantial basis.
- Encourage the faculty to grow steadily in their spiritual disciplines and to impart them into the lives of students.
- Make provision for the faculty to get involved in some form of field mission work relating to their areas of interest.
- Constantly communicate that the primary value for a theological faculty is discipline in personal and spiritual life.
- Encourage the faculty to be innovative about their teaching and assessment styles.
- Open up concrete avenues for faculty development formally and informally. They need to grow in flexibility, adaptability and tranquility while engaging in teaching and mentoring. Faculty will never want to leave a school where they enjoy peace with God, serenity with colleagues, joy with students and growth in their inner selves.

4

Wholeness in the Overall Learning Experience

Thinking *Integration* when Priorities Clash

Education is meant to nurture the total formation of the person. In other words, its aim is the healthy integration of the learner's self. This calls us to design the learning experiences in view of the whole person. Unless the knowledge gained from our academic programs reflects itself in a life of agape love, wholeness cannot be achieved. After discussing the competing paradigms in theological education, such as Academic, Monastic, Training, Business and Discipleship paradigms, Cheesman arrives at the approach that he calls the Holistic Formation of the person. He says,

> This person-related, holistic approach has at least three advantages. Firstly it requires humility on behalf of the teachers. We cannot dole out spiritual maturity, fitness for ministry, or knowledge of God as we can lecture notes; it is the work of God. Secondly, it provides a unifying focus for what is now a very diverse and fragmented task. Thirdly, we are then able to distinguish clearly between the means and the end. If the prepared person is the end, the various activities of the college become the means rather than ends in themselves, and each will have its place as it contributes to the ultimate objectives.[1]

---

1. Graham Cheesman, "Competing Paradigms in Theological Education Today," 1-11, *Journal of Theological Education and Mission (JOTEAM)* 2, no. 1 (2011): 10–28 (here, 26).

In connection with the integration of the learning experiences of a student, Figure 14 depicts the result of Thomas's 2007 survey conducted in selected theological colleges in India.[2] This survey attempted to identify from students, seminaries and churches their priorities in terms of what is practically expected of the student. The three groups of respondents were given the same ten attributes to arrange in order of priority.

Figure 14: Divergence of Priorities in Theological Education

	Church's Priorities for Graduates	Seminary's Priorities for Graduates	Priorities of Graduates
1	Person of prayer	Theological knowledge	Inspiring preacher
2	Person of character	Administrative ability	Successful in church/evangelism
3	Role model	Leadership skills	Interpersonal skills
4	Successful in church/evangelism	Interpersonal skills	Theological knowledge
5	Loving concern for people	Inspiring preacher	Leadership skills
6	Inspiring preacher	Successful in church/evangelism	Role model
7	Interpersonal skills	Person of character	Administrative ability
8	Leadership skills	Person of prayer	Person of character
9	Administrative ability	Role model	Person of prayer
10	Theological knowledge	Loving concern for people	Loving concern for people

This presents us with a bizarre vision for wholeness in a learning context where different constituencies have distinct priorities. In the midst of ever-increasing complexities and ambiguities, it is the school that has to envision the most appropriate learning environment for the students. What aspects of wholeness do we take into account as the fresh candidate steps in with the baggage of developmental assumptions and aspirations? Should not the developmental values set by the school for the students be made known to them? Obviously, every student should know what the institution stands for, and this awareness has to be accentuated from the first week of student orientation to campus life. The survey report in Figure 14 was not meant to

---

2. Jaison Thomas, "Church-Ministry Formation in Theological Education in India," PhD thesis, Queen's University, Belfast, 2008.

be generalized; yet it raises the question: How, then, can an institution set the formational priorities for the students? How should we design the learning environment so that the person's development takes place with the spiritual, intellectual, physical, mental and social dimensions held in balance? Every learning experience can and must play a significant part in attaining this goal. The ConneXions Model[3] of Holistic Formation (Figure 15) that portrays the four key dynamics that facilitate formative efficiency and wholeness is worth considering. The essential dynamics it sets in balance in a learning experience are: spiritual – connecting with God; experiential – connecting with life; relational – connecting with others; and instructional – connecting with truth. An example list of indicators for each of the four dynamics is given in Appendix 3 to give an idea of the design.

Figure 15: ConneXions Model of Holistic Formation

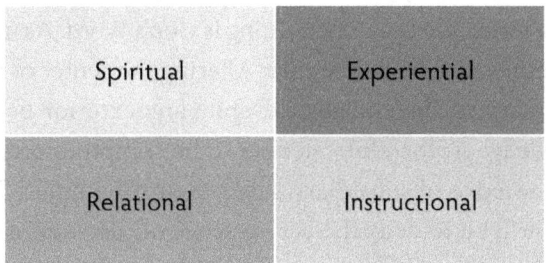

The Vitality of Knowing and Centering on God's Word

It is needless to emphasize the significance of the cognitive dimension in education. Knowledge is central. Nevertheless, we have serious concerns when

> "What drives a seminary goes beyond its mission statement. It is centered in the power of God's Spirit that ignites and persuades us to move ahead in faith... the main driving force in seminaries is this living presence of God, who is the major Stakeholder and Provider of theological wisdom, who is assumed but unfortunately neglected in the course of our educational process as we demystify the sacred materials of faith." Carnegie Samuel Calian, *The Ideal Seminary: Pursuing Excellence in Theological Education* (Louisville, KY: Westminster John Knox, 2002), 36–37.

---

3. Malcolm Webber, *Building Healthy Leaders: Spirit-Built Leadership Series 1–4* (Elkhart, IN: Strategic, 2002–2011).

it comes to theological education. Troubled by the excessive emphasis on theoretical knowledge in theological education, we sometimes raise sharp criticism at the intellectual domain as a whole. Let us be clear: cognition is the hinge domain that must be solid in its form and content and be capable of integrating every other formational domain towards the goal. This suggests that a lack of clarity in the core body of knowledge will incapacitate every domain in learning. But we are encountering a different problem. This cognitive domain is being wrongly paralleled with the abstract knowledge of theories and unlimited amounts of information available in academia. Conceivably, it is this disintegration that has created the biggest crisis in theological education. What is the knowledge we are pursuing? Who is a *scholar* in theology? What does *scholarship* signify in the context of a theological institution? If it is not the Scripture, the doctrine, the whole gospel of salvation expressing itself in holistic living and service, then what could it be? The foundational body of knowledge that forms the center of training is God's Word. As in any structure, it is very dangerous to sideline the core. Altering the center of the system will only bring damage to the endeavor despite any exterior benefits it might provide. Knowledge is, therefore, neither to be compromised, nor is it to be equaled to knowledge of subsidiary subjects or disciplines. To sideline the doctrinal core will be to deny the very essence of theological education. All subjects, theories and correlations are to be held secondary and are only to be used as supportive aids for our human minds to acquire perspectival confidence amidst our cognitive limitations. When subjects and theories take the place of the focus of the Word and doctrine, we are at fault. All our conscious and unconscious attempts to make theological education look better or sound more compatible with secular academia by moving its axis to the periphery has done immense harm to our mission. The overall learning frame in our schools must revisit this core, realizing that it is this central line that holds all components, subjects and projects in perfect balance in moving us to the goal.

Formation and transformation that are not grounded on deep knowledge of the truth of God will have only a temporary effect. Moreover, *knowledge*, as we define it theologically, is in principle holistic. Doctrine is what saturates lives, impacts the heart and enables life and action. How easily our theological educators fall into the trap of leading students to all sorts of literary resources and forget to orient them rightly to the source of all resources, the Word of God! Close observation reveals how acutely this is being reflected in the way a large number of theology students process their thinking, prepare their sermons and lead Bible studies. They often seem satisfied with a little of the Bible, with references here and there, or with having it simply as something to refer to. Today's thinking, preaching, teaching and writing seem to be progressively centering on themes and ideas substantiated with heavy *scholarly* content. As a student once confessed, "Certain contexts exert unimaginable pressure to exhibit your *scholarship*. If you make the Bible the sole or main ground of preaching, you are most likely to be labeled *not so scholarly*." This depiction calls us to revisit our form of doing theology in the light of the wholeness prospect. In a recent session on the preparatory defense of a university PhD dissertation in a seminary, a student had undertaken outstanding research on the topic across the disciplines of philosophy, sociology, history and psychology, with sporadic references to some theological books and commentaries. What the study essentially lacked was a solid theological frame of thought, or at least a reasonable section that discussed the biblical-theological view of the topic. This is understandable if the university's criteria do not require it. Still, students of theology and the faculty who guide them in research should be standing on the foundation of God's truth as their indispensable platform. We must see this as the only way to go about the learning and teaching of theology. In a sense, the absence of this coherence and firmness in our way of doing theology may have caused us to lose our rightly bestowed title in academia, "the Queen of Sciences." The subtle erasing of theology and the Bible from theological education and research has become the foremost sign of our disintegrated identity. I remember meeting a member of faculty who had a prestigious seminary-cum-university Master's degree in hand. She said, "I was compelled to write the university paper in a certain way to satisfy the theological standpoints of the number of examiners who evaluated my answer sheets. More than a particular type of words and expressions, it demanded extreme perspectives as well. In papers for internal assessment I tried to be truthful to myself and my theological convictions as much as possible. Continuing this for years has taken away my trust in myself. It meant masking myself, burying my convictions and, very often, distorting God's truth. Finally, when I completed the program, I found myself totally lost. I was unable to communicate with my people, ill-equipped to serve my church and incapable of applying any of those philosophies in my context of ministry." Training damages lives when it loses focus. Therefore, the clarion call to theology schools is to affirm and uphold their core doctrinal foundation and to make it the center of everything else that happens in education. Equally, we must hold that an exclusive and detached focus on the spiritual or ministry dimensions is as dangerous as this relegation of the cognitive foundation. Churches and missions become unhealthy in many contexts when they are led by leaders who do not know what they believe. It is the knowledge of God's Word that transforms minds, keeps on impacting lives and empowers persons and communities in true worship and service.

The Formal, Informal and Non-formal Learning Domains[4]

Planning and designing the learning exercise begins with the goal and ethos of the school. Then it addresses the curriculum, faculty, students, learning outcomes and its impact in the larger context of ministry. One of the key reasons identified for the multiple dissonances in training is the lack of awareness of the critical need for weaving these dimensions together. As a preliminary step forward, we might reflect on the major domains in a learning environment.

The Formal Learning Domain

Formal education is the largely organized, ladder-like and sequential mode with prerequisites and credentials; it tends to be teacher- and curriculum-centered, theoretical and campus-based education. This domain consists of the explicit content, sequential learning, admission requirements, examinations, grading and awarding of degrees, and anything else that holds a rightful place in the form of what we mean generally by "education." Classroom teaching, assignments, class tests, paper presentations and examinations are integral elements, although approaches may vary. Sadly, a number of theology schools are still following the age-old conventional knowledge-weighing tests assessed from a fixed total of marks as the only method of evaluation. This is also done by dividing grade percentages among the final examination and internal learning activities such as assignments, presentation of papers, attendance and group work. Schools that have a more detailed design for formal assessment

---

4. Victor Babajide Cole, *Training of the Ministry* (Bangalore: Theological Book Trust, 2001), 130–135. See also Brian C. Wintle, "Theological Education in Contemporary India: How Do We Make It Relevant?" in *Called to Teach: Essays in Honour of Peter S. C. Pothan; A Festschrift*, edited by Siga Arles (Bangalore: CFCC, 2011), 18–19.

sometimes disregard subsequent follow-up of the procedures. One prevalent concern is the limited impact of this domain on the future of the learners, in spite of the large amount of time and energy devoted to it.

The Informal Learning Domain

Informal education is the most natural mode of education, by which individuals acquire basic life education, core values, attitude development, and spiritual and character formation. Learning in this domain is not organized or systematically planned. People learn informally and naturally from the environment and the community in which they live. They absorb the good or bad models of behavior, attitude, values, and worldviews. For example, responsible behavior, time management, a disciplined work style, prayer habits and solitude are learned informally from campus life or mission exposure. Informal learning happens without us realizing or crediting it, because the learning environment expedites it. In order to enhance holistic formation, theology schools should pay closer attention to their informal learning environment, where most of the actual shaping of life and ministry occurs.

The Non-formal Learning Domain

Non-formal education is largely off-campus short-term residential training where learning occurs in a consciously planned environment. It includes small groups, seminars, workshops, short courses on skills development, reading selected books for learning, being mentored by another person and group discussions. Much learning is done, but there are no credits. It can also be done by a faculty as part of a curricular plan for personal development, but it may not be perceptible to others. Our schools can make significant progress in non-formal learning under the guidance of deans or members on faculty who are experts in educational networking and academic administrative design.

Developing a Learning Climate Conducive to Holistic Formation

Spiritual Formation, Chapel and the Chaplaincy Team

The theological community is essentially a faith community. It is designed to be a worshipping community. A school that disregards the spiritual dimension in training is dead in spite of all the great things that happen there. Theology schools should espouse this vision as central to their calling as communities where God's truth is sought with great spiritual fervor and personal devotion. When we stop experiencing life and peace on our campuses, the first thing we should do is thoughtfully revisit worship, prayer and the ministry of God's Word. Excellence in chapel services and spiritual nurture makes a theology school excellent at its core. Schools' constituencies may not deem this to be vital and accreditation bodies may not be keen about it. For some members in the school community, chapel may be a routine; for others it is the most boring exercise of the regular prayers. But the leadership of every institution, by virtue of its calling, has to ensure that each service at the chapel and each of the formational plans of the chaplain generates within the community a deep-felt thirst for God. Everyone in the community should find prayer and worship the most vital and beneficial facet in their training.

One of the imminent tasks for our schools is to redefine the role of the chapel and the chaplain. The role definition and appointment of the staff in charge of the hostel is sometimes even more crucial in the spiritual formation of the community. These are areas that primarily form the student personally and spiritually. In Calian's words, "There may be a 'chapel' vs. 'classroom' struggle for some members of seminary communities, who have yet to integrate these two experiences harmoniously. Consequently, some theological campuses are no longer communities of expectation. Prayer life has become sterile. We are too busily engaged in cognitive learning, neglecting the spiritual dimension to complement our intellectual pursuits."[5] Paul Cornelius speaks of seminary as primarily a worshipping community in his account of the transformational model of theological education. Nothing can be more vital in integrating and impacting lives than a lifestyle that is devoted to true worship. He asserts, "Worship at its core is intrinsically transformational and affects every aspect of human life and relationships. It is in the context of worship, therefore, that spiritual, intellectual, ministerial and community formation must take place. *Worship does not simply become part of the curriculum; rather it is the foundation on which both the explicit and implicit curriculum is developed.*"[6] Above all,

---

5. Carnegie Samuel Calian, *The Ideal Seminary: Pursuing Excellence in Theological Education* (Louisville, KY: Westminster John Knox, 2002), 99.

6. Paul Cornelius, "Transforming Theological Education to Be Transformational," *Journal of Theological Education and Mission (JOTEAM)* 6, no. 6 (2015): 36.

we know that spiritual orientation builds up the community in oneness and character. When spiritual formation is focused and intentional, persons grow strong both in *being* and in *doing*.

Being Different from the Secular University Model

In a secular university model, the student, as an independent learner, does not necessarily obtain personal or spiritual mentoring. That form of education does not mandate these aspects, either. But a theology school is essentially different from that model. In saying this, we are not aiming at or conveying an anti-university notion. Our focus is simply wholeness in theological education. These words are, therefore, specific cautions at the dangerous slide of theological education into a mere academic exercise. Both the model of modern university education and the increased tendency of theology schools to seek university affiliation raise important questions. What drives many of our schools to embark on an endless striving for university accreditation or to gain university status for themselves? Is the reason theological, educational, economic, political or structural? Are there theological institutions that endanger their calling by seeking accreditation? Regarding theological schools' tendency to use the modern university as the model of a training structure, Jones commented,

> There is nothing theological about the structure of the seminary institution. Instead of reflecting some theological convictions or virtues, seminaries are entirely reflective of secular universities. The schools are run by presidents, provosts, and deans. Professors (stratified into adjunct, assistant, associate, and full) compete for tenure by writing abstruse monographs for their own guilds. And students are run through the gauntlet of papers, exams, and compulsory – if marginalized – field education.[7]

There is nothing inherently bad about these offices or the educational processes. The question here is whether such moves help us retain the vital wholeness of theological education through spiritual, ministerial or personal formation. In other words: In what way is this model more conducive to and compatible

---

7. Tony Jones, *The New Christians: Dispatches from the Emergent Frontier* (San Francisco, Jossey-Bass, 2008), 209.

with the holistic formation of persons in faith and discipleship? Will any of our safeguards have long-term control over the association? To be concise, the issue here is not the university or the way it functions; rather, it is the conscious and unconscious shifts in theology that yields itself to the abstract accumulation of knowledge, misidentifying it with the pursuit of divine truth.

Balancing Solid Theological Grounding and Ministry Skill Development

Read the following fascinating paraphrase of 1 Corinthians 13 written by a theology student. The writer is articulating the theme of vital balance in theological education:

> If I have language ever so perfect and speak like a pundit, and have not the knack of love that grips the heart, I am nothing.
>
> If I have decorations and diplomas and am proficient in up-to-date methods, and have not the touch of an understanding love, I am nothing.
>
> If I am able to worst my opponents in argument so as to make fools of them, and have not the wooing note, I am nothing.
>
> If I have all faith and great ideals and magnificent plans and wonderful visions, and have not the love that sweats and bleeds, and weeps and prays and pleads, I am nothing.
>
> If I surrender all prospects and, leaving home and friends and comforts, give myself to the self-evident sacrifice of a missionary career, and turn sour and selfish amid the daily annoyances and personal slights of a missionary life, and though I give my body to be consumed in the heat and sweat and mildew of India, if I have not the love that yields its rights, its coveted leisure, its pet plans, I am nothing, nothing. Virtue has ceased to go out of me.
>
> If I can heal all manner of sickness and disease, but wound hearts and hurt feelings for want of love that is kind, I am nothing.

> If I can write books and publish articles that set the world agog,
> and fail to transcribe the word of the cross in the language of love,
> I am nothing.[8]

The dichotomy of academics and ministry is sadly percolating the theological settings. Holding theological thinking and ministerial praxis in balance has always been a puzzle for theology schools. We either promote critical academics, risking ministerial formation, or we resort to an exclusive focus on ministry skill development, disregarding the theological grounding. Barsness and Kim describe a particular instructional form as the "Pedagogy of Engagement," which is "an experiential approach to education that invites faculty to meaningfully engage students in interpersonal relationships, rooted in the values of mutuality and dignity."[9] Cultures in which education still takes the "spoon-feeding" approach will have a long way to go in realizing this notion. When we acquire its primary skills, it progressively permeates the learning process where field education and reflective praxis are eminently blended across all study programs.

An ideal theological institution is one where students grow as "community creators, not classroom sages; they become integrative practitioners, not just scholars."[10] It is from there that students grow in their calling and competency to engage authentically with the community. Nonetheless, over the past decades, theology schools have procured the bad reputation of isolating students from their own contexts, and, more specifically, from any authentic community. Holistic learning assumes that we keep our feet on the ground; we are able to listen closely to the voices around; we observe every heart-beat of our communities and effectively engage in life.

> "And Jesus ordained the twelve, that they should be with him, and that He might send them forth to preach, and to have power to heal sickness and to cast out devils." Mark 3:14-15

---

8. Paraphrase of 1 Corinthians 13 by an Indian theological student, quoted in Philip Duce and Daniel Strange (eds.), *Keeping Your Balance: Approaching Theological and Religious Studies* (Leicester: IVP, 2001).
9. Roy E. Barsness and Richard D. Kim, "A Pedagogy of Engagement for the Changing Character of the 21st Century Classroom," *Theological Education* 49, no. 2 (2015): 91.
10. Steven Studebaker and Lee Beach, "Friend Or Foe? The Role of the Scholar in Emerging Christianity," *Theological Education* 48, no. 2 (2014): 43–56.

Well-designed research and empirical procedures in theological programs can potentially assist the schools in realizing this vision.

Informal Theological Talks, Mentoring and Pastoral Direction

The learning environment in theology schools has to constantly nurture the holistic reflection of theology. Theology is not transformative when done in isolation. It is essentially relational and communal, and is best realized in a context where mentoring and pastoral interaction are intrinsic to the learning process. Theology done this way gives life to the community. We also assert that as a relevant teaching-learning approach, "theological reflection" has great potential to facilitate wholeness in the theological endeavor. John Paver maintains that theological reflection, beginning with experience, is a method of integration and that pastoral supervision is a vehicle for it. Establishing this, he demonstrates that the model and method have potential to be a catalyst for reform within theological colleges and seminaries. From the ministerial, cultural and personal integration, he goes on to make bold recommendations for structural integration within the philosophy and practice of the theological institution. Theological reflection in the training environment of Jesus's disciples happened in normal life situations in which listening, conversing, caring, mentoring, rebuking, correcting, motivating and edifying happened simultaneously.

Mentoring has profound significance in transformative education. Students, later in their lives, may or may not use their study notes or the copies of theological treatises they gathered during the program. But the relational impact of the community on a learner is long-lasting. Everything that a community is and has makes a permanent impression on students' lives. A lifelong impact is made by genuine mentoring. Effective mentors facilitate holistic learning in theological education, argue Chiroma and Cloete in their article titled "Mentoring as a Supportive Pedagogy in Theological Training."[11] In spite of the fact that mentoring is time-consuming, requires patience and commitment, presumes added responsibility, and presupposes a credible level of coaching and accountability, every school may discover and develop the

---

11. Nathan Chiroma and Anitha Cloete, "Mentoring as a Supportive Pedagogy in Theological Training," *HTS Teologiese Studies/Theological Studies* 71, no. 3 (2015), Art. #2695, 8 pages, http://dx.doi.org/10.4102/hts.v71i3.2695.

unlimited potential of mentoring in student formation. It should eventually become the normal pattern of training and discipleship on our campuses. However, this requires committed, Spirit-led, compassion-driven, well-informed members on faculty and staff.

Group-Centered and Individualized Methods of Learning

The following are examples of group-centered learning methods:

- *Simulation learning:* "Simulation" refers to imitation, re-creation, mock-up, reproduction and replication or model, with a focus more on the process than the outcome of the activity. It is not something like a game or contest where the outcome is anticipated, such as winning or accomplishing a certain task. Simulation, which is sometimes called instructive play, has five major elements: activity, realism, intellectual content, an emotional or volitional aspect, and participation. Simulation should be used sparingly as it involves a lot of preparation and time.
- *Synergogy:* This term denotes cooperative learning. The trend of making education more competitive or combative is slowly being replaced with collaborative and cooperative learning which is called "synergogy" or learning together. In this method the students work together to achieve mutually desirable goals. This kind of study is usually not for the purpose of getting grades but to achieve a group task and gain the multiple benefits from it.
- *Senior colloquium:*[12] Relevant theological topics are discussed by a panel that consists of members from all academic departments, aiming at further learning, reflection and formal documentation. Each department brings unique insights from its scholarship to nurture a whole understanding of the topic. This coordinates departmental scholarship and advances integration, and, above all, creates within the students (and faculty) a deep sense of belonging to one another and the need for mutual edification.

---

12. This method was explored and successfully implemented by Dr Saphir Athyal, the distinguished theological educator and mission strategist from India. Further references to this learning method are given in chapter 7 on the interworking of departments.

- *Panel discussion:* Panel discussion is most appropriate when there is limited knowledge on a topic, when the teachers' exposure to the subject is limited or when the learning requires people with different levels of expertise on the topic. Most of the time the questions are pre-determined, being asked or circulated to those who are experienced.

  How to use the panel discussion method:
  - Determine the learning outcome
  - Formulate well-worded questions
  - Make a list of potential panel members
  - Discuss with panel members what you are going to discuss
  - Set the room for the panel in advance
  - Introduce the topic, panel members and rules
  - Summarize the outcome and thank the panelists

There are many other useful group-centered learning methods. Since learning is multi-dimensional in theological settings, we need to include a variety of experiences, such as group spiritual exercises, sporting events, casual discussions and so on. The following are a few more such experiences that improve learning:

- *Debates:* A debate is a formal discussion between two groups on a particular topic. Defined propositions are put into a public discourse.
- *Skits and role plays:* When standard debates become stale in the class, skits and role plays can help learners to improve their metacognition capacity by reflecting on differences of opinion and perspective. These advance intellectual, physical and social learning capacities.
- *Group projects:* In group projects, students learn leadership skills and the essential dynamics of working effectively in a team. Learning from each member's particular specialties in knowledge and skill, the group grows to become its best in a team context, at the same time gaining personal significance.
- *Buzz groups:* These are small intensive discussion groups with the objective of developing a specific task, such as idea generation or problem solving. The group is expected to reach a thoughtful consensus on the task within a given time. Students learn how to manage differences of opinion and how to arrive at logical consensus.

- *Comprehensive papers and presentations:* Certain themes or issues of contemporary relevance are chosen for comprehensive deliberation. Students will employ deep reflective thinking and synthesizing skills in formulating a whole perspective on the issue, using knowledge and capacities gained from multiple courses in the program.
- *Sports:* Sporting events are profound opportunities for learning physical, social, technical and emotional skills and competencies.
- *Casual conversations:* These just happen. Most of the time, they can be sources of great interactive learning. We also need to be aware that they might produce undesirable results when conversional direction is wrong and the persons engaging in them are poorly informed. This method can reveal persons in the community with hidden treasures of knowledge who, because of their personalities, contribute most effectively to closer or small circles.
- *Informal talks in groups on real-life issues:* Every member in the community will have issues, crises and queries. Informal group situations help us to tackle those issues that are important to the members in the community. With effective moderation of talk, this always proves to be a significant learning methodology.
- *Small-group prayer times and Bible reflections:* Praying through issues and concurrently conversing on the biblical grounds or views on them are powerful methods of group learning.
- *Corporate days of meditating on God's Word, fasting and waiting on God:* This is a more focused group-learning spiritual exercise that combines meditative learning of the Scripture and the practical discipline of fasting and seeking the face of God.

There are individualized methods that focus on creative efforts and seek more specific application. Tailored learning experiences make far-reaching impacts on the lives of students.

The following are examples of individualized methods in learning:
- Journaling: the discipline of recording one's personal story regularly; a highly effective tool for personal growth and development
- Assignments, projects, interviews
- Research, reports and thought papers
- Creative writing
- Role-play design, art, craft, music and extra-curricular activities

- Innovative personal projects
- Field trips
- Ministry internships

Maximizing the Non-formal Learning Opportunities

We have seen that non-formal learning refers to learning exposure outside of the formal programs of the school. These are special opportunities for the student to obtain distinct understanding of the subject. In Jesus's practice, even immediate life events were rapidly transformed into the profoundest learning opportunities that impacted the learner's spirituality, intelligence, emotion and personality in unison. Theology schools that limit learning to technical lecturing in the classrooms through unexamined, monotonous talking, assisted by some age-old study materials, obstruct learning and prevent students from gaining holistic formation. The learning environment in a theology school may undergo methodical scrutiny to ensure coherence and wholeness. Accreditation can doubtless assist an institution to attain higher standards; nevertheless, a theology school should have its own aims of excellence, aims that are higher than the measures normally set for them in the accreditation standards. The most negative message a school can give to its students is that "everything done here is just to secure or maintain our status of accreditation." Students in such learning environments will noticeably tend to develop the attitude that they will not do anything if not for grade or credit. These are signs of unhealthy institutions. Such attitudes hamper the personal development of the students during the program and even more so in subsequent ministry involvement. Learning must become the habit of life for the faculty and student alike. In a transformative learning environment everyone will see life as a constant collection of worthwhile learning experiences designed in the will of God. The campus needs to nurture an attitude of humility that enables students to make the best use of every opportunity of life and service.

A School's Self-Assessment Guide on Overall Learning Experience

- What factors prevent the school from initiating methodological variety in learning, outside of typical classrooms lecturing?

- What are the annual plans of the chaplaincy team for the community's spiritual formation?
- How much of the school's time is devoted to annual planning and modification of these practices?
- What level of thinking and learning is going on at the school regarding worship and spiritual disciplines?
- How can students be mentored into a lifelong passion for exploring the truth of God?
- How solidly are students trained in the personal disciplines of learning, reflection and prayer?
- What specific measures are taken at the school to be distinct from a secular university model of education that is devoid of spiritual and ministerial formation?
- What accreditations and developments for the school are currently being worked on?
- Are the ongoing developmental prospects *helps* or *hindrances* to the school's vision and mission?
- Are group-learning opportunities provided or initiated on campus?
- Do students receive training that balances theological grounding with ministry skill development? What are helpful indicators of this?
- Are students able to make relevant and biblically grounded theological reflections on contemporary issues? What opportunities are specifically created to develop students in this capacity?

Practical Recommendations: Overall Learning Experience

- Pay utmost attention to the appointment of the chaplain of the school. Consider that office as the most central one in the life of the school and set apart a substantial amount of time and effort to pray, plan and prepare for the spiritual development of the community.
- Provide focused discipleship sessions at different levels to assist students who join the school at different stages of their walk in faith and discipleship.
- Practice the Lord's Table as the central practice of community of faith.

- Set apart well-designed and effectively oriented times for devotions, quiet times, journaling, corporate prayer and fasting.
- Plan to form the community as a deeply caring and hospitable body. Be determined not to breed individualistic, selfish patterns of life.
- Have a few persons on campus whom the students can approach for prayer and personal counsel. These people do not have to be full-time staff of the school, but those who have won the hearts of the community by being godly listeners and friends.
- Discuss among the faculty and staff the most effective ways to identify and encourage the talents and aptitudes of the students.
- Create opportunities for students to engage in meaningful theological talks formally and informally. Faculty's participation in this can provide great theological interaction as well as coaching.
- Do a critical self-assessment on the balance of theological formation and ministry skill development in the school. Explore strategic ways to address any problem that surfaces.
- Conduct occasional qualitative surveys among students and alumni to see what type and level of transformation is most needed in the teaching-learning method at the school.

5

Wholeness in the Community Life of the School

The influence of community life on a student's formation is enormous. Theology schools often experience difficulty in being a real community. They also struggle to be real to the community around them. Hopewell observes, "In the usual setting, the symbiotic environment of the candidate is not the world, but rather an artificial theological community. In this usual setting, the world is the calisthenics, not theology. We pepper the traditional theological course with spot announcements about the world, catchy phrases about involvement and canned observations of social involvement."[1] He talks about the withdrawal of a student to a seminary as a "three year vacation, so to speak, from the life he would live before and after." This undoubtedly poses a big challenge to the holistic formation of the students. The theology community needs to shift from an artificial to a real community that cares for those within and radiates that experience outward to the larger community of the world. This chapter discusses certain desirable characteristics of the theological community.

---

1. James Hopewell, "Mission and Seminary Structure," *International Review of Missions* 56, no. 222 (April 1967): 158.

Community That Balances Love and Discipline

We start this session with a seemingly strange dimension, that is, discipline. Most of my academic mentors as well as colleagues seem judiciously concerned about the need for personal discipline and habit formation in theological institutions. On the other hand, in recent years we have witnessed an increase in the number of theological educators who argue for the student community to enjoy an *unconditional love* on campus, meaning "no guidelines or measures of discipline." The blatant ideological differences regarding the need for discipline on theological campuses are surprising. Deeply burdened by this matter, an experienced theological educator raised the following questions in a recent conversation:

1. Are we divided on the need for moral discipline on seminary campuses?
2. How do our campuses perceive and address issues such as alcohol, drugs and illicit relationships?
3. Are we inaudibly backing up hedonistic individualism and ultimate personal freedom?
4. Have we established close ties with the church, such that the students' character issues will have implications for their future tenure of ministry within the church? In other words, how do we train persons to be accountable?
5. Do we have a healthy, ongoing reporting pattern between the church and the school on student formation?
6. Do our students act as *independent comers and goers* who do not need to maintain accountability with a ministry oversight?

"As he was scattering the seed, some fell along the path, and the birds came and ate it up. Some fell on rocky places, where it did not have much soil. It sprang up quickly, because the soil was shallow. But when the sun came up, the plants were scorched, and they withered because they had no root. Other seed fell among the thorns, which grew up and choked the plants, so that they did not bear grain. Still other seed fell on good soil. It came up, grew and produced a crop, multiplying thirty, sixty, or even a hundred times." Mark 4:4–8

These questions are pointers to awaken the theology schools' self-concept in formational vision. As our conversation went on, the renowned educator seemed greatly disturbed about the *independent, indifferent and unaccountable* student constituency that makes many theology schools unstable and very vulnerable. Not many in the theological system today are cautious or concerned to see disciplinary issues left unattended or neglected. When students engage in endless social networking and other addictions in life, it is increasingly explained as their "private space" or a matter of "individual freedom." Outlining the unlimited scope and the challenges set for theological education by digitization and the social media revolution, Jaison says,

> When these innovations turn out to be the greatest passion or the guiding feature in the life of the students and faculty, they are harmful. Learners who recognize the need to get rid of the addictive behavior often suffer from lack of skillful and informed assistance. Absorption of too many habits from media and digital technology eventually seems to become an inhibition to the spiritual discipline and formation of students.[2]

We maintain that theological schools should never cease being discipleship communities. Discipline is integral to discipleship. Salt cannot lose its saltiness. Student deans and other responsible persons may need to ensure that these seedbeds do not foster alcoholism, excessive use of social networks/browsing, gossiping, substance abuse, immoral sexual relationships, sexual harassment or elitism. Our institutions follow the model set by a Master whose primary traits were humility, community, purity and absolute devotion to his Father. Nothing less should characterize the atmosphere of a theology school.

In his editorial in the *Journal of Malankara Orthodox Theological Studies*, Thomas expressed his deep-felt realization of the need for wholesomeness in academic and spiritual dimensions of theological education. Due to the relevance of the content, a relatively large section of his writing is added to benefit our self-assessment:

> There may be students studying theology with different motivations. But the majority are in one way or other related to

---

2. Jessy Jaison, "Digitization and Social Media Revolution: Training Prospects and Spiritual Formational Challenges in Theological Schools," *OTI Journal* 3, no. 1 (2016): 18.

the ministry of the church. Therefore in the process of theological education, academics and spirituality are not in juxtaposition but are complementary. From the perspective of the pastoral ministry of the church mediocre spirituality is more adversely affecting the quality of ministry than any academic decadence. This observation does not underestimate the need of academic excellence because the intellectuals in all congregations are not happy with the mediocre knowledge of pastors. The false dichotomy that university is concerned about the academics and the churches are concerned about the spirituality should also be avoided. We should have a converging point to enhance both elements. In that process, theological colleges have got a great responsibility in enhancing both academics and spirituality. Though theological colleges differ in faith perspectives and priorities, there are of course a few common factors to which theological seminaries should have a commitment.

1. Experiencing God: Knowing God does not just happen in theological education. It comes through a personal relationship with God. Therefore all theological students should be encouraged to develop a habit of personal prayer, Bible reading and meditation. The community worship in theological colleges should help them to develop a daily personal devotion to God wherever they are even after they leave the seminaries.

2. Personal discipline, including a healthy time schedule, eating habit, simple life style, should be inculcated in students while they are in theological colleges.

3. Too much involvement in emotionally pleasurable programs that appear in WhatsApp, Facebook and other social media are to be avoided and the students should be engaged in serious studies as well as spending more time in libraries. It does not mean that they should not have any activities for physical exercise and mental relaxation.

4. Commitment and vocation to the ministry of our Lord Jesus Christ to be deepened while they engage in theological studies. Self-interest should not be a motivation for academic excellence.

5. Integrity in using the public money and resources should be developed while they are theological students. Misappropriation of money and funds is a common scandal pointed out in many churches against the priestly hierarchy.

6. Speaking about justice is a fashion in all theological discourses, but quite often it is not seen in action while the same people hold responsible positions. Theological students should be able to develop a sense of justice in all their actions particularly towards the concerns of the marginalized people and environment.

7. Recently in a theological teachers' meeting, an elderly lady Professor commented that women students are not safe with their teachers (men) even in theological institutions. Nobody in that august meeting either questioned or negated the comment. A complete silence spread over there as if acknowledging it as a reality. There were whispers that a few theological teachers as well as students have the vices of smoking, drinking etc. If it is so, which is more dangerous between academic mediocrity and spiritual degradation?[3]

> "Students are not just ecclesially formed by what happens in the classroom but also, and maybe equally importantly, in the relationships that are being formed in the communal life on campus." Edwin Chr. van Driel, "Online Theological Education: Three Undertheorized Issues," *Theological Education* 50, no. 1 (2015): 76.

In brief, theological colleges cannot escape from the responsibility of enhancing academics and spirituality hand-in-hand because they are doing it for God's glory and for his kingdom. Theology schools in the twenty-first

---

3. O. Thomas, "Editorial," *The Journal of Malankara Orthodox Theological Studies* 3, no. 1 (August 2015): 3–5. Used with permission.

century need to be reminded to be fearless in fulfilling their task of discipleship and transformation.

At times we like to perceive personal and character formation as more of an individual choice and not something that occurs essentially from exterior pressures. Nonetheless, we know that attending to this is the manifest obligation of theology schools. The theological institution is essentially a believing and worshipping community that simply cannot divorce matters of behavioral and character formation from its body of scholarship. As the soil in which the seeds are sown and grown, this community is to be spiritually, cognitively, ministerially, morally and behaviorally formative and transformative.

Growing into an Accepting, Loving and Caring Community

Life on campus should build the students holistically. Perhaps the biggest challenge for schools is the demonstration of a true Christian lifestyle in an educational setting. As theological institutions, we must look at ourselves to see if we walk on campus masking ourselves, not being *real people in the real world*. An ideal theology community is one where persons are loved in spite of their limitations. It is where acceptance, care and smiles of courteous recognition are the norm. Intellectual heaviness and self-exaltation find no place. Developing this type of community takes humility and intentionality.

The term *community* paints the picture of talking, loving, sharing, caring, laughing, eating, playing, agreeing, disagreeing, helping, problem-solving and much more. Communities are formed by relationships and sharing, not by infinite reading and research. Every experience, big or small, in the community becomes the means of learning for the members, who naturally absorb it through the relational dynamics and verbal and non-verbal communication. When all theories, books, articles and dissertations are forgotten, people will still remember their informal talks and the experiential moments they captured from their communities. This affects the classroom, too. It is not the mere content of the teaching, but also the motivations and conduct of the teacher and formative interactions in the small classroom community that impact the student. Since the relational inputs are highly formative, theology schools may need to be more intentional in shaping this dimension in training.

Students try to make sense of what they see and experience on campus. It is not only what one hears, but also what one observes and feels about the campus that makes a significant effect on formation. Shaw referred to Hardy, who said, "One of the most subtle but influential elements of the hidden curriculum is the culture and structure of the school . . . Where 'important' members of faculty do minimal preparation and teach the same material year after year, students quickly pick up the message that once you have reached a position of status, you no longer need to grow as a leader (Hardy 2012)."[4] Such negative impressions will be deeply engraved on the minds of the learners and therefore need to be guarded against. The social environment in a theology school should stand out from all the students' previous community experiences. It should be the one they want to nurture for themselves and emulate in future ministry.

The holistic formational task in theological education is complex in many respects. Students come together to a particular place with their own deep-rooted convictions of God, definitions of spirituality, different cognitive capacities, wide-ranging hopes for ministry, linguistic and cultural diversities, and dissimilarities in calling and gifting. Every aspect of social interaction on campus will have a substantial influence on students. Moreover, the way each person translates the meaning of experiences, attitudes or events on campus will differ starkly. This makes the formational task even more composite. Formation denotes much more than *learning*. It points further to the impact of learning on one's life so that the matrix of perspective, behavior, values and personhood is transformed. This sort of dynamic transformation takes place with deeper levels of motivation, internalization and integration. No two individuals develop the same way. This persuades us to shape our community into a place of true acceptance, love and care that enriches all its members at their particular points of need in life.

Managing and Developing Individual Talents of Students

Another dimension often overlooked in holistic formation is the ongoing assessment and follow-up of the talents or gifts of the students. Do our schools value the students as persons in whom God has disseminated the special grace-gifts for the building up of his kingdom? As theological educators, we should patiently and persistently remind ourselves that all great men and women of God had humble beginnings and that they encountered someone on their

---

4. Quoted in Perry Shaw, *Transforming Theological Education: A Practical Handbook for Integrative Learning* (Carlisle: Langham Global Library, 2014), 87.

journey who discovered and nurtured their talents. Not all students will have benefited in their past from a strong foundation in Sunday school, discipleship in their church or Christian nurture in their families. For many, the theology school may be the first place that made them wonder about their calling in ministry and giftedness for service. In spite of the diverse backgrounds represented, theological communities can substantively foster the talents of all members – students, faculty and staff. The significance of a theology school does not rely on its remarkable academic rating, but on so much more: on the type of gifted and committed leaders it contributes to the church and to the world. As communities of faith, we may need to explore the most effective ways of mentoring and providing talent management so that every capacity and giftedness will be maximized for God's mission. Every organization that aims to be highly effective is highly focused in talent management and development. Moreover, all members in those communities will grow in their God-given talents with deep contentment and appreciation for what they are in the plan of God.

Physical Care and Hospitality in a Genuine Community Climate

Any educational setting needs sports and physical fitness facilities as an essential part of campus life. This may be branded as "less spiritual" when it comes to the context of the church or theology school. We, however, affirm that physical wellbeing is indisputably central to wholeness. Certain theology schools have manifestly included this *physical component* in their ethos, ensuring that ample attention is given to this dimension. This component will define the provision of nutritious food, necessary medical support and facilities for exercise and sport depending on what is viable within the economic parameters of the school. Educational contexts that retain the faulty concept that overloaded academic and social requirements make good learning may have to modify their patterns so as to provide an adequate amount of rest and relaxation for learners. Physical wholeness contributes towards enhancing intellectual, spiritual and emotional formation. When schools overlook the importance of the disciplines of rest, physical exercise, quietness, contemplation and journaling, students will be trained in the worldly pattern of an achievement-driven lifestyle. Unhealthy persons formed in theology schools will make unhealthy leaders for churches and missions because they will always lack holistic habits in life and service.

Hospitality in the learning environment is key to healthy relationships and this has been the central integrative element in many historical models of theological education. In the quest to identifying a unifying principle for theological education, Nouwen's key was the analogy of hospitality. For him, the element of hospitality in theological education was a deeply theological solution whereby students and faculty can interact as guests and hosts in "a free and fearless space where mental, emotional and spiritual development can take place."[5] Alongside Nouwen's "host and guest" analogy, Shaw's "Paracletic stance"[6] also portrays the significance of relational formation in theological education. The question is not what pattern of hospitality the leadership of a school claims to have been practicing, but how hospitable is our campus as the learner experiences it? A hospitable learning environment is powerful in advancing the total growth of a person. It resembles Jesus's model in training, in which persons were accepted, valued, encouraged and empowered irrespective of their background, knowledge level, identity or achievements.

Without the context of a *community*, formation and transformation would remain invalid and irresponsive. *Learning community* does not refer to a group that is locked up in a classroom or library for reading and writing. It is the body that lives, learns and grows together in the knowledge of God. The theological campus is a learning community that passionately pursues God and practices the Bible's "one another" commands to love, forgive, comfort and encourage with total commitment. Constant reminders should be given that the entire process of learning in our schools is intended to be collaborative and multi-dimensional. Even the term "scholarship," in the Association of Theological Schools (ATS) Standards, denotes "the interrelated activities of learning, teaching, and research."[7] "The collaborative nature of theological scholarship requires that people teach and learn from one another in communal settings;

---

5. Graham Cheesman, "Spiritual Formation as a Goal of Theological Education." PDF from http://theologicaleducation.net, pg. 34. Accessed on 11 April 2017. Cheesman refers to the work of Henry Nouwen, *The Way of the Heart: Desert Spirituality and Contemporary Ministry* (San Francisco: HarperCollins, 1991). Nouwen's analogy of hospitality was taken up by Margaret Guenther in *Holy Listening* (London: Darton, Longman & Todd, 1992), 6–41.
6. Shaw, *Transforming Theological Education*, 117.
7. Association of Theological Schools, General Institutional Standards, "Standard 3: The Theological Curriculum: Learning, Teaching and Research," 30 April 2015, 5; http://www.ats.edu/uploads/accrediting/documents/general-institutional-standards.pdf; accessed 29 March 2017.

and that research is integral to the quality of both learning and teaching."[8] The unhealthy divide between the cognitive, physical, mental, emotional and spiritual adversely affects the formation of students. For further thinking on this topic, the following section presents certain themes from Robert Walter on "Community."[9]

Desirable Characteristics of a Community

- Acceptance: a place where differences are accepted and celebrated. Judgment is rare.
- Authenticity: a place where people can take off their masks. Pretending is rare.
- Confidentiality: a place where it is safe to share openly. Gossip and slander are rare.
- Honor: a place where people are encouraged. Shame is rare.
- Honesty: a place where everyone speaks truth in love. Flattery and avoidance are rare.
- Interdependency: a place where people rely on one another. Isolation is rare.
- Growth: a place where people are moving towards maturity. Stagnation is rare.
- Purposefulness: a place where people know how they fit together and enjoy their role. Complacency is rare.
- Centeredness: a place where people are depending on Christ in order to love and serve one another. Selfishness is rare.
- Love: a place where people practice the biblical "One Another" commands. Superiority is rare.

Defining the general indicators of a healthy community is a vitally important exercise for a theology school. For Walter, a healthy community, be it a family, educational institution, workplace or faith community, will consistently enjoy the following benefits:

- Partnership

---

8. Quoted in Linda Cannell, *Theological Education Matters: Leadership Education for the Church* (Newburgh, IN: EDCOT, 2006), 300.
9. Robert Walter, "Community in Theological Education," seminar materials in the ConneXions Model of Healthy Leader Development. Accessed from the Leader Development and Research Center, New India Bible Seminary, Kerala, India, 29 March 2017.

- Protection
- Support in temptation
- Support in crisis
- Character development
- Lasting fruit

Factors That Make a Community Weak

What makes poor communities? By having too many students and staff, a theology school will not make a true community. A crowd does not make a community. In spite of our claims to be great communities, we often see individualism and separateness being catered for on the campuses in hazardous measures. This is worsened by the unlimited inflow of the new technological privacies. The urgent call on us is to be intentional about the formation of real communities on our campuses by carefully shunning those factors that make unhealthy communities. Communities become unhealthy because of:

- Fear of weaknesses being exposed;
- Fear of being rejected or hurt in some way;
- Fear of control and accountability;
- Fear of losing power and being surpassed;
- Pride;
- Insecurity;
- Technological distractions;
- Busyness;
- A super-spiritual attitude that believes, "I don't need people."

A School's Self-Assessment Guide on Community Life

- Is the campus a lovely place where individuals find space to grow their talents and skills in the service of God?
- How can the school be a deeply hospitable and caring place that students will passionately imitate later in their ministry?
- Are men and women treated as God's chosen people who enjoy full acceptance and participation in the school community?
- What sorts of counseling and guidance support can a student readily make use of at the school?
- What are the specific mentoring methods at the school?

- How well are the students taken care of physically? Which areas need improvement: food, rest, sports facilities, exercise, medical assistance?
- Is there a culture of fear spreading on the campus, making students develop unhealthy behavioral patterns and attitudes?
- Does the leadership at the school consciously or otherwise overlook disciplinary issues?
- Are the many complaints, worries and questions within the community left unaddressed?
- What is the outstanding testimony (about campus community life) of the school among the alumni and the current students?

Practical Recommendations: Community Life

- Build a social climate where elitism is not encouraged.
- Build a social climate where shame will not cripple lives.
- Build a social climate where fear is not enslaving hearts.
- Build a social climate where favoritism is done away with.
- Build a social climate of humility and mutual respect.
- Build a social climate where leaders and faculty are duly honored.
- Build a social climate of acceptance, smiles and recognition of others.
- Build a social climate that at its core honors and feeds into the vision of the church.
- Build a social climate that balances intellectual pursuits and spiritual disciplines.
- Build a social climate where departments genuinely respect one another.
- Build a social climate where policies are implemented on alcohol, drugs and behavioral issues.
- Build a social climate that speaks clearly against behavioral and technological addictions.
- Build a social climate where gender relations follow the biblical mandate.
- Build a social climate that breathes in and out prayer and meditation of God's Word.

6

Wholeness in the Interworking of Departments

The Dilemma of Departmental Disconnect

It is deeply agonizing to see theology getting downgraded as a group of scientific disciplines that exist without the love and experience of God. The way academic departments in theology schools sometimes operate like opponents is regrettable. In certain places there is nothing explicitly negative between departments, but there is nothing positive either. There are no power clashes or crises, because they are independent entities existing far apart on the same campus, with virtually no interaction, mutual learning or support. Everyone is busy achieving individual goals and making an impact! Can we imagine *pride* or *rivalry* in the ministry of God's Word within a community that is constantly pursuing maturity in Christ? Chrispal wrote,

> Biblical Studies, Historical Christianity, Development of Christian Theology and Practical Theology need to be seen as integral to one another . . . The fragmentation of theological education into various disciplines does not have the inter-relational dimension; on the contrary, it threatens to lose the very identity that it tries to preserve. What we need is a critical reflection on the meaning

and truth of the Christian faith to maintain the consilience of theological education.[1]

> "Competitiveness and pride disturb the unity of theology. Theoretical theology is placed on one side, of a distinct line to distinguish it from practical theology. Old Testament is across a line from the New Testament. Even within a subdivision of theology, other lines are drawn. For example, in homiletics oratorical skills and exegetical skills seem to have lost their interdependence; here and elsewhere the bits and pieces are attended to in some sort of blind hope that somewhere along the line someone will put the pieces back together and make sense out of the whole. Thus we have learnt to live with piecemeal education." Ted W. Ward, "The Lines People Draw," *Common Ground Journal* 10, no. 1 (Fall 2012): 28.

Theological schools generally seem unconcerned about the long-term consequences of the unhealthy hierarchy of disciplines and departments within the system. Departmental rivalries, detrimental academic competition, hurting and humiliating comments, contrasting emphases in academics and practical ministry, insulated reflections and discussions adversely affect the vision of wholeness in theological education. The departments that set the toughest proficiency requirements tend to look down upon others that allow learning to happen more through forms of reflective exercises and empirical research, which are generally labeled as "not of the hard-core academic guild." Setting one against the other as exclusively reflective-practical or academic-theoretical forms division and competition instead of wholeness in the learning climate. The historical frame was four-dimensional learning, namely Biblical Studies, Theology, Church History and Practical Theology. Eventually, in the path of transition, it was reduced to three, leaving out Practical Theology. Then Biblical Studies and Theology became the two major disciplines, as Church History too got pushed into the margins. Everything else got relegated to the sidelines, except for Missions, which started appearing as a distinctive force.

Edward Farley, in *Theologia*, stated,

---

1. Ashish Chrispal, "Prospects and Retrospects of Theological Education in the Twenty-First Century," in *Educating for Tomorrow: Theological Leadership for the Asian Context*, edited by Manfred Waldemar Kohl and A. N. Lal Senanayake (Bangalore: SAIACS, 2007), 252.

The organization of studies still taken for granted in most theological schools falls into the four basic disciplines of Bible, Systematic Theology, Church History and Practical Theology, with an overlaid pattern of theoretical and practical disciplines. This four-fold pattern, anticipated as early as Hyperius (1556), actually originated with the theological encyclopedic movement in Germany in the second half of the eighteenth century.[2]

Elsewhere Farley said,

Schools have a great need for faculty in the "practical areas," which constitute a large part of the curriculum, but there are few credible graduate programs in areas like Homiletics and Pastoral Ministry. And each of the practical fields is struggling for identity and is undergoing transitions. The very concept of "Practical Theology" is unclear. This makes it very difficult for seminaries to staff themselves and develop faculty in the "practical" fields.[3]

> "The body is a unit, though it is made up of many parts; and though all its parts are many, they form one body... The eye cannot say to the hand, 'I don't need you!' And the head cannot say to the feet, 'I don't need you!' On the contrary, those parts of the body that seem to be weaker are indispensable, and the parts we think are less honorable we treat with special honor." 1 Corinthians 12:12, 21-23

Although the questions of identity and the contribution of each department are crucial matters for discussion, the key issue here is the amount of division and disintegration within the learning context. Claiming that knowledge is attainable through a single means or in a particular discipline is perceptibly disadvantageous in education.

Departmental disunity and competition:
- Breeds pride and rivalry;

---

2. Edward Farley, *Theologia: The Fragmentation and Unity of Theological Education* (Philadelphia, PA: Fortress, 1983), 49.
3. "Toward Theological Understanding: An Interview with Edward Farley," *The Christian Century* 115, no. 4 (February 1998): 149. See also http://www.religion-online.org/showarticle.asp?title=366; accessed 29 March 2017.

- Spreads negative energy in the learning environment;
- Causes personal and emotional divisions between faculty and students;
- Knocks down the core vision of church-oriented ministry formation;
- Sets a wrong paradigm of a *faith community*;
- Promotes elitism and segregations;
- Spoils the very purpose of theological education in the kingdom prospect;
- Gives an impression to future leaders that these divisions and clashes are natural and acceptable; that they are to be tolerated and not addressed;
- Undermines the entire mission of theology schools.

How can we redeem theological education from its pattern of piecemeal training? The following section considers the fractional dimensions of education and attempts to explore relevant interventions.

Lack of Research Fostering Inter–Intradepartmental Connectedness

There have been perspectival inadequacies in recognizing *research projects* as potential elements in unifying the multiple dimensions of learning. A research student once wrote that the four aspects of formation he expected to take place during the tenure of research were personality formation, faith formation, theological-intellectual formation and ministry formation. In the intricate path of research, interdepartmental support becomes indispensable and can offer unanticipated discoveries and innovative paths in the learning process. Done with appropriate planning, this will facilitate holistic formation to the learner and generate interactive confidence among the departments.

Throughout his career in theological and mission leadership nationally and internationally, Saphir Athyal made outstanding efforts in exploring ways to enhance reciprocity among the departments in theological education.[4] As mentioned previously in connection with group-centered methods in learning, his design of the "Senior colloquium" is a unique form of research orientation towards the vision of integration. The colloquium meets at fixed frequencies to

---

4. Series of personal interviews with Saphir Athyal, 2014–2016, Tiruvalla, Kerala.

deliberate on selected theological topics of contemporary relevance in a panel made of faculty representatives from several departments. Each colloquium could be followed up by further learning and reflection as required by the topic. Senior faculty colloquiums can be converted to a senior students' colloquium that is facilitated by faculty members. Holistic research and learning happen naturally in the colloquium for both the faculty and the students through the following steps:

- Select a theologically and practically relevant topic that concerns the learning community.
- Select a panel of faculty and/or students from different departments to lead the discussion.
- Approach the topic from the angles of relevant departments for effective integration of thinking.
- Have a question and answer time.
- Form a team of students to write and publish summative papers on the topic, supervised by the faculty panel.

When courteous and fearless learning interactions occur in a theology school, areas of intellectual rivalry, dominance and indifference are normally eroded. Space is offered for open interactions that build the community of theological educators. A senior colloquium of this type encourages the practitioners to progress theoretically and the theorists to appreciate placing their feet on the ground of reality. It promotes mutuality and humility, and hence sets before the learners the challenge of growing into lifelong learning and the possibility of powerful informal conversations in theology. This turns differences into pointers for greater coherence rather than larger divisions.

Unhealthy Divide between Academic and Ministerial Formation

Knowledge and practice are virtually inseparable. Yet theological education, in its delivery, seems to be developing and preserving them as separate elements in a harmful divide. Ted Ward wrote insistently against the way unhealthy divisions are brought in and tolerated by theological educators. For him,

> If the drawing of academic lines were merely a matter of organizational expediency, it might be easier to justify; but such

lines give rise to all sorts of prideful and pompous disgraces. The "professional" disciplines, Christian Education and Missions, for example, are seen as less prestigious than the "academic" disciplines. Consequently, the closer one comes actually to serving the church in a concrete, contemporary, action-oriented learning process, the more likely one is to find resistance allegedly based in standards of accreditation and institutional tradition. One must wonder if the ultimate value of erudite theology is assumed to be exclusively in the brain.[5]

Certain contexts are experiencing the damaging effects of this to the extent that churches and missions resist offering placements to theology graduates in their ministries. Knowledge detached from real life is of little transformative impact and therefore churches and missions judiciously opt to equip their ministers in a more holistic mode.

Focus Shifting Away from God-Centeredness

The highest goal envisioned in theological education is and has to be God himself. This very fact guarantees the ultimate unity and wholeness in theological education. In other words, the enterprise is, in its very soul, God-centered. At the heart of its definition and purpose, theological education has only one goal: to know God and do his will. Everything about a theology school is essentially theological. Cunningham frames it this way: "it [theological education] is theological because its philosophical underpinnings and its goals are theocentric in addition to its content."[6] Not just in the local but also in the global scene, our hope should be to demonstrate this unity wisely between schools and within programs, departments and procedures. When it moves away from being anchored to its essential God-centeredness, theological education becomes a mere cluster of courses and a theology school, a sheer association of programs.

Obviously, no single department in theology can accomplish the formational task alone. As the apostle Paul says about members in the church

---

5. Ted W. Ward, "The Lines People Draw," *Common Ground Journal* 10, no. 1 (Fall 2012): 28.
6. Scott Cunningham, "Who Is a Theological Educator?", *Africa Journal of Evangelical Theology* 16, no. 2 (1997): 80.

being the body of Christ, theology is one body. No department should say or think that "because I am this, I am not a member of this body," or "because you are not this, we don't need you." The God-centered, holistic formation of the student presupposes a balanced input from all departments in the school. What forms a whole person is the unity of theological and practical wisdom that holds the departments together. This wholeness is achieved, not by standing aloof or advancing in one's own vertical pursuit of knowledge, but rather by being reformed and nourished by the community in lateral expansion.

Inadequate Vision of Interdisciplinary Collaboration in Teaching

By *interdisciplinary collaboration* we mean theological discipline's partnering with disciplines that are normally outside of its consideration, such as sociology, philosophy, psychology, politics or other fields of science. Teaching is an art that always has hidden powers to advance wholeness in the learner. Interdisciplinary collaboration in teaching has inherent potential in spite of the fact that many of us wonder how to go about it. We often lack careful insight into what Robert Banks speaks of as "teaching as active as well as reflective practice." This points above all to the teachers' commitment in augmenting wholeness:

> 1. Alongside technical knowledge of their subject area, teachers require an intimate acquaintance of the One who is present in it and animates it.

> 2. As well as doing justice to their particular subject areas, teachers should be able to situate their learners within the overall picture of God's purposes and dealings.

> 3. Apart from explaining the substance of what they are conveying, teachers should find ways of demonstrating the practical outcome of this and how it contributes to God's ongoing purposes.

> 4. So then, passion, vision and action are all involved.[7]

---

7. Robert Banks, *Re-envisioning Theological Education: Exploring a Missional Alternative to Current Models* (Grand Rapids, MI: Eerdmans, 1999), 174–175. See that section for detailed explanation of these points.

Interdisciplinary collaboration in teaching underpins the need for theology to interact and correspond with disciplines outside the field. Due to the prevalent fear that science is contrary to faith and they are always in conflict with each other, we naturally prefer to avoid any possibility for closer interaction. An erudite approach to education seeks just the reverse. It calls us to explore, engage, listen, respond, clarify, encounter and disagree appropriately. We eventually acquire the scholarly insight to not see a point of disagreement as a tragedy, a criticism as antagonism, or the lack of knowledge in a particular area as a catastrophe. But we reaffirm that, without being vulnerable and truthful at the same time, holistic learning is close to impossible.

Absence of Collaborative Course Designs

Collaborative course designs denotes the learning networks between a theological course and a practical mission/ministry base. This seems to be a largely neglected idea, perhaps due to the surplus planning, expenditure and efforts involved in a thoughtful balancing of theory and praxis. Banks's description of bridging the gap between instruction and action seems helpful in this discussion on departmental unity. Theology schools, however, should deepen their thinking on wholeness from the departmental design to the course-design level and learning-assessment level to facilitate a transformative teaching-learning experience. Each course's learning can be built in the integrated model of education, thereby enabling students to gain an interdepartmental thinking and action orientation. Banks's major categories of courses in the "missional model of theological education" are Integrative courses, Cross-divisional courses, Collaborative courses and "Live-action" courses.[8] Collaborative courses are designed between a teacher in any of the theological fields and a practical theologian or reflective practitioner serving in a specific local setting, preferably over semester-length courses that allow more time for feedback. Banks gives the following examples:

- A course on the prophets involving an OT professor and someone involved in urban ministry, in which teacher and students work directly with people in the neighborhood on issues raised by their study.

---

8. For elaboration of each point, see Banks, *Re-envisioning Theological Education*, 176–179.

- An exegetical course involving a NT scholar and instructor in preaching, a course that has as its main assignment preparing, giving, and evaluating a relevant sermon in the student's home church.
- A course on the early expansion of Christianity in the early centuries led by a church history professor and a person founding a church, where the material studied throws light on the development of the congregation.
- A course on the person and work of Christ, co-taught by a systematic theologian and a professor of evangelism, in conjunction with a mission involving both them and their students.[9]

The relevant question at this point is: What prevents us from considering this in our contexts of training? It is well recognized that this idea receives much resistance from theology schools. Common refutations reflect interestingly diverse responses, such as the following:

- It is impossible practically for faculty, mainly due to time constraints.
- It is not feasible to work out the amount of additional funds and effort required.
- The summer ministry plans of the practical ministry department will make this up.
- We do not have reliable church/mission agencies to connect with for this purpose. They fall behind the required academic standards.
- We do not know how to do it.
- The assessment of learning is cumbersome.
- Faculty members express a lack of interest. They are content with what they are doing now.
- It is nowhere required in the accreditation manual.
- Students will resist the additional work load.

The concern that echoes here is not so much about the authenticity of this approach. Closer scrutiny of each of the above statements reveals that these are excuses primarily in terms of nonparticipation. The school and its faculty may need to be committed to instigating it. Departmental interworking becomes central in facilitating such prototypes and assessing the learning.

---

9. Ibid., 178.

Neglect of Live-Action-Reflection Model in Education

This pattern is central to Practical Theology. Action, reflection in multiple theory-praxis frames, theological hermeneutic and modified action form the cycle of learning. Departmental networking and mutuality are crucial to this form of learning. In the "Live-action course" in Banks's thought, "a professor undertakes mission outside the local congregation, so that the class can both observe how course content is shaped by and translated into action, as well as engage in joint ministry with the professor." The examples below might deepen our thinking in this direction.

- In biblical studies, an instructor could apply various Old Testament wisdom writings to administrative aspects of a Christian organization she assists or look at how certain New Testament letters could give direction to the congregation she attends.
- In church history, a class studying heretical movements could involve a teacher modeling to learners how to relate to similar people today, or a course surveying major theological movements could include dialogue with people who have different theological convictions.
- In theology, courses in apologetics or philosophy of religion could include or take their rise from encounters with seekers or unbelievers, or courses in ethics could encourage students to deal with some of their own concrete, everyday issues, such as busyness, mobility and consumerism in modern society.
- In practical theology – evangelism, homiletics, counseling, Christian education or pastoral ministry – this is relatively straightforward.[10]

Departments meet in formal gatherings and make formal interactions. Yet they function almost independently due to the natural inclination to maintain isolation to retain their unique achievements. In such contexts, this live-action-reflection model invites a dynamic change.

---

10. Ibid., 178–179.

A School's Self-Assessment Guide on Interworking of Departments

- Is there an academic team at the school working on the interworking of learning advancements among the departments?
- How does each department in the school contribute to the whole of the educational goal in theology?
- Are certain departments considered to be superior to others?
- What particular features cause some departments to be seen as superior to others at the school?
- Do departmental conflicts reflect life in the community, or is it just that departments function as separate entities except for formal meetings?
- Are there evident or subtle signs of departmental rivalries polarizing faculty and students? Is there any explicit practice at the school in which several departments undertake corporate learning tasks?
- Are there conceptual divisions between the doctrinal and ministerial courses? What specific, feasible steps could the school take to integrate?
- In perspectival terms, are Biblical Studies and Mission poles apart? Make a few suggestions to lessen the gap in the specific context of the school.
- In what ways could the Theology and Pastoral Studies departments strengthen their interaction and responsiveness?

Practical Recommendations: Departmental Connectedness

- Organize round-table discussions among the faculty and staff on the centrality and purpose of each department in the holistic theological construction.
- Make the student-orientation week at the beginning of the study program much more than an introduction to the campus, community and rules and regulations. Plan to provide the students with a concrete introduction to learning which is fundamental to a healthy perception of the learning environment and aim. Clearly

communicate the unity of the disciplines and departments in theology and the need for an attitudinal balance in approaching these multiple fields for best outcomes.
- Plan monthly or bi-monthly senior colloquiums in which a theological concept or issue is discussed in public by a panel of faculty consisting of departmental representatives. This contributes both to facilitating the networking and integration of departments and to cultivating a culture of ongoing learning and reflection among students and faculty. Senior-student colloquiums can also be formed, preferably followed up by writing comprehensive papers on the topic, mentored by the faculty members concerned.
- Provide space for interest groups to be formed on the basis of shared missional and social concerns under the supervision of appropriate faculty members.
- Encourage different levels and types of research projects in the practical-theological method to enhance the holistic formation of students: attempts to bridge gaps between biblical norms and contextual realities; theology and culture; action and reflection; and needs and resources.
- Build active bonds with like-minded churches and missions to ensure that students enrolled on various courses will have authentic ministry internships with them.
- Conduct internal viva voce examinations in an interdepartmental setting. Prior to the formal viva voce of higher degrees, the school can conduct this internal presentation of the thesis with a faculty panel representing departments that have relevant and diverse perspectives to contribute. While the chief examiners come from the department of specialization, faculty from other departments can guide thinking to help the research achieve balanced significance in theological education.
- Faculty and senior students should engage together in inter-departmental research, writing and practical ministry projects.

7

Wholeness in Quality Assessment

Assessment matters. It determines, decides, develops and directs an institution's effectiveness. Addressing the vital theme of effectiveness and impact from a biblical perspective, Chris Wright identified three biblical guidelines for theological education: "*'committed to mission'* (reflecting the teaching mandate God gave to Abraham in Genesis 18:18–19); *'faithful to biblical monotheism'* (reflecting the teaching commanded by Moses as a bulwark against idolatry in Deut. 4 etc); and *'marked by maturity'* in understanding, ethics and perseverance (reflecting Paul's insistence on teaching within the church, e.g. in Col. 1:9–11 and the Pastoral Epistles)."[1] The call for theological educators is for us to assess the results of our actions and intentions in theological education. The question at the core of our practice of theological education is, in Wrights' words: "So, is that indeed the kind of goal we have in mind as we shape our curricula and construct our syllabi, and develop our lecture courses and hold our seminars and workshops? . . . are we being *effective* in producing such graduates, and how can we find out whether we are or not?"[2] His talk emphasized that theological education, being a highly consequential activity, needs to know the results. Planned actions have intended consequences, and the Bible supports the task of evaluation.

---

1. Chris Wright, Keynote address based on Proverbs 16:3 "Commit to the Lord whatever you do and he will establish your plans." Summary of "Scholars Talk in Turkey," International Consultation for Theological Education, ICETE C-15, 2015; http://nz.langham.org/scholars-talk-in-turkey/; accessed 30 March 2017.
2. Ibid.

> "Qualitative methods of assessment are as good as, sometimes better than, quantitative methods. 'Assessment' is not synonymous with 'quantitative,' even though there is increasing pressure on accrediting agencies to value numerical assessment over qualitative assessment. This would be tragic in theological education. At the heart of ministerial work are practices that are more like art than technical skill. While the performing arts have always been evaluated, they have seldom been evaluated by numbers. Theological education needs efforts of assessment that are useful, truthful, and qualitative, and not necessarily metric."
> Daniel O. Aleshire, "The Character and Assessment of Learning for Religious Vocation," *Theological Education* 39, no. 1 (2003): 10.

Identifying assessment as a complex, multi-layered process, Wright affirmed that in the midst of our legitimate concern to count and measure and verify our effectiveness and impact, we *do not neglect the power of testimony and story*. Assessment is crucial to anything that assumes growth. The apostle Paul said, "I do not run like a man running aimlessly; I do not fight like a man beating the air" (1 Cor 9:26). As purpose-driven individuals and institutions, we must keep assessing our growth and impact to ensure that the direction taken is right. Assessment is not a one-time activity; it is not an end in itself. It is the gathering of facts that helps us to see with clarity the strengths and weaknesses, and therefore it is the primary step in the long path of sustainable development. "When you have assembled what you call your 'facts' in logical order, it is like an oil-lamp you have fashioned, filled, and trimmed; but which will shed no light unless first you light it" (Saint-Exupéry).[3]

Let us briefly address the importance of assessment in theological education.

Changing Gear from Routine Reporting

We report regularly. What is our report based on? What does it lead us to? Reporting can become a meaningless act that repeats mundane activities without assessments, observations or prospective planning. Most of our reports are not based on validated assessments. We are used to conventional reporting

---

3. Quoted in William R. Myers, *Closing the Assessment "Loop": Nurturing Healthy, On-going Self-Evaluation in Theological Schools* (Chicago: Exploration, 2006), 65. According to Myers, institutional assessment and strategic planning form the two main interwoven strands.

which summarizes activities, lists needs and shares hopes. This is beneficial in many ways. However, much more than that is assumed in an *assessment*.

The potential downsides of *conventional-type reporting* are the following:
- It may not be based on what Myers would call in theological education assessment, "discernment, witnessing and truth-telling."[4]
- It may be a basic summary of activities.
- It may be a mere attempt to justify the completion of tasks assigned.
- It may not be concerned about the quality of the work accomplished.
- It sometimes focuses entirely on the projection of numerical data.
- It could be done with an inclination to impress the recipients with exterior facts.

This chapter uses the terms *assessment* and *evaluation* interchangeably to denote *a careful appraisal*. The task of assessment is often neglected due to its inevitable complexity. Assessment is not something that happens perfunctorily in an educational system. We must choose to do it. In spite of the global wave of awakening of this rubric in educational philosophy, it sets huge challenges before the educators and leadership.

The Challenge of Assessment and Integration

Only when we look at education as a developmental process do we realize the importance of assessment. *Evaluate* or *assess* means to *ascertain the value of something* or *appraise carefully*. It is not essentially the same as measuring, which is done in terms of some fixed and absolute standards. Assessment includes measurement, but adds to it factors which are intangible and not subject to quantitative determination. "Our choice is either to learn to do this kind of educational work *grumpily* because it has been externally mandated, or to learn how to do it *faithfully* because we care about the work our graduates do and the communities they serve."[5]

---

4. Ibid., 1.
5. Daniel O. Aleshire, "The Character and Assessment of Learning for Religious Vocation: M.Div Education and Numbering the Levites," *Theological Education* 39, no. 1 (2013): 1–17 (here, 15).

As Pieter Theron and the ABS family argue,[6] theology schools need to develop organizational cultures where continuous assessment for continuous quality improvement is part of everyday practice in the school. Assessment in an educational institution takes place in multiple forms and extents because development is holistic and has multiple dimensions. For example, assessment of learning in classrooms[7] has the following essential characteristics:

- Effective assessment is a continuous, ongoing process. Much more than determining the outcome of learning, it is rather a way of gauging learning over time. Learning and assessment are never completed; they are always evolving and developing.
- A variety of tools and approaches is necessary to provide the most accurate assessment of students' learning and progress. Dependence on one type of tool to the exclusion of others deprives students of valuable learning opportunities and robs you of measures that help both students and the overall program grow.
- Assessment must be a collaborative activity between the faculty and students. Students must be able to assume an active role in evaluation so they can begin to develop individual responsibilities for development and self-monitoring.
- Assessment needs to be authentic. It must be based on the natural activities and processes students do both in the classroom and in their everyday lives. For example, relying solely on formalized testing procedures might send a signal to students that learning is simply a search for "right answers."

Assessment in theological training goes more deeply than what takes place in the classroom, and therefore it is necessary to take into account the shape and impact of the curriculum in its entirety. The Association of Theology Schools undertook incredible efforts towards the evaluation of theory curriculum and prepared a bulletin with standards of evaluation in the 1980s:

> "By their fruit you will recognize them."
> Matthew 7:16

---

6. Pieter F. Theron, "Continuous Assessment for Quality Improvements in Theological Education," in *Educating for Tomorrow: Theological Leadership for the Asian Context*, edited by Manfred Waldemar Kohl and A. N. Lal Senanayake (Bangalore: SAIACS, 2007), 229–234.

7. "Assessment vs. Evaluation," *TeacherVision*, https://www.teachervision.com/assessment/new-teacher/48353.html; accessed 8 July 2015.

The 1984 Standards of evaluation at ATS called for evaluation in three ways:

1. An institution shall provide for regular and ongoing evaluation of students, faculty, administration, and governing board in reference to the institution's goals and objectives.

2. Evaluation of the curriculum and of educational methodology shall be provided by students, faculty and administrative officers.

3. The institution should seek to develop a flexible style in which changes in program flow naturally from the data produced by evaluative procedures.[8]

Ascertaining strategic planning is vital for the success of any assessment. William Myers set out four key aspects of assessment in theological education which provide a similarly helpful direction: assessment of student learning, assessment of the academic program, assessment of the institutional departments and assessment of the institutional governance.[9] There is no doubt about theology schools' overall awareness of the need of assessment and its significance in formational development. Nevertheless, for a range of reasons, assessment has always been a complex undertaking for the large majority of them.

Complexity of Assessment in Theological Education

Generally, everything about assessment is considered difficult. Goals/outcomes must be made clear; standards set; value indicators specified; areas of assessment clarified; contextually appropriate tools developed; competent personnel involved; time and frequency set; procedural track fixed; follow-up of the result envisioned; record-maintaining patterns organized; continuing assessment strategies developed, and so on. The assessment movement has shifted from its purely quantitative orientation to a more comprehensive and qualitative nature. It is expanding as well. Beyond the limited sphere of

---

8. The Association of Theological Schools in the United States and Canada, *Bulletin* 36, part 3 (1984), 25; cited in Daniel O. Aleshire, "Fifty Years of Accrediting Theological Schools," *Theological Education* 49, no. 1 (2014): 68.
9. Myers, *Closing the Assessment* "Loop," 27.

student learning, it is now getting into institutional assessment, departmental assessment, program assessment, course-syllabus assessment, student-learning/formation assessment and faculty assessment, along with assessments of other offices and coordination procedures at the school. Interestingly, in each of these the assessment task encounters distinct aims, needs and challenges. It is unrealistic to do it hurriedly or to do too many things together. We must learn to do it gradually, gradually improve on our understanding and gradually embark on a pattern of life in which we find ways to do it better and grow. We acquire the skill by doing and improving.

The assessment of the internal consistency and integration of the theological curriculum itself is multi-layered:

- Authentic assessment entails innovation, commitment and perseverance.
- The task of assessment is not an end in itself; it seeks to transform the system towards deeper efficiency.
- Concrete assessment is cross-sectional and done with a variety of tools.
- The assessment task is always vast and keeps expanding. Four primary areas of school assessment are: the school (goal, objectives, mission statement, infrastructure, funding/resource partnerships), the programs (e.g. BTh, MDiv curriculum, goal, process, design), the constituencies (faculty, students, administrators, alumni, the church, stakeholders) and the outcome and impact (immediate and lasting results, each accompanied by a number of subdivisions).
- Assessment tools must reflect analytical and synthesizing skills as students represent diverse educational qualifications, ministry goals, personal objectives, commitments and competencies.
- Assessment of the curriculum covers numerous dimensions of the school, starting with the goal and philosophy of the school.
- Assessment of the theological curriculum aims for more than mere academic, discursive knowledge and grading. Specifying the indicators for spiritual and personal formation is a hurdle.
- The learning assessment is a process. Learning is never static and therefore the curriculum cannot be fixed once for all.
- Assessment of the faculty is assumed in curricular assessment. Faculty's methodological orientations in teaching and learning,

doctrinal stand, worldviews, training objectives, commitment to the holistic formation of students and much more are taken into account.
- Setting the transformational indicators requires a careful team effort from the leadership and faculty of each school. This engagement typically empowers the school to form and own the task of assessment.
- Assessment can become mechanical by the continual use of the same methods and tools. Therefore, periodical revisits and revisions become essential to keep the process meaningful and effective.
- There are phases and features in learning that are difficult to assess. This sets a critical restraint on the process. Certain facets of learning or levels of impact can only be assessed in real-life tests.

Assessing Wholeness in Theological Education

Indicators in the ICETE Manifesto[10]

- Contextualization (curriculum and content in correspondence with the context of the learner)
- Churchward orientation (ongoing interaction with church)
- Strategic flexibility (addressing the leader-development needs at varying levels)
- Theological grounding (theological bearings not altered by secular rationales or latest enthusiasms)
- Continuous assessments (ongoing culture of evaluating objectives, outcomes, design)
- Community life (not factories that produce graduates)
- Integrated program (focusing on "whole person" rather than mere cognitive growth)

---

10. A summary of the twelve key areas for renewal and critical self-assessment of theological schools as developed by the International Council for Evangelical Theological Education, "ICETE Manifesto on the Renewal of Evangelical Theological Education," 2nd ed., 1990; also found in Robert Ferris, *Renewal in Theological Education: Strategies for Change* (Wheaton, IL: Wheaton College, 1990).

- Servant molding (promoting and practicing servanthood and not elitism)
- Instructional variety (using a variety of teaching methodologies)
- A Christian mind (mind of Christ implanted in the learner)
- Equipping for growth (facilitating lifelong learning)
- Cooperation (authentically connected with the larger body of Christ)

The full document of this manifesto has been considered by theological educators as a comprehensive set of values for assessing formational wholeness in our schools. Specific indicators are implicit in each category of values. The standards and value indicators that ascertain the purpose and function of theological schools may be verbalized differently according to how the institution defines and envisions the goal. For example, some of the key characteristics of theology schools in the "Program Values and Standards for Theological Education" document of the Overseas Council International (OCI)[11] are given below. In the original detailed document, each of these characteristics are split further into determinant attributes in order to make the standards of assessment specific and tangible. See Appendix 4 for an extract of the document.

1. Existing to strengthen the church
2. Transformative within the local context
3. Generous in sharing knowledge and other resources
4. Growing as a learning institution with a global orientation
5. Pursuing excellence in spiritual and personal formation of all members
6. Committed to integrity and sustainability in institutional life
7. Enhancing visionary leadership and adaptive governance

Assessment documents for a theology school are carefully designed on the basis of the values and standards upheld in its specific context. It can certainly learn from comprehensive documents on quality assessment. Nevertheless, institutions need to be judicious in their use of evaluation tools or guides prepared elsewhere while assessing the objectives and outcomes.

Large-scale assessments are carried out on the global theological education enterprise. With judiciously prepared indicators, credible procedures and truthful intentions, these procedures can obtain reliable results.

---

11. Overseas Council International, "Program Values and Standards for Theological Education," 2014.

The main findings of the Global Survey of Theological Education 2011–2013[12] were as follows:

1. There are not enough theological schools in the regions of the world where Christianity is growing rapidly (Africa, Latin America and parts of Asia). In Europe and North America there is a much better match between the need for theological education and the number of institutions and programs.
2. Theological education is financially unstable in many parts of the world. However, when all factors are taken into account, the majority in all parts of the world considers the state of theological education to be at least somewhat stable.
3. Growth is seen in evangelical and Pentecostal/Charismatic theological education. Decline is seen in mainline Protestant and Roman Catholic traditions.
4. The number of women students is growing in every denomination and in every region.
5. There is significant interest in online theological education in some parts of the world, but many theological educators consider traditional formats more appropriate.
6. Cross-cultural communication and practical skills related to ministry are the subjects respondents would most like to see added or strengthened in theological education.
7. Experiential learning is a critical component in preparation for Christian ministry. Learning in the location of ministry (congregation and community) must be integrated with spiritual formation and academic programs.
8. The "integrity of senior leaders" is seen as the most important element in determining quality in theological education.
9. Vision, collaboration, integrity of leadership and relevance are named as the most important factors for the future of theological education.
10. Innovation in theological education can be found in all parts of the world and in every denomination and tradition.

---

12. World Council of Churches, "Global Survey on Theological Education 2011–2013: Summary of the Main Findings," presented at WCC 10th Assembly, Busan, 30 October–8 November 2013; https://www.oikoumene.org/en/resources/documents/wcc-programmes/education-and-ecumenical-formation/ete/global-survey-on-theological-education.

11. Denominations and local congregations are seen as having the most responsibility for funding theological education.
12. The age of theological students varies by geographical region.
13. Regular institutional self-study and accreditation by regional bodies are seen as the most important aspects of ongoing institutional improvement.
14. Institutional capacity building and the provision of scholarships are seen as the primary roles for international bodies with regard to theological education.
15. Theological education is seen as "most important" for world Christianity.

Genuine assessment is an eye-opener. It is a penetrating beam that can show us the current path, the shifts and the flaws, while also being a clear beacon to direct us forward in the right direction.

School Assessment

We can know the effectiveness of the school by weighing internal wholeness, external outcome and the long-term impact. Internal Effectiveness + External Results = Organizational Effectiveness.[13] Everything is assessed against the stated goal and mission of the school. The most-used technical terms in school assessment are *input*, *output*, *outcome* and *impact* (see Figure 16).

Figure 16: Facets of School Assessment

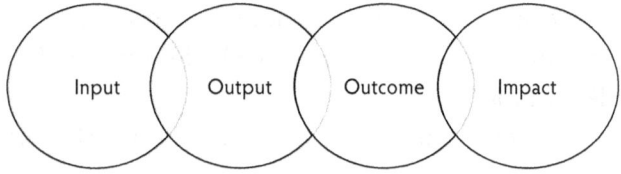

Input: This describes the amount of all kinds of resources used to conduct the training. Estimating this part is vital to a comprehensive assessment of the output, and, further, the outcome and impact. However, most designs of assessment seem to exclude this facet as relatively more attention goes to the results.

---
13. Kay Sprinkel Grace, Amy McClellan and John A. Yankey, "Evaluations," Chapter 9 of *The Nonprofit Board's Role in Mission, Planning and Evaluation* (Washington, DC: Boardsource, 2009).

Output: The services provided and activities conducted by the school are the output – for example, the training provided, number of classes held, books distributed, number enrolled, attendance and so on, showing the quantity and cost of the service provided by the school. This usually absorbs much of the space in our assessment reports. However, it cannot indicate whether any real benefits result.[14] For example, a number of students attending a class does not guarantee that they have learned the subject.

Outcome: Outcomes are short-term and intermediate changes that occur in the students' lives and ministries. The degree to which the training improves the spiritual life, ministry capacity or thinking competency in students is the outcome.[15] This vital component in assessment is only rarely found in reports.

Impact: Impact refers to the broader long-term changes that occur within the church, community or nation as a result of the ministry of the school. This would largely be assessed against our stated goal and vision statement. The ConneXions Model of Leader Development, shown in Figure 17, portrays the interrelation and definition of output-outcomes-impact (see also Figure 18).

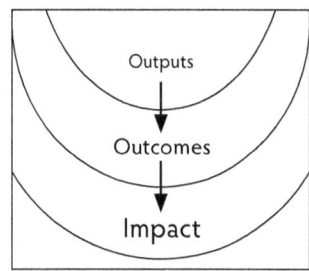

Figure 17: ConneXions Design of Assessment[16]

Outputs	Outcomes	Impact
Immediate	Short-term	Long-term
Easy to count	Harder to measure	Very difficult to measure
Attribution is straightforward	Attribution is harder to prove	Attribution is quite challenging
Ministry activities	Effects on participants	Ultimate effects on a broader scale

---

14. Tom Atema, "A Perfect Match: Leading and Measuring Belong Together," *Outcomes* (Spring 2014): 18–22. www.outcomesmagazine.com.

15. Malcolm Webber, *Healthy Evaluation Course Manual* (Elkhart, IN: Strategic, 2010), 38–39. Training materials by LeaderSource (www.leadersource.org / info@LeaderSource.org); accessed from the Leader Development and Research Center Collections at New India Bible Seminary, Kerala, 28 March, 2017.

16. Ibid.

Figure 18: A Systematic and Comprehensive Approach to Assessment LDQ®[17]

	Design — **The Map**		Process — **The Journey**	Goal — **The Destination**	
	Capacity — What We Will Need	Design — What We Will Do	Implementation — What Happens	Outcomes — What Results	Impact — What Lasts
Time Frame...	Before implementation		During implementation	After implementation	
Answers the Question...	Should it work?		Is it working?	Did it work?	
Evaluation of... (Some examples are given)	What is God already doing? Needs analysis Resources Internal operations Learning & innovation	Program design (context) Instructional design (content)	Quantitative & qualitative metrics Responses Learning Alignment	Quantitative & qualitative metrics Life transformation Ministry fruitfulness	Quantitative & qualitative metrics (depth & breadth) 4 dimensions of impact: The leader, the work, the community, God's glory

Outcome–impact assessment has gray areas that make the task challenging. This assessment is done primarily on the grounds of how effectively the results in the school corresponded to its goals. In this endeavor, we may use the formal documents and mission statements of the school and listen to the churches, missions and the larger society, gather information on the contributions of the alumni, and observe how students impact their own worlds during their study. We also recognize that the impact of a school could be reflected in the enrollment of students, enthusiasm of the feeder churches or organizations, placement offers for the graduates, increased interest and commitment on the part of funding bodies and long-term commitment of the faculty and staff.

---

17. Malcolm Webber, "Systematic and Comprehensive Approach: LDQ®: A Systematic and Comprehensive Approach to Leader Development Evaluation," in Webber, *Healthy Evaluation Course Manual*. Diagram used with permission.

Program Assessment

Program assessments are done on the stated goals and objectives of the programs. In Mager's view, "When clearly defined goals are lacking, it is impossible to evaluate a course or program efficiently, and there is no sound basis for selecting appropriate materials, content, or instructional methods."[18]

Theology schools offer educational programs distinctively titled as the Diploma, Bachelor, Master and Doctoral divisions. The following are certain principles which govern the program assessment:

- Having established our objectives, the first step in the process of assessment is the appraisal of objectives – or the determination of the amount of progress made by the program towards one or more of the established goals.
- The objectives established for a theological educational program should be specific and concrete, and articulated in terms of knowledge, attitudes, behaviors and skills.
- The instruments to assess an educational program should be characterized by validity, reliability and objectivity. Validity is the degree to which a tool evaluates what it is intended to assess. It should measure the aims sought or objectives set up. Reliability refers to the accuracy of the evaluative power of the tool. A reliable tool or procedure not only assesses what it is supposed to assess, it should also assess it accurately. Objectivity refers to that quality of a test which allows equally competent persons to score the test and obtain the same results.
- Assessment should be regarded as a continuous process of collecting, recording, assembling and interpreting information about each program. It is multi-layered and multi-faceted.
- Assessment of an academic program is both subjective and objective. It evaluates the progress of the goal of the school in terms of both its objective elements and the so-called "intangibles" or subjective elements.

A variety of methods is used to assess the effectiveness of a program. We can imagine a few overall indicators that will help our thought process

---

18. Robert F. Mager, *Preparing Instructional Objectives* (Palo Alto, CA: Fearon Publishers, 1962), 3.

in this, such as: students write comprehensive papers efficiently; they are steadily absorbed into appropriate roles of ministry related to the field of study; the stated outcomes of the program show credible accomplishments in the annual assessment by the academic dean; and the status of student enrollment advances year after year.

Assessments may be done in a variety of academic programs offered in a theology school in residential, full-time, distance or online formats. Surveys, questionnaires, focus groups, testimonies and informal procedures can effectively serve the program assessment. Wisconsin University's "Logic Model and Common Type Evaluation"[19] presents the importance of *assumptions* and *external factors* in assessing a program. This logic model displays the sequence of actions that describe how investments link to results through the following five core components of the program:

1. *Inputs:* resources, contributions, investments into the program
2. *Outputs:* activities, services, events and products that reach people who participate or who are targeted
3. *Outcomes:* results or changes for individuals, groups, communities, organizations, communities or systems
4. *Assumptions:* the beliefs we have about the program, the people involved, and the context and the way we think the program will work
5. *External factors:* the environment in which the program exists, which includes a variety of external factors that interact with and influence the program action

It is high time for theology schools to revisit the longstanding programs offered and appraise the input-output-impact balance. "How each program contributes to the fulfillment of the vision and mission of the school" and "how the structural assumptions and external factors impact the program" are the most non-negotiable aspects of the task.

Student-Learning Assessment

Student-learning assessment is taking a distinctly different shade from that which it assumed in the past. The fundamental alteration in the educational

---

[19]. Board of Regents of the University of Wisconsin System, "Developing a Logic Model: Teaching and Training Guide 2/29/2008," http://www.uwex.edu/ces/pdande/evaluation/evallogicmodel.html; accessed 13 May 2016.

system in recent times has been the shift in focus from teaching to learning. We have moved a long way from a mindset of quantifying everything through a particular mode of examination, now using new methods of transformative assessment. However, the process of learning assessment seems to be tackling tougher phases today, due to the inherent intricacies of "how can we evaluate formation in a person?" and "how do we ever know what causes what?" As Hardy observes, "The overall value of a good education is not easily quantifiable, nor can it easily be demonstrated which piece of the training program actually contributed to the success of one of our graduates."[20] Faculty might need training to design direct and indirect measures to assess student learning.

It is always beneficial to have the student's perception of each course taken. Faculty may enable this in their own preferred ways, yet the school can recommend a general frame to guide this task. Faculty members could also develop an observation document that assesses aspects of the formation of the student, to be handed in alongside the grade sheet. The students' curricular and non-curricular development are weighed together in this, so that their unique capacities and contributions will be validated. Such a format can use scores that will evaluate the student's formation level – for example, in categories such as Beginning, Developing, Accomplished and Exemplary. Apart from being a great source of integration, guidance and motivation, this approach will control the tendency to place disproportionate attention on certain dimensions in formation.

Learning has an impact not only on knowledge (which is mostly assessed in terms of information), but also on understanding, reflective capacities, skills, attitudes and application. Limiting student-learning assessment to tests and grades has done much harm to our educational system. When inquired about the holistic formation of their learners, schools normally defend themselves by saying that 40 or 50 percent of the grade is for the papers and tasks assigned to the students as part of the course. The point here is not about justifying or defending our positions, but to critically analyze how these assignments and tests form the student holistically. Successful completion of the stated requirements of the course assists the task of assessment; but there is always much more to it than that. These course requirements need periodical revision

---

20. Steven A. Hardy, *Excellence in Theological Education: Effective Training for Church Leaders* (Carlisle, Cumbria: Langham Global Library, 2016), 179.

for the revitalization of the learning process. The age-old formats of written assignments in certain schools are only detrimental to the entire education system. To what extent do question-paper setting, paper-presentation criteria, a practical-project format, required readings and book reviews make sense in the student's formative learning? How much of these is subject to our assessment of student-learning?

For example, let us think about the learning content. How do we know if a student has obtained comprehensive learning of the course content? Faculty's main tool in this may be question papers. Shaw's list of cognitive questions consists of analysis questions, hypothetical questions, reversal questions, synthesis questions, evaluation questions, deductive questions, inductive questions, adductive questions, refutation questions, perspective-taking questions and personality-in-context questions.[21] He explains how *question design* facilitates deep learning and argues that this variety of cognitive questions should be part of the warp and woof of everything we teach and not just for research papers. Summative or comprehensive papers are found to be exceptionally helpful in assessing the overall cognition and reflective competency of students. Quality assessment procedures always take seriously papers, projects and tests in the course. An urgent task is for faculty to revisit this aspect in education.

Formulating the *graduate profile* is crucial in the task of student assessment. A graduate profile is the ideal towards which a student is trained in a school, and therefore it is the tool that weighs the extent to which we are accomplishing our vision in training. It is neither to be used as a graduation requirement criterion nor is it a critical tool for a student's self-assessment. The learning outcomes of each course in a program and the formational outcomes in the spiritual and ministry dimensions of training together contribute to the graduate profile. The logical and practical interconnectedness of all learning exercises is vital in envisioning what a student is trained for. A school that has laid out the specific graduate profile for all its programs is likely to have a better realization of their functional quality in training.

---

21. Perry Shaw, *Transforming Theological Education: A Practical Handbook for Integrative Learning* (Carlisle: Langham Global Library, 2014), 201–209.

Figure 19: Contemporary and Traditional Ways of Student Learning Assessment (from Suskie)[22]

Contemporary Approaches to Assessment	Traditional Approaches to Assessment
Carefully aligned with learning outcomes/goals; the most important things we want students to learn	Planned and implemented without consideration of learning outcomes/goals
Focused on thinking and performance skills	Focused only on memorized knowledge
Developed from research and best practice in teaching and assessment methodologies	Often of poor quality because faculty and staff have had few formal opportunities to learn how to design and use effective assessment strategies and tools
Used to improve teaching and learning as well as to evaluate and assign grades to individual students	Used only to evaluate and grade individual students, with decisions about changes to curricula and pedagogies often based on hunch and anecdotes rather than solid evidence
Used to tell our story; what makes our institution or program distinctive and how successful we are in meeting students' societal needs	Not used to tell the story; stories are told through anecdotes rather than broader evidence from representative students

An understanding of some of the values in learning assessment will assist us in defining the specific skills required for the task. The basic principles underlying student-learning assessment are:

1. It is assumed that education is a process and that students change and grow in their behavior, attitudes, thinking, skills and competencies as a result of their educational experiences. The change or growth, in whatever area, can be assessed.
2. It is assumed that there are certain goals implied by educational objectives. These goals have to be attained by students and should be assessed. These are the acquisition of knowledge, skills, thoughts, ideas, attitudes and ideals.
3. It is assumed that human behavior is complex and that it cannot be described or measured by a single test or category, or a single grade.

---

22. Linda Suskie, "Creating a Culture of Assessment: Implementation of the Student Learning Outcomes Assessment Process," Presentation, https://www.umes.edu/cms300uploadedFiles/CREATING%20A%20CULTURE%20OF%20ASSESSMENT-Fin.pdf; accessed 17 March 2016. See also Linda Suskie, *Assessing Student Learning: A Common Sense Guide*, 2nd ed. (San Fransisco: Jossey-Bass, 2009).

Hence the program of assessment should consist of multiple types of methods/instruments, such as written tests, oral quizzes, observational and anecdotal records, questionnaires, interviews, checklists and rating scales.
4. It is assumed that assessment will influence teachers and learners alike and help them to improve in their roles.

The essential task at hand is, therefore, to uncover the meanings of these in our specific contexts and then to develop relevant methods and tools to assess students' learning and formation. Suskie's analysis (Figure 19) is of further aid in this discussion.

Initial, Formative and Summative Assessments[23]

Assessment is often divided into initial, formative and summative categories for the purpose of considering different objectives in the learning process.

Initial Assessment of Student Capacity

This uncredited assessment is done prior to teaching to establish the baseline for learning assessment for the student. How much did the student know before he or she joined this new situation of learning? Initial assessment helps the faculty to realize the knowledge level and skill level of the student and to teach accordingly. It also enables the teacher to relate well to the student.

Formative Assessment of Student Learning

This is carried out throughout the course of study. It helps the faculty to assess the growth of the student in the particular learning environment and aid learning as needed. Formative assessments are done in the form of standardized tests, oral examinations or practical projects simultaneously with instruction. Not all formative assessments will necessarily be added to the grades of the student, but they are significant in the learning assessment.

---

23. Jay McTighe and Ken O'Connor, "Seven Practices for Effective Learning," *Educational Leadership* 63, no. 3 (2005): 10–17.

Summative Assessment of Student Development

This is usually done at the end of a course of study and from it a grade is assigned to the student. Summative assessment takes the form of formal tests, final examinations or a major project and is evaluative. This will determine if a student passes or fails the course. When faculty members are slow in formative assessments and providing subsequent help to students, summative assessment will be too late to provide scope for learning improvement to students.

Diagnostic Assessment of the Entire Learning Process

This assesses all the hurdles and challenges that occur during the learning process.

Learning assessment is, however, only one area in the broad task of assessment.

A School's Self-Assessment Guide on Quality Assessment

- Who is in charge of developing and refining the assessment procedures at the school?
- Is assessment an inbuilt, integral and ongoing practice at the school?
- Which of the following areas are being seriously assessed at the school?
  - The school's function and effectiveness
  - The quality of an academic program
  - The effectiveness of a course
  - Student-learning and formational development
  - The contribution of faculty
  - The ecclesial and societal impacts of the ministry of the school
  - Alumni's contributions to the church and wider society
- What formal and informal assessment procedures are in place for the school's development?
- What would be a typical assessment tool/technique to determine the school's contribution to the church?
- How do we evaluate the teaching content, methodology, course assessment patterns and impact of the faculty?

- How do we assess the impact of the life of faculty and staff on the formation of the community?
- Who assesses the academic programs of the school? What standards and values are central to this task?
- How often are the examinations, tests, practical assignments and grading system of the school assessed and revised?
- How is an assessment report followed up by the school? Give specific example of changes introduced as the result of an assessment process.
- What impact has the school made in the past five years (on the church, missions, academia and the larger society)?
- What control measures are used to ensure that the assessment tools and procedures are valid and reliable?
- Which of the following are major attitudinal obstacles to the development of an ongoing assessment procedure at the school?
  - We don't have time
  - We don't have competent people
  - We don't have funds
  - We don't see the need
  - We don't know how to prepare and administer tools
  - Nobody is interested
  - Results will not be used
  - It is a lot of unnecessary work
  - It will hinder cordial and healthy interactions

Practical Recommendations: Quality Assessment

- Agree on the most vital areas for assessment in the school. Never overwhelm the staff and faculty with excessive evaluation tasks; narrow the scope to what is truly important and what is relatively easy to obtain.
- Organize short learning sessions among the leadership, faculty and staff on the need, role and impact of assessment in maintaining the integrity and sustainability of the school.
- Plan seminars and strategic discussions on the expected outcomes and impact of theological education.

- Learn and draw from the standards of assessment followed in other educational institutions.
- For each area of assessment – e.g. school, academic program, course, student formation, faculty – prepare a format with goals, standards and expected outcomes.
- Entrust the vital task of preparing value indicators and assessment techniques/tools to an insightful and competent team.
- Have a clear plan for the use of the assessment techniques/tools and for the method of processing, recording and following up the results.
- Explore ways to enhance authentic evaluation, which is the key to excellence. Initiate group learning and research in the field of assessment – e.g. building a firm literature base on this topic in the library, faculty members researching and publishing on the theme, formal and informal training for faculty in quality assessment and intentional deliberations on the cultural concerns relating to ongoing assessments.
- Create awareness within the community of the importance of authentic assessment and involve members of the campus community appropriately in various aspects and forms of assessment.

8

Wholeness in the Governance of the School

Theological colleges are not islands standing firm and unchanging in the midst of a troubled sea. They are the little boats floating on the sea of society, susceptible to its influence, pushed this way and that . . . the key issue as to whether the college prospers or dies is in the hands of the one who is steering the boat," wrote Cheesman.[1] *Governance* denotes the overall responsibility for the institution, indicating a higher level of accountability regarding the goal, direction and mission of the school. It also relates to terms such as "power," "authority" and "ownership." Schools use this term with particular connotations in their functional realm, such as the overall governance, daily administration or academic governance. However, this chapter uses the term *governance* to designate either the executive body with authority over the school or the administrative leadership which carries the school's internal day-to-day leadership function (see also below under "Working Definitions").

> "I planted the seed, Apollos watered it, but God made it grow." 1 Corinthians 3:6

School governance takes multiple forms. Church leadership governs denominational schools. In spite of an idealistic outlook, this pattern encounters multiple challenges, including those concerning the identity and professional standing of the school. Schools may find themselves helpless in addressing many of these challenges and hence tend to become either mediocre or resilient.

---

1. Graham Cheesman, "Why Do Seminaries Prosper? Why Do Seminaries Die?", *Journal of Theological Education and Mission (JOTEAM)* 3, no. 1 (2012): 1.

In another paradigm, schools choose their own governing structure, while strictly subscribing to the doctrinal and missional foundations of the church. Schools that function in more nondenominational and interdenominational patterns are likely to follow their own independent formula in governance. An inherent problem with this is the possible lack of doctrinal and ecclesial firmness in spite of the sovereignty and the assumed scope for wider influence. Arles observed seven types of governance of theological education at the overall level of authority: "foreign board, family board, denominational board, ecumenical/interdenominational board, ministry partners, representative board and consortium members' board."[2] Each structure and set of terminology will have distinct meanings and applications in context. Likewise, each field of governance has distinct expectations and responsibilities. For example, Nordbeck says about academic governance,

> There are at least four kinds of people who should not become chief academic officers: those who are happiest among stacks of books and at classroom lecterns; those who relish the satisfying sense of work completed; those who thrive on calm and predictability in their daily routines; those who agonize fiercely over conflict and criticism. Being an administrator is neither more nor less difficult than being a professor. It is, however, different.[3]

Any form of governance is vitally significant to the life of a theology school. When the act of *governance* is reduced to casual board meetings, signing papers and having a good meal, the sustainability of the institution is at stake. Such institutions are likely to be stripped of their life within half a generation.

The administrative functions of the school face several tensions. Some schools assign senior faculty to take turns in governance or in top administrative tasks. It is sometimes a cause of regret to members of the faculty that their years were wasted in that role. While recognizing the importance of the calling to teach, we acknowledge that administration and governance are also vital callings in ministry. Setting academics and governance/administration against each other will hamper the composure of the training environment.

---

2. Siga Arles, "Governance of Theological Education: Patterns and Prospects," *Journal of Asian Evangelical Theology (JAET)* 14 (2006): 58–60.

3. Elizabeth C. Nordbeck, "The Once and Future Dean: Reflections on Being a Chief Academic Officer," *Theological Education* 33, Supplement (1996): 21–23.

Operational–ministerial reciprocity is essential for wholeness. According to David Ford, "Nothing is irrelevant to our vocation. We may have what feel like 'hidden years,' spent on apparently disconnected activities and 'details' without any great sense of integrating purpose, only to find later that the quality of those details has been crucial for fulfilling a life's work."[4]

This chapter focuses more on the philosophical and relational dimensions than the structural concerns. We now consider the meanings of the terms "governance" and "administration."

Working Definitions of "Governance" and "Administration"

In general, theology schools use the terms "governance" and "administration" interchangeably, denoting the leadership functions customarily outside the teaching-learning circles that engage in multiple roles around the vision of the school and/or its daily management. This chapter uses both terms, allowing the context to determine the intended meaning. The supreme *governance*, what we call the Executive Board or Board of Directors in certain contexts, refers to the visionary, adaptive and generative body that is responsible for the developmental sustainability and future direction of the school. *Administration* generally refers to the team that manages the daily technical and academic functions of the school. There is a fairly noticeable overlap between the functions of the two in many contexts of theological education. For instance, the governing board may be well represented in the administrative team of the school to facilitate policy making and decision making, and the chief administrative members of the school may have an important say on the governing board. Traditional demeanors of the school and the cultural expectations of the place where it is situated usually impact on the formulation of the governing and administrative patterns. If a theological institution is part of a larger ministry setting, guided by an Executive Board of Directors and other officials, such as a Chief Executive Officer or Chief Administrative Officer, normally the governing body will comprise these directors along with the President/Principal and other key

---

4. David F. Ford, quoted in Stephen R. Graham, "The Vocation of the Academic Dean," in *C(H) AOS Theory: Reflections of Chief Academic Officers in Theological Education*, edited by Kathleen D. Billman and Bruce C. Birch (Grand Rapids, MI: Eerdmans, 2011), 67.

leaders at the school. When the theology school operates entirely on its own governance, the administrative team will consist of the executive leaders of the school, such as the President/Principal, the Dean(s), and the administrative leaders at all levels. The governing body of a theology school is expected to be unique, because it is a body of spiritual leadership with distinctive qualities.

Desirable Characteristics of the Governing Board

The governing board of a theology school fulfills strategic roles that are not always known to the larger community. Describing the governing function, Thomas says,

> The uniting factors of Board members should be the ethos, values, goals and objectives of the seminary. It is desirable that Board members should be those who themselves are involved in ministry and are willing to spend time and effort in discussing the concerns of the institution and participating in the life of the seminary. Goals and objectives are key tools in coordinating efforts. It is, therefore, important that the principal, every faculty member and all the members of the board know, own, and appreciate the vision and mission statement of the seminary.[5]

The governance of theological education should be profoundly theological, constantly radiating the divine attributes in every facet of service. The form of this governance and administration is in no way a tyranny; rather, it is the "love–grace–counsel mix" of the Trinity. Every member in the governing leadership of a healthy institution will comprehend that a theology school has both formal and informal domains of function. It is the healthy intermingling of discipline and grace. For wholeness in training, the governing body has to:

- Understand and appreciate the goal and mission of the school and frequently communicate it within the school community.
- Make strategic and innovative plans for development with a global vision in the church's mission.
- Explore ways and means to collaborate with the church, like-minded schools, missions and accrediting bodies.

---

5. Jaison Thomas, "Church-Ministry Formation in Theological Education," PhD thesis, Queen's University, Belfast, 2008.

- Plan for consistent and meaningful assessment of the outcome and impact of training.
- Offer visionary leadership that is adaptive and generative to maximize training innovation to impact service to the church locally and globally.
- Provide strategic opportunities to all members on the team to advance their unique strengths for the growth of the school.
- Ensure appropriate opportunities for faculty sabbaticals and higher-level collaborative learning.
- Make prayerful and careful planning for the economic viability of the school.
- Improve resources for the academic, ministerial and spiritual development of the community and facilitate sustainability.
- Take the academic, spiritual and ministerial formation of the community seriously and engage as actively as possible.
- Think strategically into leader development and succession plans for the school.

One of the major flaws in the practice of theological education has been its long-term polarization of *administration* and *academics* in the local settings of the schools. The *administrative staff* on team normally contribute little to the formation of the community. Their voices are not seen as crucial in policy-making and their service is limited to the technical jobs they are entrusted with. We need to examine this mindset closely and look for ways in which administrative staff can be made active participants in the holistic formation of the institution. Theological education is not about knowing but about growing a life that is lived in the fullness of the knowledge of Christ; it cannot be reduced to an information explosion or data-dumping in classrooms. It is about values, attitudes, hopes and visions lived out by a community of faith representing the kingdom of God. Everyone has vital roles to fulfill; every member is important in this body. Therefore, a major task of theological institutions is to build up its staff and faculty holistically. This will naturally result in the healthy formation of students and a deepened spiritual–social impact on the community. In other words, the theological vision and educational passion of the institution must be owned by all members in the governing and administrative bodies.

Awareness of the Shifts in Theological Education

The governing bodies of theology schools might need to realize the significant changes that are occurring in the practice and philosophy of theological education. Such perspectival transferences include a shift of focus:

- From teaching to learning;
- From the teacher to the student in his or her context;
- From monologues to reciprocal learning;
- From books to research, narrations and traditions;
- From programs to people;
- From large numbers to quality enhancement;
- From routine reports to genuine assessments;
- From daily functions to enhancement of wholeness in community living;
- From more buildings to active community interactions;
- From more programs to more indepth dialogues.

Contributing to the Holistic Formation of the Faith Community

In a healthy community all members realize and act their rightful roles. The governing/administrative bodies should be committed to ways in which they can bring life and instill hope in every member of the community. Very often, however, traditional administrative styles unintentionally exert undesirable restraints in the growth of the community towards wholeness. Denominational, interdenominational and nondenominational institutions have their own distinct styles of governance, adapted to suit the structure of the institution. Even within the denominational seminaries, there are variants in administrative structures. The failure of administrative bodies to offer transformative leadership has been a troublesome reality for many theology schools. The role of effective administrative patterns in advancing the impact of training is crucial. The following are a few examples of concerns regarding administrative function in theology schools.

- The administrative team functions as a separate, disconnected entity from the academic body.

- The administrative team operates as a secular professional system with no Christian values/outlook.
- The administrative team comprises persons that are theologically illiterate, missiologically numb and ministerially indifferent.
- The administrative team detaches itself from the corporate learning activities and spiritual fellowship within the school community.
- The administrative team members consider their role as a job rather than a ministry of service to the kingdom of God.

> "Crucial here is the issue of power, for whoever has this or is willing to distribute it among the various stakeholders in theological education, will largely determine the fate of any of the proposals in the debate, at least within existing theological institutions. The crucial question here is not so much: 'What should theological education be?' as 'Who determines what theological education should be?'" Lynn N. Rhodes and Nancy D. Richardson, *Mending Severed Connections: Theological Education for Communal Transformation* (San Franscisco: Network Ministries, 1991), 43.

There is a felt need for deeper thinking, vision and commitment in the theological institution's governance/administration. Too much and too long engaged in it conventionally, we become unable to see things clearly.

Both the supreme governance and the internal administration should ensure that the community stays rejuvenated in spiritual life, theological wisdom and ministry. They are to keep watching and responding to the way the institution grows into a functional whole. As those who set the right direction, they are to consider how the parts are integrated and how well those parts align with the whole. This implies that they must constantly attend to the interworking of the:

- Goal;
- Objectives;
- Mission statement;
- Administrative structure;
- Admission requirements;
- Recruitment policies;
- Needs in the church and society;
- Role of the faculty;

- Overall curriculum;
- Curricular design and process;
- Syllabi revisions;
- Community life;
- Ongoing assessment;
- Outcomes and impact;
- Institution's future in the plan of God.

We can safely argue that the governing teams must be continuing learners and persons who exhibit integrity in setting the right agenda for the institution, seeking God's direction. A theological community will not grow just because students are provided with excellent facilities and profound scholarship. It grows as a community if all members nourish one another and pursue maturity in faith and service. The governance/administration plays a vital role in facilitating this growth by enhancing unity and quality of life. In a growing community, the governing and administrative members participate as full members and take active roles in the formation of all other members.

Providing an Adaptive and Visionary Leadership

In many countries, the major need of theology schools is for a theologically informed and ministerially committed leadership. Along with the members of the governing body, the entire team of internal administration provides the visionary leadership of the school. As faculty members fulfill their duties, administrative staff do their jobs and students complete their assignments, the institution's overall vision can get buried in the hurriedness of fragmented activities. A theological college can function with reasonably good intentions but simultaneously lack a solid theological vision. People embark on starting a theology school for various reasons, not realizing what is involved in the long run *in leading a theology school*. What essential role is assumed in the governance/administration of the theological institution? Four "habits of successful governing leaders"[6] are:

- They must ask the right questions;
- They must balance tradition and innovation;

---

6. Charles E. Bouchard, Susan Thistlethwaite and Timothy Weber, "The President's Role as Academic Leader," in *A Handbook for Seminary Presidents*, edited by G. Douglass Lewis and Lovett H. Weems Jr. (Grand Rapids, MI: Eerdmans, 2006), 83.

- They must be persons of evident learning; and
- They must cultivate courage.

The governance/administrative role in a theology school is to make sure that wholeness is breathed into the formation of persons, to the entire community and beyond, to the larger society around. These leadership teams are those who can view things simultaneously from above and from on the ground. Moreover, by seeing the future by faith in God, they instill courage and hope for the sustainable growth of the institution. This is essentially a generative leadership. It takes the institution to the next level. It epitomizes many observable, executable, learnable and improvable distinctions, which produce outcomes that are associated with effective leadership.

Adaptability is a rare quality. It refers to the commitment and courage to take steps to meet new challenges and needs in ministry using relevant resources and taking unusual pathways. A rigid implementation of rules and traditions seems much easier than offering an adaptive leadership. However, given our changing selves, churches and society, a responsive-adaptive leader will look at the situation and ask, "What should we do differently to be relevant while remaining true to the Word of God?" Adaptable leadership discovers innovative ways to deliver a contextually relevant theological education and makes thoughtful decisions on the accreditation policies of the school in line with its goal and mission. Many schools seem to be focusing heavily on improving the infrastructural and technical administrative facilities. The missing leadership element, in general, is an responsive-inquisitive perception to capture the prophetic vision for our schools. Adaptive leadership denotes a move from a conventional to a responsive functioning, where new vision is gained; we explore new approaches and nurture new relationships to meet the challenging needs of the times. Cannell writes as follows about the significance of adaptive leadership in times of transition: "Adaptive leadership is rooted in the recognition that people, not systems, are the engine for organizational development; and, second, planning processes require leaders and members of the organization to suspend tendencies to preserve what is or, at the very least, to make changes that are of such a nature that what is will not be significantly affected."[7] Every theology school needs an administrative

---

7. Linda Cannell, "Adaptive Leadership: Planning in a Time of Transition," *Theological Education* 46, no. 2 (2011): 25–45.

body that is sensitive and adaptive to the needs, aspirations and challenges of its members. Administrative leadership should focus on developing our theological communities to be more concerned about people than systems; about calling than capacities; about kingdom prospects than human strategies.

Role-Modeling as Christlike Servant-Leaders

Affirming a high level of order and discipline is embedded in the calling of directorial teams. However, extremely rigid hierarchical performances in governance/administration will transmit to the school community an unhealthy image and perception of leadership. This will have adverse effects for the rest of the lives of its members. When body, mind and soul are cared for in an educational system, students grow into wholeness to live, love and serve in the fullness of the divine nature. Even while meager provision is causing huge internal concerns for theological institutions in certain regions in the Majority World, a servant-leadership modeled by the governing/administrative body would still assure a warm, hospitable and conducive climate for teaching and learning. This servant-modeling in leadership should not be limited to a few areas, but should saturate all levels of service in a theology school. "Staff trained in hospitality and service are an essential ingredient in a welcoming program. The first contact is a key persona in the process and should be gracious and welcoming, as well as knowledgeable. Housekeeping, maintenance, and food service personnel may have more contact with guests than so-called executive staff. All need training in hospitality and service."[8] We tend to overlook the significant role of the governing/administrative team in shaping the community by leading in the Christlike servant model. This crucial dimension has unlimited potential in facilitating transformation in persons, who, in turn, become catalysts for the transformation of the world.

---

8. Carolyn Henninger Oehler, "Welcoming the Whole Person," in *A Lifelong Call to Learn: Continuing Education for Religious Leaders*, edited by Robert E. Reber and D. Bruce Roberts (Herndon, VA: The Alban Institute, 2010), 349.

Extending Formal–Technical Performance to Active Participation

The dream of journeying to wholeness must be embraced and captured by every member in the governing and administrative teams. It is their indispensable mission, beyond all their demanding and mostly stressful responsibilities. From their formal roles, these leaders have to become active participants in introducing reforms and newer directions in which the entire community joins dynamically. People do not easily accept or welcome changes or new ideas for reform. While introducing or recommending changes, the administrative leadership may foresee certain concerns, such as the following:

- Incompatible responses among the faculty;
- Resistance at different levels from academic departments;
- Lack of clarity on the part of administration about the change introduced and its further prospects;
- Lack of cooperation from various constituencies to pursue the dream further;
- Lack of the financial assistance needed for the change.

Synchronizing the strengths of everyone in the community is essential for functional wholeness. We have seen in recent decades how Human Resource (HR) departments function as the central source of power in successful organizations. Jesus's team was made up of excitingly diverse personalities, contributing to the emergence of greater learning and many clashes. In Acts, the first ever church problem was a situation in which one team felt it was being neglected by the other group that was considered to be *the real ministry team*. Formation happens with the active participation of the leadership in the strategic dimensions of the community life. In a theology school the leadership should aim to maintain manifest cordiality in relationships so that wholeness can be truly experienced in community living.

The governing and administrative teams at a theology school presume courage to partner with God in transforming lives. They have to become active participants in the life of the school in all ways possible. Administration has to grow far beyond mere financial or other official transactions, as it is conceived and practiced currently in many of our schools. Our pattern of leadership has to ensure that every program, every member and every event/plan contributes to wholeness in training and, therefore, advances the mission of God's kingdom.

Exploiting Resources to Sustain the School's Mission

Leadership holds both qualitative and quantitative obligations. Resource development is a key task of the governing and administrative bodies of the school. The need for resources for general funds, student scholarships, the library, infrastructural developments, the teaching needs of the church, practical ministry placements, faculty sabbaticals, research and publications, and alumni associations all make this a massive responsibility. A variety of resources in terms of skills, materials and capacities is required to advance networking and growth for the institution. Advancing the stability of an institution is the primary mission of the governing body and this is possible only when the school is transformative within its context and expands its life in collaboration with the churches and missions around. The sustainability of its mission is attained only by addressing multiple areas of governance/administration, such as centering the community on the school's vision, exploring financial resources, improving the paths of communication and public relations, making global connections and planning strategically for leadership succession. Single-owner institutions might show an outstanding level of growth for a particular period. With the lack of sustainable resources and a structured governance, these institutions become vulnerable and might encounter sudden crises. When the visionary leader moves away from the scene through ill-health, transition or demise, the efforts and investments of a lifetime are lost forever. Large campuses become vacant, huge buildings unused and learning resources wasted. As someone once said pessimistically, our seminaries may soon become cemeteries if we neglect the significance of sustainable leadership practices and patterns. Certain contexts are already realizing this dreadful reality. In view of the changing scenes within theological education, we need not only a structured, visionary governance, but also for this governance to lead the institution towards sustainable development for the future, foreseeing opportunities and threats.

A School's Self-Assessment Guide on Governance

- Draw on paper the complete structure of the executive governance and the internal administration of the school. What in this plan is working well, and what is not?

- Of whom does the central team of administration at the school consist?
- Are they persons with theological direction, field-ministry exposure, personal testimony and social vibrancy?
- What strategic planning has this team made over the past two to three years in leading the school to its central goal and to foster growth into newer avenues?
- What procedures are initiated at the school to motivate the governing/administrative teams so that they can actively participate and offer the best service to the campus community?
- How often does someone at the school solidly assess the effectiveness of the administrative functions within?
- Does the governance/administrative team tend to be narrowly concerned with certain aspects in the school's life – e.g. buildings, fundraising, daily functioning, non-formal learning and university affiliation?
- What might be the two main strengths and two main weaknesses in the school's administrative model?
- Are members of the governing and administrative team normally found detached from the life of the school?
- Are the administrative staff loved by the community or seen as disconnected officials/disciplinarians?
- Do members in the governing body impact the community in formational dimensions in any way?
- Are the administrative team members encouraged to participate in fellowship or ministry events in the school community?
- Are they given opportunities to minister the Word of God in the community?
- Who is the key person in the institution, anchoring the networks between faculty, administration and public relations?
- How often does the governance/administrative team meet for reflection, evaluation and planning for the development of the school?
- How strong is the community life of the school? Who in the leadership team is the strongest link in building up care and hospitality in the community?

- Does the school exemplify professional vigor in its planning, learning and functioning?
- What specific measures may be used to ensure that the members in the governing/administrative bodies attend core activities of growth towards wholeness in training?
- What specific steps are necessary to strengthen or revitalize the administration team to help the institution grow holistically in the plan of God?

Practical Recommendations: Governance

- Governing-body executives who are part of the administrative team of the school should fervently communicate the core theological vision of the school.
- Actively and intentionally involve the governance and administrative team members in the spiritual and ministry activities of the school. Prayer times and days for waiting upon God are indispensable for a theological institution to grow in God's vision. What the institution sets before the community as *most significant, unavoidable* or *non-negotiable* will continue to be so through members' lives on campus and in the future.
- Form a core administrative team of visionaries and strategists who are united in purpose for the institution to grow more deeply and widely in God's mission as a community of disciples.
- Develop strategic planning for the professional development of the school's leadership team in communications, public relations, networking, funding, academic-resource development, and leader development and succession.
- Involve the administrative staff appropriately in teams that assess the formational impact of the school in spiritual, intellectual, physical, ministerial, social and cultural dimensions.
- The governance/administrative team should discuss together how each event or experience on campus contributes to the holistic formation of the school community – e.g. chapel, the classroom, library, hostels, family apartments, dining hall, recreational areas, gym, fellowship groups, outreach teams, celebrations, cultural events.

- Have systems in place to bring faculty and administrative staff to grow together in their knowledge of God and experience of his grace. Make specific strategic plans in this direction.
- Provide space for the administrative team to plan new methods to assist the faculty team to grow in their calling, contributions, potential, ambitions, needs, struggles and ministry commitments.

9

Transformative Methodological Trends in Teaching and Learning

Changing Patterns in Theological Education

The following are changes that have been taking place within theological education:
- Increase in ethnic diversity
- Online higher education
- More varied teaching methodologies
- Churches seeking focused/specialized programs
- Increase in the number of women students
- Increase in the number of part-time students
- Increasing internationalization and transnational higher education
- Increase in the number of independent students with no accountability to the church
- A greater influx of mature students
- Substantial grants and scholarships in higher education
- Schools' increasing interest in secular university affiliation or becoming global universities
- More varied doctrinal stands
- Advanced use of technologies
- New fully-fledged disciplines of psychology, business, family education, sex education

- New competency programs such as administration, management
- New ministry programs such as Bible translation, youth ministry

> "For we are God's fellow workers; you are God's field, God's building... no one can lay any foundation other than the one already laid, which is Jesus Christ. If any man builds on this foundation using gold, silver, costly stones, wood, hay or straw, his work will be shown for what it is, because the Day will bring it to light." 1 Corinthians 3:9, 11–13

Change: A Necessity, Opportunity and Paradigm

Amidst these multiple changes and challenges, theological education is called to pursue wholeness. The central task is wisely to synchronize these changes towards the advancement of formational wholeness. In fact, this new situation offers us enormous opportunities to grow. At the same time, a downward paradigm is also observable in many contexts, where these changes are birthing more disconnects in theological education. Flip Buys advocated a thorough biblical and practical training for ministers and missionaries against this educational background. At the Bible school consultation hosted by Mukhanyo Theological Seminary, at which were gathered seventy participants representing twenty Bible colleges from South Africa, he set out the following "Seven Tombstones of Theological Seminaries":[1]

1. Academic intellectual knowledge is given a higher priority than character-transformation skills.
2. The highest priority of lecturers is to impress academic colleagues and not to form, mold and shape students to be men of God and effective pastors.
3. Excellence assessed merely on academic terms and learning through field experience are not integrated.
4. Lecturers have no vision of the church as God's primary instrument for transformation of society.

---

1. P. J. Flip Buys, at the South African Bible School Consultation, hosted by Mukhanyo Theological Seminary; "How Can Bible Schools Become More Effective?" Frontline Fellowship, http://www.frontline.org.za/index.php?option=com_content&view=article&id=99999991:how-can-bible-schools-become-more-effective&catid=23:contemporary-cat&Itemid=193#sthash.gB7z4DpE.dpuf; accessed 3 July 2016.

5. The curriculum is determined by secular accreditation agencies.
6. The forming of character and skills is marginalized in training.
7. Theological education is being priced out of the market and made unaffordable.

Changes happen. An effective institutional leader or theological educator will be highly cognizant of the forces of fragmentation and will mend them back to wholeness. Threats of disintegration sometimes take subtle forms, such as cultural detachment within classrooms or dormitories, ideological divisions among the faculty and emotional distance between members from different denominational backgrounds. Theological training as practiced today needs to be empowered with a definite focus on holistic formation, shared learning in a community and contextual orientation. This presumes a commitment to ongoing assessment. The aptitude to assess and address strengths and weaknesses is an exceptional quality in transformational teaching and learning. It grants us the power to turn obstacles into opportunities in training. Assessment, in this sense, is the beginning of active growth towards wholeness. Our call is simply to preserve and nurture the wholeness that is innate in theology. Despite sporadic deliberations and writings on the unity of theological education on the global scene, our theological communities still seem far from truly realizing the need for wholeness. Next we discuss a few dynamics that are critical power sources for the revitalization of theological education in the changing era.

Four Key Dynamics in Teaching-Learning Methodology

There are dynamics that set certain challenges as well as promises before the forward trajectory of wholeness in theological education. Their impact will depend on how we respond to them. The four facets addressed below are significant in assisting the task of transformation (see Figure 20).

Spiritual Formation as Fundamental to Theological Education

Without spiritual formation holding the central space, theological education is nothing more than a vain pursuit. All learning in a theology school must be built upon the foundation and within the solid frame of spiritual formation. Defining spiritual formation as "the transformation of people into what C. S.

Lewis calls 'little Christs,'"[2] Mark Maddix explains its key aspects as "a focus on being 'formed' and 'transformed,' a focus on human participation with God, a lifelong process that takes place in the context of community and a focus that includes the nurturing of self in relationship to others." We are often at fault by relegating this component in training to the neglected peripheries. It would appear that adding yet another course on "spiritual formation" may not resolve the problem. There should be a comprehensive aspect in training that addresses the deep spiritual needs and issues of the students as individuals and as a community. Both individual and group methods can be designed to help them to grow in healthy spiritual formation. This, however, goes beyond programs and activities; it has to be embedded in the learning environment.

Figure 20: Dynamics in Teaching-Learning Methodology

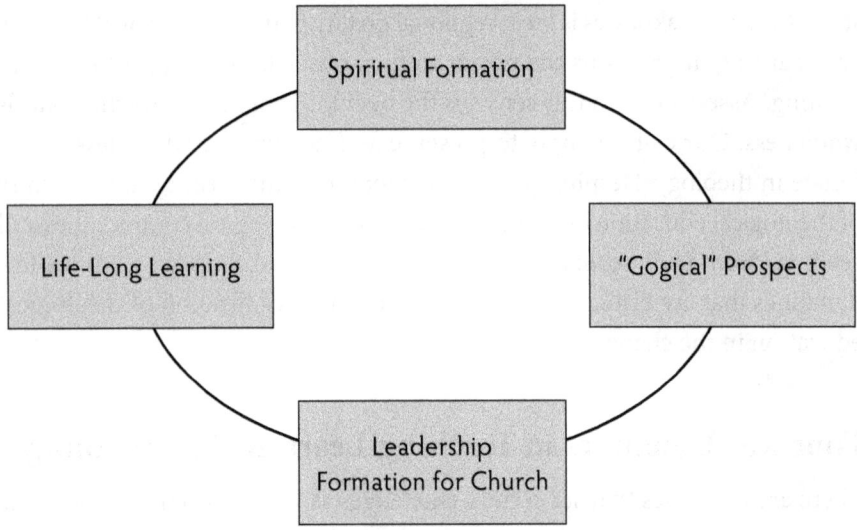

Every individual's worth as beloved of God and everyone's unique calling in life in the plan of God forms the foundation for spiritual formation, be it that of students, leadership, faculty or staff. A considerable number of students in our schools seem to have suffered a lack of authentic discipleship and mentoring in life. Even more tragically, many are raised in cultural and ecclesial traditions

---

2. Mark A. Maddix, "Living the Life: Spiritual Formation Defined," in *Spiritual Formation: A Wesleyan Paradigm*, edited by Diane Leclerc and Mark A. Maddix (Kansas City: Beacon Hill, 2011), 11–16.

that have somehow damaged their perception of God and spiritual formation. Schools that are sensitive to this vital dimension will certainly provide space for mentoring, journaling, sharing life stories, individual prayer habits, committed participation at the communion table, fasting, Scripture meditation, and so on. Group spiritual formational activities are also powerful means for personal growth. Group Bible studies and reflection, extra-curricular interactive sessions, informal talks on personal struggles and challenges, question and answer sessions, focused times of corporate prayer and team-based artistic spiritual expressions of spirituality can be truly transformational.

Spiritual formation is about developing a lifestyle that is increasingly transparent to God, committed to others and true to self. For a Christian, there is intrinsic value in daily meditation of the Bible, contemplative prayer, fasting, service to the community, love for the poor and disadvantaged, holiness in personal life and integrity at work. For instance, an assessment of a spiritual-formation program[3] listed about thirty-one core areas, including ability to pray about one's heart's desires, practice of silence and solitude, integration of prayer in daily life, integration of prayer in studies, exercise of the spiritual gift of discernment, contribution to mercy and justice in the world, genuine fraternity with fellow students and ability to receive God's grace in weaknesses. Different formats could be developed according to the school's tradition and vision. While certain schools make student participation in spiritual activities compulsory, others opt to provide opportunities for spiritual growth, expecting students to make choices for themselves. Students may be given spiritual-formation questionnaires at the points of entry and exit (or perhaps at the end of every year). This helps the student to realize his or her status in spiritual life and the need for growth. It also guides the school to offer relevant guidance and support to the student. Lifelong disciplines of personal spiritual habits should be nurtured in theology schools. But most institutions are far from this ideal. As a minister jokingly commented, "In the seminary we didn't pray due to heavy assignments; in the ministry field we don't pray due to heavy work."

Cheesman identifies spiritual formation and mentoring as the distinct strengths of the evangelical tradition:

---

3. Karen Kangas Dwyer and Edward M. Hogan, "Assessing a Program of Spiritual Formation Using Pre and Post Self-Report Measures," *Theological Education* 48, no. 1 (2013): 31–33.

> There has been a shift from the assumption that prayer and a good relationship with God will make personal problems insignificant in a Christian, or give them "victory" over these things, to structured provision for hurting students of "amateur" help from their personal tutors and referrals on to professional counseling where needed. Combining this with an increasing interest in the spiritual direction of all students (rather than merely counseling those with personal problems) has seen the rise of the concept of "mentoring" – a significant program of care and development of students in small groups, sometimes the fellowship group of all those assigned to a particular tutor and individually.[4]

The student is the focus, not the teacher. Not only in the classroom and in assessment, but also in the whole of training, the learner becomes the center. All our mentoring and discipleship needs to seize this awareness firmly.

> Theological educators must know and use the power of mentoring if theological education is to make the most of transforming them. To adopt "an academically distant superior lecturer" or an unmodified "guru-shishya" model of relationship will rob young leaders of the support, challenge and mutuality in discipleship that they and the church need. Mentoring is an essential part of transformative education.[5]

There are zones in spiritual formation that are best realizable through the discipleship model. This model, as we learn from Jesus, touches every dimension of life and enhances holistic formation in inimitable ways.

> Discipling is a particular mode or "model" of teaching, as distinct from other models such as parenting or schooling. A disciple may utilize any number of different methods in the teaching process including narrative, explanation, discussion,

---

[4]. Graham Cheesman, "A History of Spiritual Formation in Evangelical Theological Education," *Journal of Theological Education and Mission (JOTEAM)* 6, no. 6 (February 2015): 24. A useful introduction to this topic is Keith R. Anderson and Randy D. Reese, *Spiritual Mentoring: A Guide for Seeking and Giving Direction* (Guildford: Eagle, 2000).

[5]. Ian Payne, "Reproducing Leaders through Mentoring," *Journal of Theological Education and Mission (JOTEAM)* 6, no. 6 (2015): 74–96. Also in *Tending the Seedbeds: Educational Perspectives on Theological Education in Asia*, edited by Allan Harkness (Quezon City, Philippines: Asia Theological Association, 2010), 167–192.

instruction, preaching, question and answer, demonstration, modeling, practice, small groups or action reflection, but he/she will use them within the context of a discipling relationship. The working definition is, "Discipling is a voluntary, personal relationship between two individuals, in community or alone, in which the disciple commits him or herself to learn from the other, by imitation, oral communication and sharing in the life and work of the disciple" . . . Many would not consider that the discipling model of teaching used by Jesus has any relevance at the level of tertiary education today. Joe Bayly has commented cynically that the only similarity between modern theological training and Jesus' training of the Twelve is that both take three years.[6]

Spiritual formation always has multiple impacts on the community. Thoughtful individual care that is spiritually formative can resolve many of the intensifying disciplinary issues on theology campuses. The learning climate in theology schools is changing drastically. Enormous effort is required to keep up with the rapidly changing social and technological pressures. Most of the questions brought to me personally in 2015, at a feedback session of a paper presentation with theological educators in India, were about ways to tackle the ethical disciplinary issues on campuses. These issues were not present a decade before. The postmodern mindset of individual freedom and anti-foundationalism seems to be capturing the lifestyles of students. Cultural values of creating genuine space for one another and respecting others' opinions are breaking down and unlimited use of technology and the Internet is feeding into this. We cannot address these issues merely by establishing a set of "rules and regulations" and announcing them over and over. The only way to help is to design a thoughtful path for spiritual formation which transforms persons inside out by the power of God's Word and inspirational real-life examples. To lead this track, schools may need to identify and deploy members from within the community who are devoted to the spiritual formation on campus, creative in their interpersonal ministry capacities and fervent pursuers of personal spiritual formation in their own lives. They alone can become patient listeners to and co-travelers with the troubled souls around them.

---

6. Sylvia Wilkey Collinson, *Making Disciples* (Milton Keynes: Paternoster, 2004), 4.

Hospitality is the hallmark of a school that believes in spiritual formation and student-centered learning. "No one cares how much you know, until they know how much you care," said Theodore Roosevelt. Theological education has to shift gears from the banking model, and a focus on the relational dynamic has to saturate our mission. When course content fails to correspond to the relational facets of life, it lacks transformative power. Charles Foster quotes Henry Nouwen's description of hospitality as

> The creation of a free space where the stranger can enter and become a friend instead of an enemy. Hospitality is not to change people, but to offer them space where change can take place. It is not to bring men and women over to our side, but to offer freedom not disturbed by dividing lines. It is not to lead our neighbor into a corner where there are no alternatives left but to open a wide spectrum of options for choice and commitment.[7]

Davina's study addressed the need for hospitality in theological higher education. In the works of Henry Nouwen and Parker Palmer she identified the motif of hospitality as a viable concept for theological education and investigated how teachers in theological institutions can use it to create an environment for facilitating the holistic formation of students.[8]

Theological education is a committed way of life that requires determined practices of self-discipline, long hours of reading, biblically guided reflection, indepth times of prayer, fasting and devotion, reading and re-reading, thinking and rethinking, writing and rewriting, and serving in anticipation of the ultimate establishment of God's kingdom. According to Neibuhr,

> theological students are personally involved in their work to an unusual degree. The study of the determination of the personal and human destiny by the mystery of being beyond being, of the tragedy and victory of the Son of Man, of the life-giving, healing power immanent in personal and social existence, of the

---

7. Charles R. Foster, *Educating Congregations: The Future of Christian Education* (Nashville, TN: Abingdon, 1994), 66.
8. Soh Hui Leng Davina, *The Motif of Hospitality in Theological Education: A Critical Appraisal with Implications for Application in Theological Education*, ICETE Series (Carlisle: Langham Global Library, 2016). She also addresses the concept of hospitality in higher education from the perspective of an Asian female living in Singapore.

parasitic forces of destruction that infest the spiritual as well as the biological organism, of the means of grace and the hope of glory – this cannot be carried on without a personal involvement greater than what seems to be demanded by the study of history, nature or literature.[9]

Nothing justifies the neglect of spiritual formation on our campuses. It is the non-negotiable facet in the study of theology, and it should take place in a context where mentoring, discipleship, community and hospitality form the normal style of living.

Re-imagining "Gogical" Varieties in Theological Education

Theological *teaching* is encountering a rapid change. We now realize that reading and literature analysis is only one type of learning among many others. Also, we understand that each student learns differently and applies knowledge differently. The best form of education is that which best equips the students to meet the needs of the contexts in which they live and serve. The emerging fields of art and orality in theological education are great examples of this. As people of theology we, more than anyone else, should appreciate the importance of an educational philosophy that impacts all distinct forms of human cognition. The teacher's role as "a sage on the stage" is changing into "the facilitator and assessor of learning." The student becomes the agent of learning and transformation in his or her context. Educational institutions are to facilitate the paradigm that "Education is about learning, not teaching."[10] Learning, in its true definition, is deeper than memorizing ideas or theories. It assumes that *knowledge* is to be used rather than accumulated.

Let us consider the five major "gogical" terms – the five stages[11] in teaching and learning:

---

9. H. Richard Niebuhr, *The Purpose of the Church and Its Ministry* (New York: Harper & Bros, 1956), 118.
10. Perry Shaw, *Transforming Theological Education: A Practical Handbook for Integrative Learning* (Carlisle: Langham Global Library, 2014), 134.
11. Dave Laton, Joe Raynolds, Ted Davis and Dave Stringer, "From Pedagogy to Heutagogy: A Teaching and Learning Continuum," 13, where the first four stages are discussed. Unpublished paper; http://studylib.net/doc/7584003/from-pedagogy-to-heutagogy---a-teaching-and-learning-cont; accessed 15 March 2016.

- *Pedagogy* is the process of influencing introductory-level learners so that they acquire basic knowledge, skills and/or attitudes; it serves as a baseline from which further learning can occur. In a *pedagogical environment*, the emphasis is on the teacher, while the student is viewed as a passive and dependent receiver.
- *Mesagogy* is the process of influencing intermediate-level learners to further their acquisition of knowledge, skills and/or attitudes; it serves as the enabling link between pedagogy and andragogy. Teachers in a *mesagogical environment* engage the learner in the process of becoming active and independent.
- *Andragogy* is the process of influencing learners to acquire higher levels of learning employed in life-centered applications. In an *andragogical environment* the teacher's role clearly shifts towards facilitating or mentoring, and the learner often takes the lead in acquiring information.
- *Heutagogy* is the process of learners personally acquiring advanced levels of learning through self-discovery and creativity. A learner in a *heutagogical environment* has responsibility for direction and application of information, while the teacher (if present) assumes the role as a full partner in learning.
- *Synergogy* is cooperative learning that focuses on the learning and problem-solving by using group activities and joint projects. It has been shown to be active for most of the educational process. This is identified as the best method of learning for adults because adults retain more information through this method than through any other.

Fostering Andragogy Principles

As the facilitator in learning, the teacher should create the most influential learning environment. As mentioned before, andragogy is an adult learning theory in which the educator's role remains meaningful but less instructive, involving coaching, facilitating and guiding. In contrast to the hierarchical, traditional pedagogy, adult learning ensures that the learners are fully engaged in the process, to the extent that they, in turn, influence the curriculum and help redefine the learning objectives. The term "andragogy" was first coined by Alexander Capp (1833), a German high-school teacher, but it lay unused for many decades.[12] Malcolm Knowles, who is known as the chief proponent of andragogy, in his work *The Modern Practice of Adult Education* (1970) presented a practical "technology" of andragogy built on the primary assumptions of adult learning mentioned above. According to Carlson, adult educators should accomplish the following seven-step process with their students in a healthy learning environment:

1. Set a cooperative learning climate.
2. Create mechanisms for mutual planning.
3. Arrange for a diagnosis of learners' needs and interests.
4. Enable the formulation of learning objectives based on the diagnosed needs and interests.
5. Design sequential activities for achieving the objectives.
6. Execute the design by selecting methods, materials and resources.
7. Evaluate the quality of the learning experience while re-diagnosing needs for further learning.[13]

> "For students who come from an evangelical background, in the very first year, their faith gets disturbed; in the second year, instead of proclaiming God, we end up questioning the existence of God and deny God [him]self. In the third year, after... analyses and questioning, we realize God is present, and only in the fourth year, we come back to normal and discover the true God... With these entangled psychological outbreak[s], students... endeavor somehow with great struggle to complete their theological education and a few tragically end up discounting their theological education." Beena Priyadarshini, "What Do We Expect from Theological Educators: A BD Student's Point of View," in *Theological Education: Ploughing the Field for New Life to Sprout*, edited by G. Lawrence Jebadoss and P. Mohan Larbeer (Bangalore: BTESSC; Chennai: CLS, 2014), 205-211.

---

12. J. Reischmann, "Andragogy: History, Meaning, Context and Function," in *International Encyclopedia of Adult Education*, edited by L. M. English (Houndsville, NY: Palgrave Macmillan, 2005), 58-63.

13. R. Carlson, "Malcolm Knowles: Apostle of Andragogy," *Vitae Scholasticae* 8, no. 1 (Spring 1989): 217-233. Retrieved from http://www.nl.edu/ace/Resources/Knowles.html; accessed 22 March 2007. See also Malcolm S. Knowles, *The Modern Practice of Adult Education: Andragogy versus Pedagogy* (Chicago: Follett, 1980).

By 1980, Knowles had refined his definition of andragogy and clarified its relation to pedagogy, formulating a distinctive set of assumptions about mature learners:

1. Their self-concept moves from dependency to independency or self-directedness. Although pedagogy may have made learners dependent, the adult educator (or andragogue) can help to move adults to self-directed learning in which they assume primary responsibility for their learning and its direction.
2. They accumulate "a growing reservoir of experiences" that can be used as a basis on which to build learning. The adult's life experience becomes an invaluable learning resource, as valid a mine of riches as an academic library.
3. Their readiness to learn becomes increasingly associated with the "developmental tasks of social roles." In other words, adults are not as motivated as children to learn due to external academic pressure; rather, they learn best in response to their own sense of what they need to know in order to grow.
4. Their time and curricular perspectives change from postponed to immediate application of knowledge and from subject-centeredness to problem-centeredness.
5. Their motivation to learn becomes internal.[14]

The undeniable power of this methodology in theological education can be explored within our unique training contexts. Knowles set out the following six assumptions of adult learning (see Figure 21):[15]

1. Adults can respond better to internal than to external motivators.
2. Adults are most interested in learning subjects, having experience in work and more experience in life.

---

[14]. R. Hiemstra and B. Sisco, "Moving from Pedagogy to Andragogy (Adapted and Updated from *Individualizing Instruction: Making Learning Personal, Empowering and Successful*, San Francisco: Jossey-Bass, 1990)," Paper retrieved from http://home.twcny.rr.com/hiemstra/pedtoand.html; accessed 19 March 2007. See also Knowles, *Modern Practice of Adult Education*, 44–45.

[15]. Malcolm S. Knowles, Elwood F. Holton III and Richard A. Swanson, *The Adult Learner: The Definitive Classic in Adult Education and Human Resource Development*, 6th ed. (Burlington, MA: Elsevier, 2005). See also Malcolm S. Knowles, *The Modern Practice of Adult Education: From Pedagogy to Andragogy* (Wilton, CT: Association Press, 1980).

3. The basis of learning activities is experience. Adults have more experience to reflect on.
4. Adults want to know the need and reason for learning something.
5. Adults are contributors of their own involvement in the planning and evaluation of their instruction; they should also be responsible for decisions on their education.
6. Adult learning should be more problem-centered than content-centered.

Figure 21: Knowles' Six Assumptions of Adult Learning

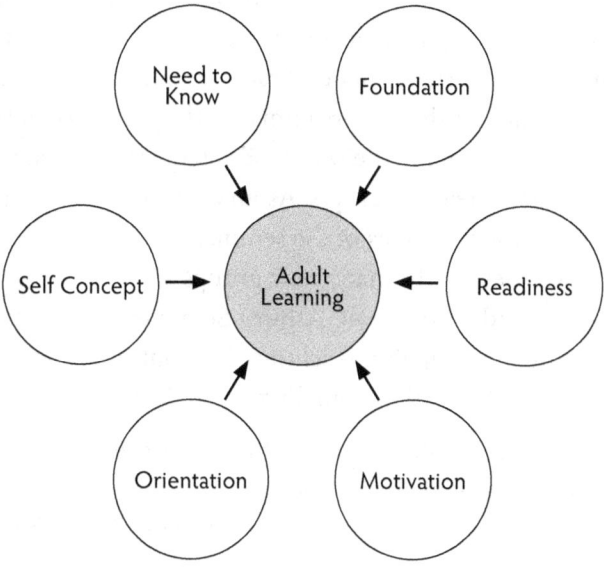

Learning as Lifelong Vocation

Formation is a lifelong process. Therefore, we continue learning. "A teacher's task is inherently future oriented," wrote Ward.[16] Perceiving graduation as the end of learning is a major cause of many of the problems in ministry later on. Therefore, we maintain that schools that fail to instill in students a true commitment to grow as lifelong learners have essentially missed their purpose. "The greatest defect in theological education today is that it is too

---

16. Ted W. Ward, "With an Eye on the Future," in *With an Eye on the Future: Development and Mission in the 21st Century*, edited by Duane Elmer and Louis McKinney (Monrovia, CA: MARC Publications, 1996), 13.

much an affair of piecemeal transmission of knowledge and skills, and that, in consequence, it offers too little challenge to the student to develop his own resources and to become an independent, lifelong inquirer, growing constantly while he is engaged in the work of the ministry."[17] We can draw examples from theology schools that have a set specific focus on lifelong learning. One of the "Core Values" of Asbury Theological Seminary is its commitment to lifelong learning for pastors and church leaders. The "Strategic Map" of the seminary describes this value thus:

> The rapid pace of change in the world requires that we no longer conceptualize a two or three-year program as an isolated period of training which equips someone for a lifetime ministry. Rather we affirm the importance of developing an ongoing relationship with our alumni for their entire ministry. The growing challenges and fast-paced change in the world today require that pastors and leaders become lifelong learners. Asbury Seminary is committed to extending the resources of the seminary as a bridge not only to the graduates but to many new groups who will look to us for training and instruction. Asbury Seminary will become a vital resource for ongoing teaching, distribution of resources, networking, collaboration, retooling and reflection.[18]

Stated with clarity and specific indicators, this value gives a firm pointer to the goal and criterion for effective assessment.

The vision of "Coaching as Continuing Education" at Auburn seminary climaxed in the establishment of the Auburn Coaching Institute (ACI)[19] and grew into residential components as well as ongoing coaching for clergy and church leaders in "real time." There is a felt need for ongoing coaching today as the distance between learning theory and doing ministry is increasing in formal theological settings. "Theological education can no longer simply be a

---

17. H. Richard Niebuhr, Daniel Day Williams and James M. Gustafson, *The Advancement of Theological Education* (New York: Harper, 1957), 209.

18. See Asbury Theological Seminary, "2023 Strategic Map: Ten Core Values of Strategic Planning," http://asburyseminary.edu/wp-content/uploads/2023StrategicMap011012.pdf. For a summary of this document, see Appendix 2.

19. Laurie J. Ferguson and Frederick W. Weidmann, "Coaching As Continuing Education: The Auburn Seminary Experience," in *A Lifelong Call to Learn: Continuing Education for Religious Leaders*, edited by Robert E. Reber and D. Bruce Roberts (Herndon, VA: The Alban Institute, 2010), 183.

fragmented course of studies in a school. The future of theological education in its several modes is found in a commitment to lifelong learning for the whole people of God."[20] When the vision of ongoing personal formation and lifelong inquiry enlightens a student of theology, learning breaks out of the four walls of the classroom, taking on the vast vistas of formation. Meri MacLeod writes extensively on the rapid acceleration of mobile technologies that move from *learning individually* to the *stimulation of learning in dialogue with others* located anywhere in the world. She says, "The rapid, and unrelenting adoption of new technologies (mobile phones, rural wireless networks, and solar powered technologies) is changing how people learn, and more importantly, how they want to learn."[21] These new technologies are also making a noticeable impact in the trends of online and cohort learning methods, as discussed below.

Online learning

The current whirlwinds of change in education and life invite us to patiently analyze the good and the bad of online learning. Although the debate requires a rather detailed engagement, in order to keep things simple we limit this discussion to a brief mention of the two major views. The fundamental pedagogical assumptions in theological education are being challenged by well-structured online learning programs. The online educational philosophy holds certain assumptions that credits our unbiased attention. Affirming the advantages of online education, Christopher Hammon wrote,

> The new information and communication technologies include technologies for voice, video, data creation, storage and presentation as well as communication networks such as internet and wireless networks . . . Our approach to using connected learning for lifelong learning for ministry has brought congregational leaders, chaplains and counselors together online . . . For a world that realizes the value of diverse perspectives for constructing understanding of problems and developing solutions, forming learning communities in cyberspace presents several key opportunities. One is the chance to form an ongoing community among practitioners who are in

---

20. Linda Cannell, *Theological Education Matters: Leadership Education for the Church* (Newburgh, IN: EDCOT, 2006), 317.
21. Meri MacLeod, "The Future Is Here: Changing the Way People Learn," *Common Ground Journal* 11, no. 2 (Spring 2014): 72–76 (here, 74).

the field working and moving from place to place throughout their careers. While the seminary campus provides a special learning community environment during a minister's basic professional training, ministers tend to relocate several times during their careers typically from small, rural congregations progressively toward larger metropolitan congregations.[22]

The following are some of the arguments in favor of online education:
1. Classroom teaching, which tends to be mostly "talking," isn't the method of any good learning situation. Consider the methods Jesus used with his hearers.
2. Teaching unending theories by "talk" in the classroom setting, even when they seem sensible and relevant, does not provide room for the students to think for themselves.
3. Online learning in theology is not simply watching videos of someone talking about topics. Neither is it all about reading books online. There is space for relational bonding and mentoring, interactive academic development and mutual edification.
4. Collaborative learning designs can take place effectively online. Learning online is not to be written off as "practice in isolation."
5. Considering the economy of time, space and human resources, one can facilitate learning holistically if the student takes the process seriously. Written and online resources can make a personal impact on the students as real teachers are designing the materials.
6. Usually, personal affective qualities are not magically created in a theology classroom; rather students come to learning with these qualities.
7. Rigidity in pedagogical philosophy is done away with in the online learning process. The student in well-designed online learning does not need to complete numerous courses that are rigidly built into the program. There is room to choose programs that specifically address a student's needs and interests.
8. Such personal and spiritual formation can be done effectively with a well-designed online learning program. Therefore, claims of

---

22. A. Christopher Hammon, "Connected Learning for Ministry in a Technological Age," in *A Lifelong Call to Learn: Continuing Education for Religious Leaders*, edited by Robert E. Reber and D. Bruce Roberts (Herndon, VA: The Alban Institute, 2010), 288, 290.

guaranteed spiritual and personal formation through online learning may not always be questionable.
9. Personal mentoring and ministry formation can be provided effectively with online learning. This depends on how the learning process is designed and how self-motivated the group of learners is.
10. Through online learning, the student as the agent of learning is capable of internally processing information, ideas and concepts in ways that are most relevant for his or her context.
11. The online transformative sharing of experiences and information is not inferior to that of the classroom, if the learning process is thoughtfully structured and facilitated. In fact, this safeguards the students from unhealthy "power dynamics" played out in the classroom that negatively impact them.
12. If there are questions about "community" with online learning, the same may be true with seminary settings, where the "crowd" is often mistakenly understood as a community.
13. Online learning can offer the best space to facilitate learning in the students' own preferred ways.

The unlimited possibilities of online learning and its scope in blending together the global wealth of wisdom are worth considering in our world today, where keen learners who are restricted by time and mobility can still receive transformative theological education.

Could we opt for online learning as a transformative paradigm and an opportunity that addresses the pressing issues of time, availability and distance? Is what the online theological programs offer useful when ecclesial and social needs are taken into account? Certain fundamental assumptions of online learning could be challenged. Van Driel points out three formative aspects of theological education that are undertheorized in online education:

- Education as a form of apprenticeship;
- Essential place of worship; and
- Ecclesial formation.[23]

The difficult question raised over the whole idea of virtual learning has been on the holistic formation of learners. The argument is that, without the

---

23. Edwin Chr. van Driel, "Online Theological Education: Three Undertheorized Issues," *Theological Education* 50, no. 1 (2015): 69–79.

context of a community and real mentoring and learning interaction, we cannot realize the spiritual, personal and ministry formation of learners. However, as long as the program does not degenerate into a commercial enterprise (which is also applicable to campus training), the design is holistically transformative, the process viable, learners pursue with utmost seriousness, the local church provides the context of worship, ministry and mentoring, and, fundamentally, a holistic assessment process for formational development is in place, online learning can be a potential methodology for lifelong learning.

Peer-Learning Cohorts

A *peer-learning cohort* in theological education signifies a group in which members share particular characteristics and commitments in learning and ministry. In the paradigm of continuing education, these cohorts are recognized as a very positive model for motivated learning and practice.[24] There are emergent emphases on group learning in theological education today. Classroom-based peer-learning groups are *focused learning communities* or *communities of practice*, different from the conventional pattern of student teams engaging in sporadic group assignments. Peer-learning cohorts facilitate collaborative learning, create shared knowledge and can grow into prominent forms of lifelong-learning cohorts. These cohorts can be formed in both the residential and non-residential settings of learning, with an added focus on shared knowledge and supportive dynamics, as the program intentionally fosters distinct advantages to group membership. Cohorts as active communities offer multiple means of support to candidates and provide opportunities for members to learn from one another. Hammon's concept of *connected learning*,[25] representing online collaborative learning, is an emerging trend in theology. Once faculty members acquire real experience of cohort learning for themselves and are oriented to the creative application of this methodology in teaching, it will make a significant impact on learning and action. Methodologically, teachers today are ever more aware of the fact that individuals learn differently and that different forms of interactive learning

---

24. Bruce Roberts, "Motivated Learning and Practice: A Peer Group Model," in *A Lifelong Call to Learn: Continuing Education for Religious Leaders*, edited by Robert E. Reber and D. Bruce Roberts (Herndon, VA: The Alban Institute, 2010). The discussion here is particularly on the need for innovation in congregational leadership and continuing education.
25. Hammon, "Connected Learning," 283.

produce great results in shaping them as practicing thinkers and reflective practitioners. When peer-learning cohorts grow beyond the classroom into dedicated teams of lifelong learners impacting on God's mission within and outside the church, training achieves the lasting impact it envisions.

Theological Education as Ministry Leadership Development for the Church

> Traditional forms are maintained only because they are traditional and radical forms pursued only because they are radical – and the formation of effective leadership for the church is hindered. We heartily welcome the wise critiques of evangelical theological education which have arisen in recent times, which have forced us to think much more carefully both about our purposes in theological education and about the best means for achieving those purposes.[26]

So said Bernhard Ott alongside the ICETE Manifesto of Theological Education. For the multiple reasons that have been discussed so far in this book, our patterns of training tend to resort to too many words with no silence, too much professional perfection with no character, too many programs with no reflection and too many theories with no application in ministry. This has led educators such as Saphir Athyal and Sam Simmons to talk about *the prodigal seminary that needs to return to the church*. Athyal said, "The seminaries exist to serve the church, but they have become prodigal children doing their own thing. They are often out of touch with the needs of the church in society at large."[27] The formation of ministers for the church is becoming more of a challenge in training. As Jones and Armstrong put it, "The conventional model by which a 'learned clergy' was supposed to be formed has broken down, and the church and academy have developed a mutual suspicion and even hostility rather than the synergy that is critical for shaping the clergy to

---

26. Bernhard Ott, *Understanding and Developing Theological Education*, ICETE Series (Carlisle: Langham Global Library, 2016), 23.
27. Saphir P. Athyal, "Missiological Core of Theological Education," *UBS Journal* 1, no. 2 (September 2003): 55.

be people who learn throughout their vocations."[28] Addressing the issue of fragmentation in theological education, some have proposed the matrix of "leader development for the church" as the pertinent resolution. Cannell makes a compelling appeal on this theme in *Theological Education Matters*: "God's primary interest is the church, defined as the people of God. It is doubtful that God mandated Christian schools, mission organizations, non-formal organizations or even institutional expressions of the church. These are human creations and should always be seen as supportive to the mission of the people of God in the world."[29] Calian, in *The Ideal Seminary*, raises the same concern: "Is church leadership really a neglected discussion topic on our campuses?" He establishes that "Seminaries and churches require leaders who are willing to be educated in the context of continuity and change, a never-ending tension that faces every generation of believers."[30] True formation takes place in the real context of service. Theological education is for the church. According to Cheesman, "The backbone of the church and its future direction usually rests upon the leaders who have been trained in the theological education schools and programs. Where theological education has been strong and lively, often the church has been also, and vice versa."[31] Development happens when learners engage in the real task themselves. Seminaries form seminarians; churches have a need to train their leaders. Therefore, when a theology student's real context of formation is the church, there is a tremendous impact. In the words of Graham Houghton, "our programs must be understood in terms of training for effective leadership in the church and in mission. It must be high on our agenda to produce leaders, men and women of influence, who will in the course of time take the high ground for biblical faith."[32]

---

28. L. Gregory Jones and Kevin R. Armstrong, *Resurrecting Excellence: Shaping Faithful Christian Ministry*, Pulpit and Pew Series (Grand Rapids, MI: Eerdmans, 2006), 118.

29. Cannell, *Theological Education Matters*, 278.

30. Carnegie Samuel Calian, *The Ideal Seminary: Pursuing Excellence in Theological Education* (Louisville, KY: Westminster John Knox, 2002), 10–12.

31. Graham Cheesman, "The Philosophy of Theological Education," Module 1, 2003; Teaching materials at the Centre for Theological Education (CTE) Collections, Belfast Bible College Library, Belfast.

32. Graham Houghton, "Theological Education for Leadership Development," in *Educating for Tomorrow: Theological Leadership for the Asian Context*, edited by Manfred Waldemar Kohl and A. N. Lal Senanayake (Bangalore: SAIACS, 2007), 213.

James Hopewell[33] and Joseph Hough and Barbra Wheeler[34] proposed the congregational paradigm, where the shift changes from efforts from the intellectual and character development of the student to the cognitive and character development of the church.

Participation of church in the theology school[35] and the reciprocity between the two is diminishing in many contexts. The pattern of the relationship between the church and the seminary has been a much discussed theme over the decades. Regarding the anomaly of theological education as "institutions serving an institution" Ward categorically speaks of the failure of theological schools, such that "the church has not consistently been well served by the schools and school-like institutions to which it has delegated the responsibility to prepare its own leaders."[36] Is it that the church is losing confidence in the school and, therefore, is not willing to invest in its mission? Or is it that the school is withdrawing itself from the church, thinking its mission is to be an independent professional center of knowledge doing different things?

Are theological institutions making a difference in the church? Have we gained the confidence to equip the church with theologically sound, emotionally trustworthy, morally pure and ministerially committed leaders? It is disheartening to realize the failure of theology schools in forming students in habits and passions integral to service. Ronald Vallet wrote, "Pastors, when asked how they *actually* spend their time, give an answer quite different than the answer they give when they are asked how they *should* spend their time."[37] Theology schools are to be more intentional in designing their curricula in order to train leaders for the church in the desired habits and passions. Moreover, effective assessment techniques should be used to see the impact the school makes on the ministry and leader development of the church in a given context. Spencer writes, "As the context of the church changes and new

---

33. James Hopewell, "A Congregational Paradigm for Theological Education," *Theological Education* (Autumn 1984): 60–70. This paper was a point of reference at the Consultation on the Congregation and Theological Education at the Candler School of Theology, 3–5 June 1985.

34. Joseph Hough and Barbara Wheeler, *Beyond Clericalism: The Congregation as a Focus for Theological Education* (Atlanta, GA: Scholars, 1988).

35. Samson Prabhakar and M. J. Joseph (eds.), *Church's Participation in Theological Education* (Bangalore: BTESSC/SATHRI, 2003).

36. Ted Ward, "Foreword: The Anomaly of Theological Education; Institutions Serving an Institution," in Cannell, *Theological Education Matters*, 11.

37. Ronald E. Vallet, *Stewards of the Gospel: Reforming Theological Education* (Grand Rapids: MI: Eerdmans, 2011), 189.

generations with new sensibilities and challenges arise, theological educators must respond with both conviction and creativity." Nonetheless, regarding the application of design thinking to curriculum, he observes that "it isn't just about integrating disciplines or innovating instruction, but about creating viable, sustainable, effective structures to address the student experience more broadly."[38] In order to improve ministerial preparation, Lincoln gives four pieces of advice to theology schools:

> 1. Church and seminary leaders should drop the rhetoric of excellence and replace it with the rhetoric of competencies (plural).
>
> 2. Critics and friends of theological schools need to recognize the inevitability of some slack between the work of seminaries and the actual work of pastors.
>
> 3. Researchers should conduct qualitative studies that focus on the intersection of theological education and the practice of ministry.
>
> 4. Those who care about improving theological education or about improving the vibrancy of ministry must care about both and must look over the fences that divide disciplines and professional foci.[39]

At a time when more theology schools are turning out as hybrid institutions, desperately pursuing higher-education and multiple accreditations, we need constant reminders that we exist for the church. By choice, our schools must seek to be more and more *in* the church, *by* the church and *for* the church.

A School's Self-Assessment Guide on Transformative Methodological Trends

- Do the majority on campus feel that the focus at the seminary is very different from the actual work of the church? How can this be resolved practically?

---

38. James Spencer, "Online Education and Curricular Design," *Theological Education* 49, no. 2 (2015): 30, 22.
39. Timothy D. Lincoln, "A Few Words of Advice: Linking Ministry, Research on Ministry and Theological Education," *Theological Education* 49, no. 1 (2014): 119.

Transformative Methodological Trends in Teaching and Learning 175

- How would the students and faculty describe the practice of spiritual formation as it happens on campus today? What transformative impact does it have on the student?
- What are the spiritual disciplines cultivated intentionally in this campus as distinct from other theological schools?
- Do the majority of faculty appear as "academically distant superior professionals" or as "spiritually exemplary accessible gurus"? How can we address this aspect of faculty formation consistently at the school?
- What gets deeply rooted in the student in terms of his or her personal spiritual formation, particularly in the first year of study, apart from regular chapel services and other regular prayer events?
- Which system or person at the school looks closely at the blending of academics and spirituality? How is the school improving year after year in this area of transformative training?
- Looking back over the entire history of the school, who were (or are) the faculty that presented to the campus the most influential discipleship model in training? What was outstanding in their approach, and how could the school build on their strengths today?
- What are viable ways and means by which the school could enhance the balance of academics and spirituality in the life of the faculty?
- How does the school promote the climate of corporate learning on and off campus?
- Discuss and write down the ongoing disciplinary issues on campus that could be directly resulting from the continued negligence of spiritual formation in the community. How should this be dealt with? When? And by whom?
- Other than by receiving a degree and theoretical knowledge, in what specific ways is a student personally helped for the future by the training at this school?
- What practical steps are taken by the school in the first and second year of training to develop in a student a firm commitment to lifelong learning of God's Word and theology?
- How does the school instill in the student and the faculty a genuine passion for the church and its mission?

Practical Recommendations: Transformative Methodological Trends

- Make it a practice for the faculty members and administrative leaders to gather once every two/three months to review spiritual and personal formation issues in training. Pray about, discuss and explore the most relevant ways to address them.
- Entrust this responsibility to persons/teams who are accountable, self-motivated for the task, able to implement ideas and skilled to undertake effective evaluation.
- Review the traditional definition of "spiritual formation" at the school and modify/redefine it, specifying the *goal*, *process*, *design* and *impact assessment*.
- Offer specialized support to the students to develop individual and corporate spiritual formation plans, student-initiated, problem-based research projects, and competency development that occurs in a valued mentoring context.
- Train students in basic skills of online learning so that the school can track the possibility of offering continuing education for alumni in the future, as individuals or regional cohorts.
- Formulate and practice a training design for peer-learning cohorts as part of the school's curriculum and encourage students to implement this in their ministry contexts, closely associating with local churches and missions.
- Motivate and assist the members of faculty to revisit their syllabus and incorporate newer *gogical* varieties (teaching methods) for excellence in the teaching-learning experience.
- Explore and test new approaches by which contemplative prayer, journaling, fasting and hospitality will get embedded in the daily life of the school.
- Initiate focused dialogues with churches and missions regarding the opportunities for mutual service assistance, competency nurturing, and ongoing informal and non-formal training.
- Create free space for students to share experiences, express ideas, promote team-based formational initiatives and engage in social-developmental tasks.

10

Treading the Path of Wholeness

Strategic Steps Forward

Sometimes to get a clearer view, we need to stand at a distance. At times, it is only by thinking out of the box that we see the best way forward. Our proposition is not that our system is beyond recovery; it is rather an urgent call to synchronize the excellent parts into an integrated whole in theological education. Facets of disintegration are in no way to be seen as evidence of ultimate destruction. They sound the alarm for informed decision making. The following recommendations from Cannell[1] for a critical balance invite us to such informed decision making:

- Not anti-institution, but not serving the institution for the institution's sake.
- Not anti-technology, but not letting technology drive education.
- Not anti-knowledge, but not knowledge for knowledge's sake.
- Not anti-theology, but not theology for theology's sake.
- Not against ordered learning, but not organizing learning in relation to specialized disciplines.
- Not against theological education, but not equating theological education with formal schooling.

---

1. Linda Cannell, *Theological Education Matters: Leadership Education for the Church* (Newburgh, IN: EDCOT, 2006), 331–335.

> "Virtually all of the writers who have examined the study of theology in recent times – most notably Gerhard Ebeling, Edward Farley, and Wolfhart Pannenberg – have remarked on the diversity and general disarray of the subject. And virtually all have recognized that this diversity and disarray both undermine the credibility of theology in our time and render exceedingly difficult, if not impossible, the task of reintegrating the theological disciplines in such a way that they support a cohesive and cogent ministry of the gospel." Richard Muller, *The Study of Theology*, Vol. 7 (Grand Rapids, MI: Zondervan, 1991), 26.

The hazardous disarray in certain dimensions of theological education invites our response towards deeper balance and coherence. So the primary question in assessment would be: What makes an ideal school? Calian's outline of characteristics that describe *an ideal seminary* can serve as a guidepost in this assessment task.[2] Some of these characteristics challenge the system at its core but deserve critical reflection:

- An ideal seminary will not waste time discussing the nature of community; instead, its energies will be spent on *being* the community of God, the family of love.
- The ideal seminary supports spiritual engagement that is willing to struggle with the holy mysteries of our faith. In an ideal seminary, there is no dichotomy between the classroom and the prayer room.
- The ideal seminary will do away with grades and evaluations; instead, we would be so caught up in our desire to please God that we would expect nothing less from ourselves than our best; this would be our standard.
- The ideal seminary would do away with hierarchy in any shape or form.
- The ideal seminary needs to have adequate facilities, be electronically accessible and have financial support to enable it to minimize scrambling for the scarce resources within the community.
- The ideal seminary will have ingrained in its daily culture the need to share God's love to all, expressed so powerfully in the person of Jesus Christ (John 3:16).

---

2. Carnegie Samuel Calian, *The Ideal Seminary: Pursuing Excellence in Theological Education* (Louisville, KY: Westminster John Knox, 2002), 105–111 (see the book for descriptions of each of these points).

- The ideal seminary and the ideal church will seriously consider de-emphasizing commencement and confirmation services which often convey that we have "graduated" from further learning.
- The ideal seminary will, of course, enroll ideal students.
- The ideal seminary requires an ideal faculty.
- The ideal seminary needs an exceptionally dedicated core of administrators and staff to attend to the numerous institutional workings of the seminary community.

This speaks of the essential quality of theological education and the excellence to be modeled in the functioning of the seminary. We are to do justice to our model of training that has God's Word as the immovable foundation, love of Jesus Christ as the driving force, proclamation of the gospel in word and deed as a habit, and holy living, sincere worship and the service of the kingdom of God as an act of devotion.

Where are our schools heading in the coming years? What are the essential steps for unity and wholeness in our vision and praxis? Facilitating wholeness in the context of a theology school is an active, thoughtful process. It is not attained merely by consultations or publishing. Not many would resist the call for wholeness in theological education, but certain questions are challenges on the way, such as the following:

- *What:* What would the term *wholeness* mean in the context of my school?
- *Who:* Who is the insightful leader or team to direct the school in the true vision of theological education?
- *When:* When do we start active thinking and moving in the direction of self-assessment and integration?
- *Where:* Where exactly should we start?
- *How:* How should we facilitate holistic transformation and growth in the school? What pathways will get us there?

Good questions are great guides. Schools have to grapple with these questions in their own settings in their own modes. However, certain inferences from our discussions thus far might propel us along the way. The ideas presented in the previous chapters may be condensed to four overarching aspects in the self-assessment and renewal of our school's training philosophy and practice (see Figure 22). These are central extrapolations that stand out in the task of facilitating wholeness in the learning environment.

180   Towards Vital Wholeness in Theological Education

Figure 22: Pivotal Procedural Considerations in the Path of Wholeness

ACCREDITATION STANDARDS	ASSESSMENT CULTURE
RESEARCH AND LEARNING METHODOLOGY	FACULTY FORMATION

(WHOLENESS at center)

Wholeness Steered and Enhanced by Standards of Accreditation

There are schools that suffer within the team a stark dearth of personnel who would envision formation and growth. Guidance extended from an authorized external authority can normally afford a substantial amount of transformation in such situations. While quality maintenance is by and large the responsibility of individual schools, accreditation standards can play a significant role in facilitating schools to pursue excellence. The formal influence of these bodies on the schools and the profound resource potential within their constituencies assist in maximizing their contribution. All the key areas of deliberation we have covered so far in this book fit well into the frame of service of accreditation in one way or another. The accrediting body is the quality-enhancing service. It exists to build awareness in the institution's governance on the vital need for wholeness and to strategically initiate the keenest debate on this topic within theology circles. The more we shy away from this imperative call, the more chaos we invite into our own growth.

A survey I conducted in February 2016 of principals or academic deans of eighty evangelical theological institutions in India gathered wide-ranging information on the areas they wanted the accrediting bodies to precisely focus on while evaluating the training. The ideals represented in the responses were:

- High academic standards
- Clear vision statement
- Missional impact

- Robust and focused governance
- Context-appropriate curriculum and curricular revision
- Relationship with the church
- Spiritual nurture and mentoring to students
- High moral values and disciplines
- Spiritual formation
- Practical ministry opportunities
- Ministry-based research opportunities
- Training for faculty in transformative teaching
- Facilities and methods to enhance active learning in library
- Revision of methods of examination and grading

There is nothing remarkable about this list. Schools know how to maintain their reports on all of the above areas. The difficulty is with formulating specific indicators or attributes for each of these points. For instance, what specific indicators or values would assess "a robust and focused governing body," "high moral values and disciplines" or "missional impact of the school"?

Presumably, the central task of accreditation is to strengthen the integration of the overall curriculum through quality assessment, which goes far deeper than an evaluation of the separate functions of the school. To think outside of the conventional modes, an educational system would need a generative and adaptive leadership alongside the technical administration that makes decisions and manages the daily affairs of the school. The expression *adaptive and generative leadership* means that it must be highly responsive and innovative in situations of deeper formational needs and new challenges. The felt need for this sort of leader development is perhaps a primary challenge that both accrediting bodies and the schools should be addressing in the first place.

Wholeness Sustained by an Ongoing, Inbuilt Culture of Assessment

Schools are at home with assessment in the conventional patterns of examinations and tests inherited from the banking model of education. While this limits the task of assessment to information-based grading within the classroom, our current proposal is a logical review of the entire life on campus and beyond, towards facilitating wholeness in purpose. *Assessment* in this sense is already steering the direction of theological education in many regions of the world. Assessment is not done by assumptions. It necessitates indicators, values and standards that precisely define the attributes of what is being assessed. "Indicators are to goals what windows are to a house."[3] By specifying indicators of change and growth, we are able to evaluate more concretely. However, too much assessment may spoil the spirit of the institution, and therefore identifying the most relevant aspects for evaluation is central to this vision.

Extensive studies have been undertaken on assessment in the educational scenario, always with the broader vision of holistic transformation and growth. Suskie addressed the assessment theme in detail. She maintained that "good assessments are used to inform important decisions, especially those to improve curriculum and pedagogy but also regarding planning, budgeting, and accountability." Her extensive list that follows summarizes the key characteristics of good assessment:

- Successful assessment leads to improvement. (Huba and Freed, 2000)
- The institution uses evidence of goal attainment to effect improvements in its programs. (C-RAC, 2004)
- Good assessments point to action to be taken on results. (APQC, 1999)
- Assessment evidence should be actionable. (Ewell, n.d.)
- Good assessments give us useful information. (Suskie, 2004)
- Assessment must be meaningful. It must be useful to faculty and co-curricular specialists. (Bresciani, 2003)
- Assessment must be influential. It must help institute a culture of accountability, learning, and improvement at the institution. (Bresciani, 2003)
- Effective outcomes assessment ensures that assessment data are used continuously to improve programs and services. (Banta & Associates, 2002)
- Effective outcomes assessment produces data that guide improvement on a continuing basis. (Banta & Associates, 2002)
- A good assessment program leads to reflection and action by faculty, staff, and students. (Palomba & Banta, 1999)

---

3. Leroy Ford, *A Curriculum Design Manual for Theological Education: A Learning Outcomes Focus* (Nashville, TN: Broadman, 1991), 111.

- The implementation of the institution's strategic plan accords high priority to assessment practice that determines the effectiveness with which the institution is achieving its goals and objectives. (AAC&U, 2001)
- There is an ongoing, systematic process for using assessment results to improve teaching/learning and to identify areas needing improvement (and ways to do so). (AAC&U, 2001)
- A good assessment program is linked to decision making about the curriculum. (Palomba & Banta, 1999)
- Good assessment practice includes an ongoing, systematic process for using assessment results to improve teaching, learning, and the curriculum. (Greater Expectations Project, 2004)
- Successful assessment provides feedback to students and the institution. (Huba & Freed, 2000)
- [Assessments] are best used as "problem detectors" to identify areas for attention and further exploration. (APQC, 1999)
- Clear linkages between [assessments] and resource allocation are critical, but the best linkages are indirect. (APQC, 1999)
- A good assessment program is linked to processes such as planning and budgeting. (Palomba & Banta, 1999)
- Through assessment, educators meet responsibilities to students and to the public. (AAHE, 1991)
- Effective outcomes assessment provides a vehicle for demonstrating accountability to stakeholders within and outside the institution. (Banta & Associates, 2002)
- Assessment must be accountable: inform decisions for continuous improvement or provide evidence that what you believed was being learned is, after all, being learned. (Bresciani, 2003)[4]

---

4. Linda Suskie, "Five Dimensions of Good Assessment." Document compiled by Suskie for Middle States Commission on Higher Education, 1 November 2006; https://www.pratt.edu/uploads/principles_of_good_assessment_suskie_2006.pdf; accessed 17 March 2016.

A good assessment:
- Is used
- Is valued
- Is cost-effective
- Has reasonably accurate and truthful results
- Has clear and important goals (see Figure 23)

Figure 23: Characteristics of Good Assessment (Suskie)

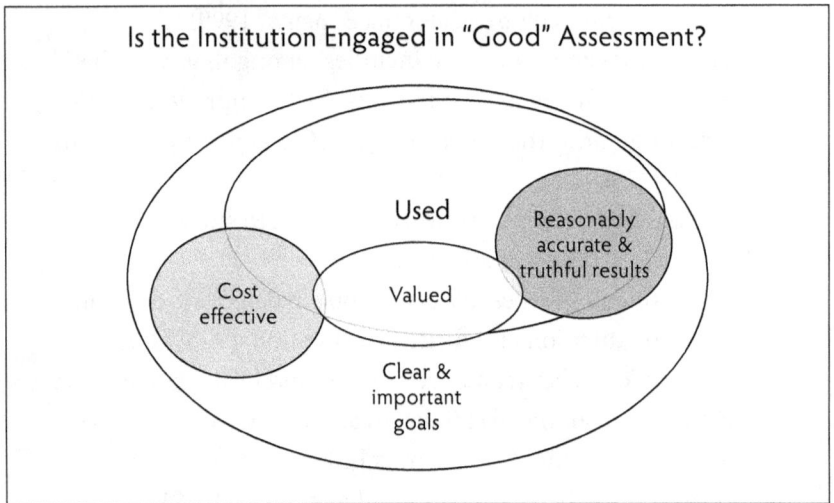

Good assessment needs to be interwoven in the culture of the school. However, it takes a long journey of rigor, steadiness, persistence and commitment to get there. Moreover, this is a progressively corporate and contextually grounded pursuit and not an individualistic, isolated achievement. The prime example of a teacher who carried out learning assessment with all its components was Jesus Christ himself. Always setting the larger vision of the kingdom of God as the chief directive, he designed the path of discipleship in the most transforming manner. At every juncture, he asked his disciples a reflective question. He enthused and challenged them with theologically sound and practically challenging questions. He performed extraordinary works and watched their response. He sensed their thinking and made comments that provoked further thinking. Assessment and follow-up was not a sporadic add-on in Jesus's training model; it was an ongoing practice and an inbuilt culture.

Schools may have to embark on deeper learning on the "what," "who," "when," "where" and "how" of assessment. In each phase of assessment, such as the assessment of the institution or program assessment, we must ask these questions constantly and consistently. Courses and programs are related. Yet, as the course is only a part of the program, the assessment of each will have a distinct focus in spite of their interconnectedness to the vision–goal level as well as the outcome–impact level. Also, as discussed elsewhere, the assessments of a curriculum and a lesson plan take on discernibly different expectations and procedures. Most of all, the results of these assessments reflect on the vision–mission foundation and must be checked against the outcome–impact goal of the school. This mobilization of the upward spiral that builds confidence in the *wholeness of the goal* is what makes the task of assessment complex; the cogent design and thinking required in the process is profound.

Wholeness Effectuated by Transformative Research and Learning Methodology

Scholars have been engaging in unending discussion on the integral core that can nurture wholeness in theological education. They have wrestled with the question of the fundamental unifying core. Is it

- Theological inquiry?
- Missiology and mission?
- Ministry/leader development for the church?
- Practical theology?
- All of the above in balance?

The tendency to give priority to one department or subject area in the task of integration might result in further intensification of gaps rather than the construction of connectors. Hierarchical prerogatives do not make a positive impact on the prospect of wholeness. Drawing from the detailed deliberations on transformative learning in this book, we might seek methodological solutions to this. One could consider moving from intradepartmental to interdepartmental and then to a comprehensive methodological frame in theological education to theoretically inform and systematically form the theme of wholeness. This should address the multiple concerns of transformative teaching-learning in theology schools discussed so far. A wholeness-envisioned transformative research methodology in theology will have the following features:

- Solid and balanced approach to theological wisdom;
- Problem-based practice in research;
- Action-oriented approach to learning;
- Critical hermeneutical approach that nurtures wholeness;
- Compact correlational-inquiry approach that facilitates ongoing learning;
- Theory–practice balance or theological wisdom and missional integration;
- Development of a lifelong habit of research and learning;
- Research as central to theological and missional wisdom;
- Faculty as facilitators of transformative research and learning;
- Learning as an experience beyond the classroom.

In spite of relentless efforts in advancing academic formation, we find many of our graduates poorly oriented in their reading, writing, thinking, reflective and responding capacities. Strategic research patterns could offer a potential resolution to this. Skills in analysis, synthesis, problem-solving, interpretation, correlation, communication and continuing reflection can be advanced through the interrelatedness of courses, programs and experiences in theological education.

Reiterating this burden for theological research and learning is simple and straightforward. All theology is/has to be holistically transformative and this must happen in the context of a community. The all-encompassing horizon of faith in God and in his unchangeable Word is the hub of this theological practice, and the church is the beneficiary of this. The essential networking and interactive style of learning strengthens reciprocal relations between the church and the school. It recognizes the unreserved commitment and intentional work plans to help students get immersed in local situations and to confidently address the global situations in which they are to minister, persisting to overcome ideological captivity and irrelevant abstractions.[5] In the transformative research and learning methodology, faculty is the facilitator and the student owns the process of learning. Each school may explore ways to

---

5. Jessy Jaison, "Practical Theology: A Transformative Praxis in Theological Education towards Holistic Formation," paper presented at SAIACS, Bangalore, 25 September 2008; online at www.theologicaleducation.org; published in *Journal of Theological Education and Mission (JOTEAM)* 1, no. 1 (2010): 76–86.

develop this holistic research paradigm that recognizes theology and ministry as a blended whole all through the learning experience.

Wholeness Rooted in and Advanced by Formation of the Faculty

Another significant movement in theological education is the formation of faculty in the teaching-learning process. Without this, no effort towards wholeness will come to fruition. The process of faculty formation can be initiated by the school, by an exterior educational association or by the accrediting body. Faculty's refresher programs should go beyond scholarship and pedagogical skills to a variety of transformative focuses, such as:

- Spiritual formation for themselves;
- Spiritual-formation services for students;
- Course design and lesson planning;
- Curricular development and revision;
- Pedagogical adaptation;
- Academic mentoring for students;
- Non-formal teaching skills;
- Theory–practice balance in teaching;
- Innovations in adult education;
- Interdisciplinary research and learning methods;
- Designing of tools for learning assessment;
- Assessment and grading expertise;
- Transformative research practice;
- Contribution and conduct in campus community;
- Role-modeling in family and church;
- Passion in service to church/mission;
- Peer-learning exposures.

Conclusion

Theological education today seems diverse and imprecise in many respects. Nevertheless, we reiterate that the aim is neither information transfer nor grades, but the holistic formation of the kind of person who will fulfill God's will in his church for his world. Scholarship and expansion are good, but the core values that make a theological community cannot be altered. Perhaps our parallelism of education's cognitive domain with abstract knowledge of theories and unlimited amounts of information in academia has triggered the biggest setback in training. The indispensable God-centeredness in theological education seems to be fading away. The Scriptures, doctrine and the whole gospel of salvation are hazardously being sidelined in many contexts. This subtle erasing of theology and the Bible from theological education and its academic research is a primary sign of our disintegrating identity.

Theological education cannot be equaled to the accumulation of information in subsidiary subjects or disciplines. The blurring of the truth of the gospel at some edges of the curriculum is simply unwarrantable. *Knowledge*, as envisioned in theological education, is dynamically holistic. This is the decisive strength from the theology school for which the church has been desperately yearning for centuries. Formation in worship, service and personal wholeness are held in a healthy blend in this axis of holistic knowing, which takes place in the context of the church and its mission field, the world. Theology is a personal and communal reality of experiencing God. It is hollow when done in isolation from the church and the church's mission. It is designed to grow and be transformed in the church's milieu in the real context of the world; therefore, it must be built on spiritual, personal and ministerial formation, firmly grounded in the Word of God.

Our argument is clear. The task of theology is intrinsically holistic; and therefore the call on theology schools is for formational wholeness. The term *wholeness* means the integration of intellectual, spiritual, emotional, physical and social development into a healthy unity of the person. When this divine agenda is denied, we fail God, his people and his mission. Any attempt to confine theological education solely to the world of abstract knowledge is critically disadvantageous. An exclusive, detached focus on spiritual or ministry dimensions is equally dangerous. Therefore, theology schools are invited to intentionally revisit the goal and mission of the school, governance, curriculum, faculty, learning experiences, community life, departmental functions and assessment procedures. With the mandate of vital wholeness, the predicament goes beyond the need to rightly outline areas of assessment; we need to embody the assessment results in action. It is hoped that theology schools will realize and take responsibility for the outcome and impact of their training, good or bad, and own the vision of assessment so that ministry can grow as an integrated whole. The four transformative methodologies recommended for the revitalization of our endeavor are spiritual formation, adult education, continuing education and church-ministry formation. The strategic directions recommended for a sustainable realization of this vision of wholeness are the standards of accreditation, the assessment culture of the school, transformative research methodology and the holistic formation of the faculty.

To put it succinctly, this is a call for nothing less than the conversion of seminaries. To conclude, it is hoped that deeper deliberation and actions will emerge on the theme of wholeness in schools in their unique settings, and that our schools will embark on candid procedures of self-assessment. Perceiving theological education as the indispensable plan of God at the core of the church's life and mission, we continue to seek his will, discern his wisdom and celebrate his worth. At the core of our existence, we recognize that theology is not something to be kept at the center of our debates; it is God's truth that shapes our lives. The standard is not survival or the utility of an institution; it is about maintaining the intrinsic value and direction of theology in our formational agenda. May our institutions solidly seek to uphold and embrace the definition of theological education as "Knowing God and loving him with all our being," from which all our incessant worship and service stream forth.

Appendix 1

Detecting Points of Innovation through Needs Assessment[1]

Guidelines: Assess the function of the school closely to see if any of the scenarios below characterize its mission at some level. Write down one or two specific innovative steps to facilitate transformation of the learning environment.

Scenario 1: Faculty
(Academics vs. Mentoring)

Realization that members of faculty provide high-standard intellectual formation but are too busy doing their own things to attend to the spiritual and ministerial mentoring needs of the students.

Scenario 2: Physical Infrastructure and Technology Innovations
(Development vs. Calling)

Realization that the school is getting sidetracked from its central goal and focusing heavily on physical/technological infrastructure.

---

1. Taken from Jessy Jaison, "Evaluation and Innovation: Possibilities of Theological Education," paper presented in Colombo, Sri Lanka, at the Overseas Council International Institute for Excellence, 8 August 2014.

Scenario 3: Community Enlargement
(Crowd vs. Community)

Realization that in spite of the growing number of people on campus, there is no *community* that shares openly, listens generously and participates sacrificially.

Scenario 4: Professional Excellence
(Professionalism vs. Spirituality)

Realization that students strive endlessly for higher grades, but are not practicing spiritual disciplines in knowing God personally.

Scenario 5: New Programs
(Programs vs. Purpose)

Realization that the school is advancing its impact with a number of new programs but they add confusion rather than strength in facilitating the core vision.

Scenario 6: Church-Ministry Formation
(Practical Ministry vs. Church Expectation)

Realization that in spite of the routine practical ministry programs and reporting, the student is not equipped for service in the multi-faceted ministries of the church.

Scenario 7: Partnerships
(Partnerships [or Leadership] vs. Advancement)

Realization that the school's governance and funding partnerships cause problematic interference and intimidation instead of constructive outcomes and vision expansion.

Scenario 8: Accreditation
(Accreditation vs. Ministry Formation)

Realization that the heavy academic expectations of the accreditation standards hinder the spiritual and ministry formation of the school community.

Appendix 2

Mission Statement, Core Values and Value Definitions: A Model

Asbury Theological Seminary 2023 Strategic Map

For the full, formal version, see http://asburyseminary.edu/wp-content/uploads/2023StrategicMap011012.pdf

MISSION STATEMENT: Asbury Theological Seminary is *a community called* to prepare theologically educated, sanctified, Spirit-filled men and women to evangelize and spread scriptural holiness throughout the world, through the love of Jesus Christ, in the power of the Holy Spirit, and to the glory of God the Father!

DEFINING VALUES: Asbury Seminary is committed to historic Christian faith in the Wesleyan tradition in a way which is globally engaged, spiritually formative and missionally alert.

Ten Core Values of Strategic Vision

Asbury Theological Seminary will be committed to:
1. Serving the global Church
2. Graduate level theological education which is faithful to God's Word
3. Personal and community formation
4. Pursuing a diverse, missionally oriented student body

5. Lifelong learning for pastors and church leaders
6. Equipping pastors for missional engagement in service to the Church
7. Serving the emerging ethnic churches
8. Developing new constituencies
9. The laity
10. Strengthening our economic model and developing our network of support

A few examples of the value descriptions:

Core Value 1

Asbury Theological Seminary will be committed to serving the global Church.

We will be ever mindful of the global Church as we develop new programs, utilize technology and innovative delivery systems, understand global trends, and partner with theological institutions around the world. We will strategically deploy faculty, student, and learning resources on every continent in a collaborative way marked by servant leadership.

Core Value 5

Asbury Theological Seminary will be committed to lifelong learning for pastors and church leaders.

The rapid pace of change in the world requires that we no longer conceptualize a two- or three-year program as an isolated period of training which equips someone for a lifetime of ministry. Rather, we affirm the importance of developing an ongoing relationship with our alumni/ae for their entire ministry. The growing challenges and fast-paced change in the world today require that pastors and leaders become lifelong learners. Asbury Seminary is committed to extending the resources of the Seminary as a bridge not only to our graduates, but to many new groups who will look to us for training and instruction. Asbury Seminary will become a vital resource for ongoing teaching, distribution of resources, networking, collaboration, retooling, and reflection.

Appendix 3

Four Dynamics of Holistic Formation: ConneXions Model[1]

Four Dynamics of Holistic Formation			
Spiritual: Connecting with God		Experiential: Connecting with Life	
• Praying/prayer walking • Being prayed for/ receiving healing and deliverance • Meditation in the Word • Memorization of Scriptures • Praying Scriptures • Confession of sin • Forgiveness • Listening inwardly • Being moved by the Holy Spirit • Power encounters • Visions, dreams, prophecies • Worship	• Praise • Waiting on God • Devotions/family devotions • Reflection • Contemplation • Journaling/writing • Fasting • Giving • Silence • Solitude • Spiritual rest • Retreats • Music	• Challenging assignments • Learning by doing • Success • Fruitfulness • Suffering • Pressure • Persecution • Crises • Responsibilities • Failure • Receiving and enforcing discipline • Ministering • Receiving ministry • Praying for others' healing and deliverance	• Exercising gifts • Career/work/job • Field trips/camp • Travel • Cross-cultural experiences • Sickness/health • Evangelism/sharing gospel and own testimony • Relief work/social work • Service projects • Deadlines • Internships • Language learning and acquisition

---

1. Malcolm Webber, "Transforming the Way Leaders are Built: The 5C–4D Model," training documents at the Leader Development and Research Collections, New India Bible Seminary, Kerala. See also Malcolm Webber, *Building Healthy Leaders: Spirit-Built Leadership* Series 1–4 (Elkhart, IN: Strategic, 2002–2011).

Relational: Connecting with Others		Instructional: Connecting with Truth	
• Friends	• Accountability	• Teaching	• Creative media
• Family	• Evaluation	• Study	• Poetry
• Spiritual mothers and fathers	• Communication	• Questions	• Songs
	• Counsel	• Dialogue	• Drama
• Examples	• Correction	• Facilitation	• Q & A
• Role models	• Enemies	• Round-table discussion	• Panel
• Mentors	• Conflict		• Debate
• Coaches	• Rejection	• Discussion groups	• Interviewing
• Team learning experiences	• Reconciliation	• Reading	• Sharing notes
	• Serving/serving together	• Problem-based learning	• Learning projects
• Working groups/ small groups	• Fun/playing	• Audio-visual/ PowerPoint	• Homework
			• Bible studies
• Cooperation	• Laughing	• Simulations	• Papers/exams
• Networking	• Recreational activities together	• Interaction with leaders and teachers	• Demonstrations
• Multicultural activities			• Speeches
	• Sports		• Show and tell
• Reflection together	• Fellowship	• Internet	• Stories and analogies
• Prayer for each other	• Eating together	• Podcasts/webinars	
• Communion and love feast/ foot-washing	• Hospitality	• CDs/DVDs	• Metaphors/parables
	• Visitation	• Radio	• Case studies
	• Care	• Role play	• Storytelling
• Support	• Facebook/Twitter	• Brainstorming	• Kinesthetic activities
• Nurture	• Phone calls/SMS	• Whiteboarding	• Conferences
• Biographies and testimonies	• Blogging	• Quizzes	• Consultations
		• Call out	• Workshops/seminars
• Informal instruction		• Puzzles/riddles	

Appendix 4

Overseas Council International Program Values and Standards for Theological Education 2014

NOTE: This is an excerpt. The original document explains each value, means of assessment and specific areas of examination.

1. We believe that theological schools exist to *strengthen the church*, and seek to enable institutions that

- Are committed to biblical, historical and orthodox Christianity.
- Train leaders who strengthen the church in all of its ministries and functions.
- Foster mutually beneficial partnerships with churches, church bodies, and Christian professionals through ongoing, dynamic dialogue.
- Have national and regional ownership, both legal and psychological.

2. We believe that theological schools must *be transformative within their context* and seek partners that

- Demonstrate significant influence for positive change within their context.
- Have a track record of producing thought leaders for church and society.

3. We believe in *collaboration and institutional generosity* and seek to enable institutions that

- Demonstrate a commitment to multidenominational ministry and the unity of the Body of Christ.
- Are willing to avoid unnecessary competition or duplication in a city or country.
- Demonstrate diversity of age, gender, language and ethnicity.

4. We seek to be a *learning organization* with a *global orientation* and seek partners that

- Are committed to ongoing learning, dialogue and change.
- Are able to thrive in complex, dynamic environments.
- Are committed to a culture of assessment.

5. We are committed to *excellence in education*, including spiritual formation, and seek to partner with institutions that

- Demonstrate concern for academic excellence, spiritual and character formation, and ministry skills in an integrated and holistic manner.
- Are willing to explore ways to provide wider access to theological education.
- Are committed to lifelong learning.
- Have quality faculty with academic expertise, educational skills, spiritual maturity and relevant ministry experience.
- Are accredited or are actively pursuing accreditation.
- Are committed to creativity and flexibility in the curriculum.
- Are committed to a learning environment where the needs and experiences of adult students are taken seriously.
- Are committed to making relevant knowledge and research more widely available.

6. We are committed to *integrity and sustainability* in all matters of institutional life and affirm institutions that

- Practice financial management that demonstrates integrity and accountability.
- Are progressing toward financial sustainability through increasing reliance on local resources.

7. We believe that *visionary leadership* and *generative governance* are essential to institutional leadership and seek to affirm institutions that

- Have leaders who rely on teams.
- Display strategic thinking regarding future opportunities and threats.
- Seek to affirm institutions where management draws on the expertise of a body with ultimate responsibility for the institution.
- Benefit from the wisdom of many counselors from governance, management, faculty and constituency.

Bibliography

Aleshire, Daniel O. "The Character and Assessment of Learning for Religious Vocation: M.Div. Education and Numbering the Levites." *Theological Education* 39, no. 1 (2003): 1–16.

———. "Fifty Years of Accrediting Theological Schools." *Theological Education* 49, no. 1 (2014): 63–80.

———. "The Future Has Arrived: Changing Theological Education in a Changed World." Lecture presented at ATS/COA Biennial Meeting, June 2010. http://www.ats.edu/uploads/resources/publications-presentations/documents/aleshire-the-future-has-arrived.pdf.

Anderson, Keith R. and Randy D. Reese. *Spiritual Mentoring: A Guide for Seeking and Giving Direction.* Guildford: Eagle, 2000.

Arles, Siga. "Governance of Theological Education: Patterns and Prospects." *Journal of Asian Evangelical Theology (JAET)* 14 (2006): 58–60.

———. *Theological Education for the Mission of the Church in India.* Frankfurt: Peter Lang, 1991.

Arles, Siga (ed.). *Called to Teach: Essays in Honor of Peter S. C. Pothan.* Bangalore: Center for Contemporary Christianity, 2011.

Asbury Theological Seminary. "2023 Strategic Map: Ten Core Values of Strategic Planning." http://asburyseminary.edu/wp-content/uploads/2023StrategicMap011012.pdf.

Asia Theological Association. "Values Esteemed by ATA Educators." Revised May 2006. http://www.ataindia.org/uploaded_files/uploads/documents_32.pdf.

"Assessment vs. Evaluation." TeacherVision. https://www.teachervision.com/assessment/new-teacher/48353.html. Accessed 8 July 2015.

The Association of Theological Schools in the United States and Canada. *Bulletin* 36, part 3 (1984).

———. *General Instituional Standards,* "Standard 3: The Theological Curriculum: Learning, Teaching and Research," 30 April 2015, 5. http://www.ats.edu/uploads/accrediting/documents/general-institutional-standards.pdf. Accessed 29 March 2017.

———. "Standard 4: The Theological Curriculum, Statement 4.1.1." *Bulletin* 45, part 1 (2002).

Atema, Tom. "A Perfect Match: Leading and Measuring Belong Together." *Outcomes* (Spring 2014): 18–22. www.outcomesmagazine.com.

Athyal, Saphir P. "Missiological Core of Theological Education." *UBS Journal* 1, no. 2 (September 2003): 50–56.

Banks, Robert. *Re-envisioning Theological Education: Exploring a Missional Alternative to Current Models*. Grand Rapids, MI: Eerdmans, 1999.

Barsness, Roy E., and Richard D. Kim. "A Pedagogy of Engagement for the Changing Character of the 21st Century Classroom." *Theological Education* 49, no. 2 (2015): 89–106.

Board of Regents of the University of Wisconsin System. "Developing a Logic Model: Teaching and Training Guide 2/29/2008." http://www.uwex.edu/ces/pdande/evaluation/evallogicmodel.html. Accessed 13 May 2016.

Bouchard, Charles E., Susan Thistlethwaite and Timothy Weber. "The President's Role as Academic Leader." In *A Handbook for Seminary Presidents*, edited by G. Douglass Lewis and Lovett H. Weems Jr., 72–88. Grand Rapids, MI: Eerdmans, 2006.

Brandt, James M. "Student Formation through Experiential and Transformative Learning: Pedagogical Insights from/for Contextual Education." In *Proleptic Pedagogy: Theological Education Anticipating the Future*, edited by Sondra Higgins Matthaei and Nancy R. Howell, 55–69. Eugene, OR: Cascade Books, 2014.

Brynjolfson, Robert, and Jonathan Lewis (eds.). *Integral Ministry Training: Design and Evaluation*. Pasadena, CA: William Carey Library, 2006.

Cahalan, Kathleen A. In *The Wiley Blackwell Companion to Practical Theology*, by Bonnie J Miller-McLemore. Chichester: Blackwell, 2012.

Calian, Carnegie Samuel. *The Ideal Seminary: Pursuing Excellence in Theological Education*. Louisville, KY: Westminster John Knox, 2002.

Cannell, Linda. "Adaptive Leadership: Planning in a Time of Transition." *Theological Education* 46, no. 2 (2011): 25–45.

———. *Theological Education Matters: Leadership Education for the Church*. Newburgh, IN: EDCOT, 2006.

Carlson, R. "Malcolm Knowles: Apostle of Andragogy." *Vitae Scholasticae* 8, no. 1 (Spring 1989): 217–233. Retrieved from http://www.nl.edu/ace/Resources/Knowles.html. Accessed 22 March 2007.

Cetuk, Virginia Samuel. *What to Expect in Seminary: Theological Education as Spiritual Formation*. Nashville, TN: Abingdon, 1998.

Cheesman, Graham. "Competing Paradigms in Theological Education Today." *Journal of Theological Education and Mission* 2, no. 1 (2011): 10–28.

———. "A History of Spiritual Formation in Evangelical Theological Education." *Journal of Theological Education and Mission* 6, no. 6 (February 2015): 8–27.

———. "Kissing and Theological Education." Blog post, 31 December 2012. http://theologicaleducation.org/category/blog/.

———. "The Philosophy of Theological Education." Module 1, 2003. Teaching materials at the Center for Theological Education (CTE) Collections, Belfast Bible College Library, Belfast.

———. "Spiritual Formation as a Goal of Theological Education." PDF from http://theologicaleducation.net, pg. 34. Accessed on 11 April 2017.

———. "Why Do Seminaries Prosper? Why Do Seminaries Die?" *Journal of Theological Education and Mission (JOTEAM)* 3, no. 1 (2012): 1–7.

Chiroma, Nathan, and Anitha Cloete. "Mentoring as a Supportive Pedagogy in Theological Training." *HTS Teologiese Studies/Theological Studies* 71, no. 3 (2015). Art. #2695, 8 pages. http://dx.doi.org/10.4102/hts.v71i3.2695.

Chopp, Rebecca S. *Saving Work: Feminist Practices of Theological Education.* Louisville, KY: Westminster John Knox, 1995.

Chrispal, Ashish. "Prospects and Retrospects of Theological Education in the Twenty-First Century." In *Educating for Tomorrow: Theological Leadership for the Asian Context*, edited by Manfred Waldemar Kohl and A. N. Lal Senanayake, 247–256. Bangalore: SAIACS, 2007.

Cole, Victor Babajide. *Training of the Ministry.* Bangalore: Theological Book Trust, 2001.

Collinson, Sylvia Wilkey. *Making Disciples.* Milton Keynes: Paternoster, 2004.

Colson, Howard P., and Raymond M. Rigdon. *Understanding Your Church's Curriculum.* Nashville, TN: Broadman, 1981.

Cornelius, Paul. "Transforming Theological Education to Be Transformational." *Journal of Theological Education and Mission* 6, no. 6 (2015): 28–43.

Cronshaw, Darren. "Reenvisioning Theological Education and Missional Spirituality." *Journal of Adult Theological Education* 9, no. 1 (2012): 9–27.

Cunningham, Scott. "Who Is a Theological Educator?" *Africa Journal of Evangelical Theology* 16, no. 2 (1997): 79–86.

Das, Rupen. *Connecting Curriculum with Context: A Handbook for Context Relevant Curriculum Development in Theological Education.* ICETE Series. Carlisle: Langham Global Library, 2015.

Davina, Soh Hui Leng. *The Motif of Hospitality in Theological Education: A Critical Appraisal with Implications for Application in Theological Education.* ICETE Series. Carlisle: Langham Global Library, 2016.

Dearborn, Tim. "Preparing New Leaders for the Church of the Future: Transforming Theological Education through Multi-Institutional Partnerships." *Transformation* 12, no. 4 (Oct.–Dec. 1995): 7–12.

Dewey, John. *The Child and the Curriculum.* Chicago: University of Chicago Press, 1902.

van Driel, Edwin Chr. "Online Theological Education: Three Undertheorized Issues." *Theological Education* 50, no. 1 (2015): 69–79.

Duce, Philip, and Daniel Strange (eds.). *Keeping Your Balance: Approaching Theological and Religious Studies.* Leicester: IVP, 2001.

Dwyer, Karen Kangas, and Edward M. Hogan. "Assessing a Program of Spiritual Formation Using Pre and Post Self-Report Measures." *Theological Education* 48, no. 1 (2013): 25–34.

Edgar, Brian. "The Theology of Theological Education." *Evangelical Review of Theology* 29, no. 3 (2005): 208–217.

Esbjörn-Hargens, Sean, Jonathan Reams and Olen Gunnlaugson (eds.). *Integral Education: New Directions for Higher Learning.* Albany, NY: SUNY, 2010.

Farley, Edward. *The Fragility of Knowledge: Theological Education in the Church and University.* Philadelphia, PA: Fortress, 1988.

———. *Theologia: The Fragmentation and Unity of Theological Education.* Philadelphia, PA: Fortress, 1983.

———. "Toward Theological Understanding: An Interview with Edward Farley." *Christian Century* (4–11 Feb. 1998): 113–115, 149.

Ferguson, Laurie J., and Frederick W. Weidmann. "Coaching As Continuing Education: The Auburn Seminary Experience." In *A Lifelong Call to Learn: Continuing Education for Religious Leaders*, edited by Robert E. Reber and D. Bruce Roberts (eds.), 181–200. Herndon, VA: The Alban Institute, 2010.

Ferris, Robert. W. *Renewal in Theological Education: Strategies for Change.* Wheaton, IL: Wheaton College, 1990.

———. "The Work of a Dean." *Evangelical Review of Theology* 32, no. 1 (2008): 65–73.

Flinders, David J., Nel Noddings and Stephen J. Thornton. "The Null Curriculum: Its Theoretical Basis and Practical Implications." *Curriculum Inquiry* 16, no. 1 (Spring 1986): 33–42. Published by Blackwell Publishing on behalf of the Ontario Institute for Studies in Education/University of Toronto Stable. URL: http://www.jstor.org/stable/1179551. Accessed on 10 July 2015.

Ford, Leroy. *A Curriculum Design Manual for Theological Education: A Learning Outcomes Focus.* Nashville, TN: Broadman, 1991.

Foster, Charles R. *Educating Congregations: The Future of Christian Education.* Nashville, TN: Abingdon, 1994.

Grace, Kay Sprinkel, Amy McClellan and John A. Yankey. *The Nonprofit Board's Role in Mission, Planning and Evaluation.* Washington, DC: Boardsource, 2009.

Graham, Stephen R. "The Vocation of the Academic Dean." In *C(H)AOS Theory: Reflections of Chief Academic Officers in Theological Education*, edited by Kathleen D. Billman and Bruce C. Birch, 63–74. Grand Rapids, MI: Eerdmans, 2011.

Gushee, David P., and Walter C. Jackson (eds.). *Preparing for Christian Ministry: An Evangelical Approach.* Grand Rapids, MI: Baker, 1998.

Hammon, A. Christopher. "Connected Learning for Ministry in a Technological Age." In *A Lifelong Call to Learn: Continuing Education for Religious Leaders*, edited by Robert E. Reber and D. Bruce Roberts, 273–300. Herndon, VA: The Alban Institute, 2010.

Hardy, Steven A. *Excellence in Theological Education: Effective Training for Church Leaders*. Carlisle, Cumbria: Langham Global Library, 2016.

———. "Strategic Planning for Theological Education." In *Educating for Tomorrow: Theological Leadership for the Asian Context*, edited by Manfred Waldemar Kohl and A. N. Lal Senanayake, 59–76. Bangalore: SAIACS, 2007.

Harkness, Allan. "Introduction." In *Tending the Seedbeds: Educational Perspectives on Theological Education in Asia*, edited by Allan Harkness, 7–22. Quezon City, Philippines: Asia Theological Association, 2010.

Hiemstra, R., and B. Sisco. "Moving from Pedagogy to Andragogy (Adapted and Updated from *Individualizing Instruction: Making Learning Personal, Empowering and Successful*. San Francisco: Jossey-Bass, 1990)." Unpublished paper. http://home.twcny.rr.com/hiemstra/pedtoand.html. Accessed 19 March 2007.

Hopewell, James. "Mission and Seminary Structure." *International Review of Missions* 56, no. 222 (April 1967): 158–163.

Hough, Joseph C. Jr., and John B. Cobb. *Christian Identity and Theological Education*. Atlanta, GA: Scholars, 1985.

Hough, Joseph, and Barbara Wheeler. *Beyond Clericalism: The Congregation as a Focus for Theological Education*. Atlanta, GA: Scholars, 1988.

Houghton, Graham. "Theological Education for Leadership Development." In *Educating for Tomorrow: Theological Leadership for the Asian Context*, edited by Manfred Waldemar Kohl and A. N. Lal Senanayake, 209–228. Bangalore: SAIACS, 2007.

International Council for Evangelical Theological Education (ICETE). "ICETE Manifesto on the Renewal of Evangelical Theological Education." 2nd ed. 1990. http://www.icete-edu.org/manifesto/. Accessed 8 April 2016.

Jaison, Jessy. "Digitization and Social Media Revolution: Training Prospects and Spiritual Formational Challenges in Theological Schools." *OTI Journal* 3, no. 1 (2016): 7–22.

———. "Evaluation and Innovation: Possibilities of Theological Education." Paper presented in Colombo, Sri Lanka, at the Overseas Council International Institute for Excellence, 8 August 2014.

———. "Excellence through Integration and Evaluation: Essentials for Curriculum Development in Theology Schools." Paper presented at the Annual General Meeting of the Asia Theological Association, UBS Pune, 26 August 2015.

———. "Faculty Formation for Revitalizing Theological Education." *Journal of Theological Education and Mission (JOTEAM)* 6, no. 6 (February 2015): 1–11.

———. "Practical Theology: A Transformative Praxis in Theological Education towards Holistic Formation." Paper presented at SAIACS, Bangalore, 25 September 2008. Online at www.theologicaleducation.org. Published in *Journal of Theological Education and Mission (JOTEAM)* 1, no. 1 (2010): 76–86.

Jayaraj, Dasan. "Theological Education for Missionary Formation." *Journal of Asian Evangelical Theology* 12, nos. 1 & 2 (June–December 2004).

Jeyaraj, J. B. *Christian Ministry: Models of Ministry and Training.* Bangalore: TBT, 2002.

Jinkins, Michael. "Mission Possible: Making Use of the School's Mission Statement in Curriculum Review." *Theological Education* 43, no. 1 (2007): 17–21.

Jones, Alan. "Are We Lovers Anymore: Spiritual Formation in the Seminaries." *Theological Education* 24, no. 1 (1987): 9–29.

Jones, L. Gregory, and Kevin R. Armstrong. *Resurrecting Excellence: Shaping Faithful Christian Ministry.* Pulpit and Pew Series. Grand Rapids, MI: Eerdmans, 2006.

Jones, Tony. *The New Christians: Dispatches from the Emergent Frontier.* San Francisco: Jossey-Bass, 2008.

Kelly, A. V. *The Curriculum: Theory and Practice.* 6th ed. London: SAGE, 2009.

Kelsey, David H. *To Understand God Truly: What's Theological about a Theology School?* Louisville, KY: Westminster John Knox, 1992.

Knowles, Malcolm S. *The Adult Learner: A Neglected Species.* 4th ed. Houston, TX: Gulf, 1990.

———. "Andragogy, Not Pedagogy!" *Adult Leadership* 16 (1968): 350–352.

———. *The Making of an Adult Educator: An Autobiographical Journey.* San Francisco: Jossey-Bass, 1989.

———. *The Modern Practice of Adult Education: Andragogy versus Pedagogy.* Chicago: Follett, 1980.

———. *The Modern Practice of Adult Education: From Pedagogy to Andragogy.* Wilton, CT: Association Press, 1980.

Knowles, Malcolm S., Elwood F. Holton III and Richard A. Swanson. *The Adult Learner: The Definitive Classic in Adult Education and Human Resource Development.* 6th ed. Burlington, MA: Elsevier, 2005.

Kohl, Manfred Waldemar, and A. N. Lal Senanayake (eds.). *Educating for Tomorrow: Theological Leadership for the Asian Context.* Bangalore: SAIACS, 2007.

Laton, Dave, Joe Raynolds, Ted Davis and Dave Stringer. "From Pedagogy to Heutagogy: A Teaching and Learning Continuum." Unpublished paper. http://studylib.net/doc/7584003/from-pedagogy-to-heutagogy---a-teaching-and-learning-cont. Accessed 30 March 2017.

Lincoln, Timothy D. "A Few Words of Advice: Linking Ministry, Research on Ministry and Theological Education." *Theological Education* 49, no. 1 (2014): 103–120.

MacLeod, Meri. "The Future Is Here: Changing the Way People Learn." *Common Ground Journal* 11, no. 2 (Spring 2014): 72–76.

Maddix, Mark A. "Living the Life: Spiritual Formation Defined." In *Spiritual Formation: A Wesleyan Paradigm*, edited by Diane Leclerc and Mark A. Maddix. Kansas City: Beacon Hill, 2011.

Mager, Robert F. *Preparing Instructional Objectives*. Palo Alto, CA: Fearon Publishers, 1962.

McFayden, Ken. *Education or Calling in Multiple Paths to Ministry*. Cleveland, OH: Pilgrim, 2004.

McGee, Patricia. "Learning Objects: Bloom's Taxonomy and Deeper Learning Principles." Paper for the Department of Interdisciplinary Studies & Curriculum and Instruction, University of Texas at San Antonio. http://faculty.coehd.utsa.edu/pmcgee/nlii/LOBloomsMcGee.doc. Accessed 23 March 2017.

McKinney, Larry J. "Evangelical Theological Education: Implementing Our Own Agenda." Paper presented at the ICETE International Consultation for Theological Educators, High Wycombe, UK, 20 August 2003. http://www.icete-edu.org/pdf/0%2003%20McKinney%20Our%20Own%20Agenda.pdf. Accessed 19 April 2016.

McTighe, Jay, and Ken O'Connor. "Seven Practices for Effective Learning." *Educational Leadership* 63, no. 3 (2005): 10–17.

Muller, Richard. *The Study of Theology*. Vol. 7. Grand Rapids, MI: Zondervan, 1991.

Myers, William R. "Antecedents to a Hopeful Future: Challenges for Theological Faculty." *Theological Education* 50, no. 1 (2015): 81–94.

———. *Closing the Assessment "Loop": Nurturing Healthy, On-going Self-Evaluation in Theological Schools*. Chicago: Exploration, 2006.

Niebuhr, H. Richard. *The Purpose of the Church and Its Ministry*. New York: Harper & Bros, 1956.

Niebuhr, H. Richard, Daniel Day Williams and James M. Gustafson. *The Advancement of Theological Education*. New York: Harper, 1957.

Nordbeck, Elizabeth C. "The Once and Future Dean: Reflections on Being a Chief Academic Officer." *Theological Education* 33, Supplement (1996): 21–23.

Nouwen, Henri J. M. *Reaching Out*. London: Harper Collins, 1976.

———. *The Way of the Heart*. New York: Ballentine, 1989.

Oehler, Carolyn Henninger. "Welcoming the Whole Person." In *A Lifelong Call to Learn: Continuing Education for Religious Leaders*, edited by Robert E. Reber and D. Bruce Roberts, 347–358. Herndon, VA: The Alban Institute, 2010.

Ott, Bernhard. *Beyond Fragmentation: Integrating Mission and Theological Education.* Oxford: Regnum, 2001.

———. *Understanding and Developing Theological Education.* Carlisle: Langham Global Library, 2016.

Overseas Council International. "Program Values and Standards for Theological Education." 2014.

Palmer, Parker J. *The Courage to Teach: Exploring the Inner Landscape of a Teacher's Life.* San Francisco: Jossey-Bass, 2007.

Paver, John E. *Theological Reflection and Education for Ministry: The Search for Integration in Theology, in Explorations in Practical, Pastoral and Empirical Theology.* Aldershot: Ashgate, 2006.

Payne, Ian. "Reproducing Leaders through Mentoring." *Journal of Theological Education and Mission* 6, no. 6 (2015): 74–96. Also in *Tending the Seedbeds: Educational Perspectives on Theological Education in Asia*, edited by Allan Harkness. Quezon City, Philippines: Asia Theological Association, 2010.

Prabhakar, Samson. and M. J. Joseph (eds.). *Church's Participation in Theological Education.* Bangalore: BTESSC/SATHRI, 2003.

Priyadarshini, Beena. "What Do We Expect from Theological Educators: A BD Student's Point of View." In *Theological Education: Ploughing the Field for New Life to Sprout*, edited by G. Lawrence Jebadoss and P. Mohan Larbeer. Bangalore: BTESSC and Chennai: CLS, 2014.

Reischmann, J. "Andragogy: History, Meaning, Context and Function." In *International Encyclopedia of Adult Education*, edited by L. M. English, 58–63. Houndsville, NY: Palgrave Macmillan, 2005.

Rhodes, Lynn N., and Nancy D. Richardson. *Mending Severed Connections: Theological Education for Communal Transformation.* San Francisco: Network Ministries, 1991.

Richardson, Will. *Blogs, Wikis, Podcasts, and Other Powerful Web Tools for Classrooms.* 3rd ed. Thousand Oaks, CA: Corwin, 2010.

Roberts, Bruce. "Motivated Learning and Practice: A Peer Group Model." In *A Lifelong Call to Learn: Continuing Education for Religious Leaders*, edited by Robert E. Reber and D. Bruce Roberts, 73–92. Herndon, VA: The Alban Institute, 2010.

Sarkar, Arun K. "Non-formal Faculty Development in Theological Seminaries." In *Tending the Seedbeds: Educational Perspectives on Theological Education in Asia*, edited by Allan Harkness, 129–144. Quezon City, Philippines: Asia Theological Association, 2010.

Shaw, Perry. *Transforming Theological Education: A Practical Handbook for Integrative Learning.* Carlisle: Langham Global Library, 2014.

Smith, Gordon T., and Charles M. Wood. "Learning Goals and Assessment of Learning in Theology Schools." *Theological Education* 39, no. 1 (2003): 17–30.
Smith, Mark K. "Curriculum Theory and Practice." The Encyclopedia of Informal Education. www.infed.org/biblio/b-curric.htm. 1996, 2000.
Spencer, James. "Online Education and Curricular Design." *Theological Education* 49, no. 2 (2015): 19–31.
Stackhouse, Max L. *Apologia: Contextualization, Globalization and Mission in Theological Education*. Grand Rapids, MI: Eerdmans, 1988.
Studebaker, Steven, and Lee Beach. "Friend Or Foe? The Role of the Scholar in Emerging Christianity." *Theological Education* 48, no. 2 (2014): 43–56.
Suskie, Linda. *Assessing Student Learning: A Common Sense Guide*. 2nd ed. San Fransisco: Jossey-Bass, 2009.
———. "Creating a Culture of Assessment: Implementation of the Student Learning Outcomes Assessment Process." Unpublished paper. https://www.umes.edu/cms300uploadedFiles/CREATING%20A%20CULTURE%20OF%20ASSESSMENT-Fin.pdf. Accessed 17 March 2016.
———. "Five Dimensions of Good Assessment." Document compiled by Suskie for Middle States Commission on Higher Education, 1 November 2006. https://www.pratt.edu/uploads/principles_of_good_assessment_suskie_2006.pdf. Accessed 17 March 2016.
Theron, Pieter F. "Continuous Assessment for Quality Improvements in Theological Education." In *Educating for Tomorrow: Theological Leadership for the Asian Context*, edited by Manfred Waldemar Kohl and A. N. Lal Senanayake. Bangalore: SAIACS, 2007.
Thomas, Jaison. "Church-Ministry Formation in Theological Education in India." PhD thesis, Queen's University, Belfast, 2008.
Thomas, O. "Editorial." *The Journal of Malankara Orthodox Theological Studies* 3, no. 1 (August 2015): 3–5.
Tidball, Derek. *Skilful Shepherds: Explorations in Pastoral Theology*. Nottingham: Apollos, 2009.
"Toward Theological Understanding: An Interview with Edward Farley." *The Christian Century* 115, no. 4 (February 1998): 113–115.
Vallet, Ronald E. *Stewards of the Gospel: Reforming Theological Education*. Grand Rapids, MI: Eerdmans, 2011.
Walter, Robert. "Community in Theological Education." Seminar materials in the ConneXions Model of Healthy Leader Development.
Wanak, Lee. "Theological Education and the Role of Teachers in the Twenty-First Century: A Look at the Asia Pacific Region." In *Educating for Tomorrow:*

Theological Leadership for the Asian Context, edited by Manfred Waldemar Kohl and A. N. Lal Senanayake, 173–194. Bangalore: SAIACS, 2007.

———. "Towards Perspective Transformation: Adopting Jesus' Use of Questions in the Seminary." In *Tending the Seedbeds: Educational Perspectives on Theological Education in Asia*, edited by Allan Harkness. Quezon City, Philippines: Asia Theological Association, 2010.

Ward, F. *Lifelong Learning: Theological Education and Supervision*. London: SCM, 2005.

Ward, Ted W. "Curriculum: The Path to High-Worth Outcomes." *Common Ground Journal* 10, no. 1 (Fall 2012): 42–44.

———. "The Lines People Draw." *Common Ground Journal* 10, no. 1 (Fall 2012): 26–35.

———. "Understanding Teaching and Learning as Inseparable Processes." *Common Ground Journal* 10, no. 1 (Fall 2012): 45–61.

———. "With an Eye on the Future." In *With an Eye on the Future: Development and Mission in the 21st Century*, edited by Duane Elmer and Louis McKinney. Monrovia, CA: MARC Publications, 1996.

Webber, Malcolm. *Building Healthy Leaders: Spirit-Built Leadership Series 1–4*. Elkhart, IN: Strategic, 2002–2011.

———. "ConneXions Model of Building Healthy Leaders." LeaderSource. www.sgai.org/ www.leadersource.org.

———. *Healthy Evaluation Course Manual* (Elkhart, IN: Strategic, 2010). Training materials. LeaderSource. www.leadersource.org / info@LeaderSource.org. Accessed from the Leader Development and Research Center Collections at New India Bible Seminary, Kerala, 28 March 2017.

Werner, Dietrich, David Esterline, Namsoon Kang and Joshva Raja. *Handbook of Theological Education in World Christianity*. Bangalore: Asian Trading Corporation, 2010.

Wheeler, Barbara G., and Edward Farley (eds.). *Shifting Boundaries: Contextual Approaches to the Structure of Theological Education*. Louisville, KY: Westminster John Knox, 1991.

Wilfred, Felix. "Foreword." In *Theological Education: Ploughing the Field for New Life to Sprout*, edited by G. Lawrence Jebadoss and P. Mohan Larbeer. Bangalore: BTESSE; Chennai: CLS, 2014.

Wintle, Brian C. "Theological Education in Contemporary India: How Do We Make It Relevant?" In *Called to Teach: Essays in Honour of Peter S. C. Pothan; A Festschrift*, edited by Siga Arles, 13–23. Bangalore: CFCC, 2011.

World Council of Churches. "Global Survey on Theological Education, 2011–2013: Summary of the Main Findings." Presented at WCC 10th Assembly, Busan, 30 October–8 November 2013. https://www.oikoumene.org/en/resources/

documents/wcc-programmes/education-and-ecumenical-formation/ete/global-survey-on-theological-education.

Wright, Chris. Keynote address based on Proverbs 16:3 "Commit to the Lord whatever you do and he will establish your plans." Summary of "Scholars Talk in Turkey." International Consultation for Theological Education, ICETE C-15, 2015. http://nz.langham.org/scholars-talk-in-turkey/. Accessed 30 March 2017.

Yong, Amos. "Beyond the Evangelical–Ecumenical Divide for Theological Education in the Twenty-First Century: A Pentecostal Assist." *Theological Education* 49, no. 1 (2014): 87–102.

Global Hub for Evangelical Theological Education

Mission

ICETE advances quality and collaboration in global theological education to strengthen and accompany the church in its mission.

Objectives

As a global hub for evangelical theological education, ICETE is recognized for its reliable capacity to:

1. Develop, disseminate, mutually validate, harmonize, and inspire quality in theological education, aimed at fostering reciprocal trust among stakeholders, including the church;
2. Cultivate worldwide relationships, stimulated through gatherings, communications for reflection, interactive dialogue, collaboration, and practice in support of the church's mission; and
3. Train, consult, and provide resources for those involved in theological education, marked by relevance, accessibility, and collaborative effectiveness.

ICETE's mission emphasizes its dual focus on quality *and* collaboration through its constituency to strengthen and accompany the church in its mission. The quality aspect of our work addresses the church-academy gap by requiring theological institutions to build strategic partnerships with churches and ministry organizations. ICETE quality assurance seeks to be an agent for change in theological institutions, and consequently in the lives of the next generation of global leaders.

Through collaborative opportunities, our impact begins with theological educators and extends exponentially to training programs, students, church leaders, and the broader community for the sake of the church. Our work targets theological educators across all sectors who prepare thousands of learners serving in hundreds of ministries.

www.icete.info

Langham Literature and its imprints are a ministry of Langham Partnership.

Langham Partnership is a global fellowship working in pursuit of the vision God entrusted to its founder John Stott –

> *to facilitate the growth of the church in maturity and Christ-likeness through raising the standards of biblical preaching and teaching.*

Our vision is to see churches in the majority world equipped for mission and growing to maturity in Christ through the ministry of pastors and leaders who believe, teach and live by the Word of God.

Our mission is to strengthen the ministry of the Word of God through:
- nurturing national movements for biblical preaching
- fostering the creation and distribution of evangelical literature
- enhancing evangelical theological education

especially in countries where churches are under-resourced.

Our ministry

Langham Preaching partners with national leaders to nurture indigenous biblical preaching movements for pastors and lay preachers all around the world. With the support of a team of trainers from many countries, a multi-level programme of seminars provides practical training, and is followed by a programme for training local facilitators. Local preachers' groups and national and regional networks ensure continuity and ongoing development, seeking to build vigorous movements committed to Bible exposition.

Langham Literature provides majority world preachers, scholars and seminary libraries with evangelical books and electronic resources through publishing and distribution, grants and discounts. The programme also fosters the creation of indigenous evangelical books in many languages, through writer's grants, strengthening local evangelical publishing houses, and investment in major regional literature projects, such as one volume Bible commentaries like *The Africa Bible Commentary* and *The South Asia Bible Commentary*.

Langham Scholars provides financial support for evangelical doctoral students from the majority world so that, when they return home, they may train pastors and other Christian leaders with sound, biblical and theological teaching. This programme equips those who equip others. Langham Scholars also works in partnership with majority world seminaries in strengthening evangelical theological education. A growing number of Langham Scholars study in high quality doctoral programmes in the majority world itself. As well as teaching the next generation of pastors, graduated Langham Scholars exercise significant influence through their writing and leadership.

To learn more about Langham Partnership and the work we do visit **langham.org**

www.ingramcontent.com/pod-product-compliance
Lightning Source LLC
Chambersburg PA
CBHW071740150426
43191CB00010B/1641